Center for Community Based Service-Learning
Career Services, San Diego State University
5500 Campanile Drive
San Diego, CA 92182-8255
http://servicelearning.sdsu.edu
email: servicelearning@mail.sdsu.edu

Escape from the Ivory Tower

Contributors

Syllabi

Xavier N. de Souza Briggs

Arturo Cherbowski

Jacqueline McEvoy

Laura Harris

Jim Pitofsky

Wendy Whitehill

Student Views

Stanford:

Curt Cortelyou

Mike Sandoval

Emily Simas

Berkeley:

Lok C. D. Siu

Kyle Stewart Miller

William Cambell

Kristin Chin

Jake Hoelter

Stephen Midgley

Harvard:

Craig Mitchell

Kim McCarty

Brown:

Thomas Abner Lewis, III

Shannon Wright

Escape from the Ivory Tower

Student Adventures in Democratic Experiential Education

David H. Lempert
in association with
Xavier N. de Souza Briggs
and Contributors

Jossey-Bass Publishers • San Francisco

Pages 222–223 reprinted from *A Model Development Plan: New Strategies and Perspectives*, D. Lempert, C. Mitchell, and K. McCarty. Westport Conn.: Greenwood, 1995. Reprinted with permission from Greenwood Publishing Group, Inc., Westport, Conn.

Substantial discounts on bulk quantities of Jossey-Bass books are available to corporations, professional associations, and other organizations. For details and discount information, contact the special sales department at Jossey-Bass Inc., Publishers. (415) 433–1740; Fax (800) 605–2665.

For sales outside the United States, please contact your local Simon & Schuster International Office.

 Manufactured in the United States of America on Lyons Falls Pathfinder Tradebook. This paper is acid-free and 100 percent totally chlorine-free.

Library of Congress Cataloging-in-Publication Data

Lempert, David H. date.
  Escape from the ivory tower : student adventures in democratic experiential education / David H. Lempert, in association with Xavier N. de Souza Briggs, and with contributions from Arturo Cherbowski . . . [et al.]. — 1st ed/
    p.   cm. —(The Jossey-Bass higher and adult education series)
  Includes bibliographical references (p.   ) and index.
  ISBN 0-7879-0136-9 (alk. paper)
  1. Education, Higher—United States—Aims and objectives. 2. Active learning—United States. 3. Field work (Educational method) 4. Education, Higher—Social aspects—United States. 5. Education, Higher—United States—Curricula. 6. Democracy—United States. I. de Souza Briggs, Xavier N. II. Title. III. Series.
LA227.4.L45 1996
378.73—dc20   95-22192

FIRST EDITION
HB Printing   10 9 8 7 6 5 4 3 2 1

The Jossey-Bass Higher and Adult Education Series

Contents

Syllabi and Materials

Course and Project Proposals

Course Syllabi and Project Descriptions

Preface

This is a small book about a large vision.

It is a vision of American education and how the educational system can serve and create a healthier and more democratic society.

It is a vision of the potential relationship between educational institutions and citizens, as well as that between American institutions of all kinds and citizens of all interests and beliefs.

Former President Jimmy Carter, now a professor at Emory University in Atlanta, recently wondered aloud when university social science departments would draw on the communities surrounding them, study those communities, and contribute to solving their pressing social and economic problems.

Whereas a former president wondered, another president has started to act. In one of his first acts of office, President Bill Clinton created the Corporation for National and Community Service to challenge colleges and universities to renew their commitment to service.

These efforts may seem like small seedlings sprouting out from America's ivory towers—foreboding institutions under assault in an era of dwindling finances and diminishing public trust. But they represent part of a continuing recognition that changes are needed in this country's universities if the United States is to remain a vital and dynamic society and if other countries—many of them following America's lead in education—will invigorate their own commitments to community, democracy, and development.

The vision this book shows is how to bring about these changes within the constraints of existing resources. It is a vision of unleashing the energies of students, teachers, and society to make learning an adventure and to set the groundwork for healthy societies of the future.

Escape from the Ivory Tower is part story, part philosophy, part illustration, and part how-to.

It has implications for American high schools and colleges, postgraduate education, adult education, and even primary schooling. It is for educators and administrators—university trustees, school board officials, principals, professors sitting on endowed chairs, and even elementary school teachers—and parents, as well as for community members who ask what their universities can do for them to meet their concerns and improve their lives. It is for educators and students not only here in the United States but also in other nations, as this country continues to be an international leader in higher education, exporting models of training and curricula through government and private programs worldwide.

In *Escape from the Ivory Tower*, we make our first report of a new and tested form of education that we call "democratic" and "experiential": a form of education that combines the best features of discussion and interaction, laboratory work and field learning, community involvement and service, democratic citizenship and skills training, and student-initiated participatory learning into courses, projects, and clinical work that goes well beyond traditional classroom education. In an environment in which there is growing recognition of the value of nonclassroom learning, the successful models that we report on here incorporate the most effective attributes of—and go beyond—internships, service learning, independent study, and seminars.

In this book, we describe a model of education that starts with the intrinsic desires of students themselves—to learn, develop skills, and contribute to society—and with the needs of the communities surrounding our universities for new ideas and tools to address real needs. It is our attention to student and community needs and participation that makes our view of education a democratic one. We have designed an educational model in which citizens are active participants and interact with each other to best negotiate their individual needs and use of their talents. In this model, educational institutions are community partners in creating a healthy and adaptive society, rather than isolated enclaves consuming hard-earned resources with little contribution in return.

For the past decade, we have taken the best features of what we found to be the most creative and inspired educational theories and have combined them with ideas of our own, of our professors, and of our students and classmates. We have applied and evaluated them in a number of different universities, in different disciplines, with students of varying interests and backgrounds.

What makes this book unique is that it offers pragmatic solutions and presents them from the perspective of perhaps the most important group in the debate on higher education and the future of American society: university and graduate students who are now becoming the next generation of scholars, citizens, and teachers.

Where other authors writing on higher education have pointed out its many flaws and have ended their arguments with exhortations to action, we take the debate one step beyond. This book goes beyond proposing a novel theory of what is wrong with higher education and how it can be improved: it presents tested solutions that have had unusual success and describes in detail how they can be adopted elsewhere as a part or full model of new curricula at the undergraduate, graduate, and professional school levels.

We have taken it upon ourselves to cut through the hyperbole and, too often, the animosity of current debates over higher education. Some of us have risked the early stages of our careers in an effort to cut to the real issues in educational reform and to develop genuine alternatives that work. We have done so with the understanding that progress might be slow and rewards might take time but that the effort would make it worthwhile and that we would see success down the road, as we do. The different efforts that this book represents are not those of scholars who started out with the intention of putting books on dusty shelves. We intended to make a difference.

This book came to be because of our efforts as students (and those of our students) at America's top universities in several different fields. We took action despite our entrance into privilege at several of the premier universities in the United States (and the world). As we and our students now rise in the ranks of the educational community as professors, consultants, and scholars at the forefront of a new generation of faculty members, many of us have continued to be fed up with the quality of education at those institutions and with the focus of current debates on educational "reform." We believe that it is time for action and not just words.

As individuals differing in our specific goals but with a common purpose, we have been concerned less with turf battles and ideological warfare than with improving learning for ourselves and others and with integrating the university with the community. In doing so, we sought to create a model for American education in general.

With no resources but time, energy, and a sense of commitment and idealism—and with help from our students and many faculty members who were inspired by our energies and who inspired us— we began to design an alternative to what appears, to put it bluntly, as a growing intellectual and spiritual wasteland inside this country's universities. It was time for a new vision.

Audience

We present our findings here in a way that makes them immediately useful and understandable for a variety of audiences in the academic community.

- *For university faculty and administrators,* in particular, this book provides a vision of how education can be more effective in imparting skills, how it can be less expensive, how it can inspire students to greater achievement, and how it can receive greater community support. Beyond general ideas, this book offers blueprints that can make even the besieged bureaucrat a community hero.

- *For universities whose reputations are based on research*, the models we present are a means of increasing and enriching research opportunities and of training future researchers. For social scientists, this book is an effort to clear away much of the rubble and ideology of Cold War social science; to produce theories that are grounded in social reality and empirical testing and that neither idealize nor mythologize because of short-term political needs. For those who seek to bridge the gaps between disciplines in universities, we present proven models for developing new interdisciplinary thinking and approaches.

- *For administrators and university trustees* who believe that universities must vigorously commit themselves to transmitting basic American values, teach basic skills necessary for citizens in a democracy, and improve American competitiveness, we present models of educational programs for communicating those values and concepts directly to communities and for teaching students the skills needed in a vital and dynamic economy and an international marketplace.

- *For students in colleges as well as in graduate and professional schools* (where some of the approaches we describe may be needed most), this book presents a how-to guide to starting exciting versions of learning within existing university programs.

- *For public servants, professionals, and ordinary citizens*—ranging from members of Congress, judges, and White House officials to business executives, union leaders, city planners, publishers, writers, entertainers, lawyers, and doctors—we extend our welcome to join in similar educational adventures and to make the most of this new form of learning. Already, there are special university seminars for executives, summer programs for adults of all interests, and government fact-finding tours. Student adventures are both a kind of "reality tour" and a means of gaining a fresh perspective and a new empathy—one that is critical and informed.

- *For ordinary citizens who ask American universities to open their doors to studies of ethnic diversity and the variety of American and world cultures,* this book does not just open doors—it welcomes those outside in and beckons those inside to step out. It is part of a vision inherent in democratic ideals and values, put into practice in small ways and in sometimes unexpected places.

With our ideas for education, we seek to expand the concepts of what students and universities can achieve; we reach out to everyone and include the best that everyone can offer within our model of education. We demonstrate what today's students can give to their communities and how they can take part in a dialogue while enhancing learning. We show how to return to a sense of morality, of sharedness and connectedness between students and the community. And we point out new ways to build skills in the type of consensus and personal responsibility that is an essential part of a working democracy.

We envision and have tested a kind of university education that can be adapted not only for university students but for all of those who retain a spark of curiosity and desire to learn and benefit their communities, whether at the local, national, or international level. We invite and encourage everyone to share in the educational courses and projects that we have developed, to participate in an educational adventure, and to experience the "unseen."

A Special Message to Students

For undergraduates and graduate students, like those who created the programs on which this book is based, *Escape from the Ivory Tower* carries a special message: you can share in the excitement of a new form of education that starts with your needs and interests, allows you to learn by doing, and enables you to make a real contribution to your community and the world in a way in which you are at the frontier of knowledge and the forefront of research. This is not another program that provides you with make-work assignments, turns you into a "gofer" or underemployed employee for credit, replaces education with work, or tries to convince you to follow a contrived and bureaucratic program.

One of the goals of this book is to take you along to share in the excitement of student adventures that we have proven to be successful at several of America's top universities and that we envision in model curricula elsewhere. To help you get started, this book provides some of the basics for setting out on your own.

Faculty members and administrators may push for projects like these and expand the boundaries of the possible, if they choose. Foundations and community organizations may help fund them. But since there are structural reasons why they may not do so without prodding from students, enlightened donors, and community groups, we advocate that you, students, follow our example and take greater responsibility in your own education in designing courses and projects that test book learning in useful projects outside the classroom. We appeal to you (and young professors who are our contemporaries as leaders and designers of the projects in this book) to take courage and to make your own experiential democratic contributions to your college curricula.

As leaders and students, you have a unique advantage over the authors of this book, the student-entrepreneurs who designed these projects and sacrificed to implement them. You have precedents and successful models to draw from.

Within this book are examples of approved syllabi, application questions for detailed projects, statements of the philosophy of democratic experiential education, sample student "contracts," and answers to the most commonly asked questions about innovative courses and projects. We present a few tips, along with a few warnings about problems to avoid.

The message of this book is simple.

Like all of the best ideas, those we present here with our practical suggestions and sample materials are "self-activating." If you follow the instructions, you will essentially be teaching yourselves everything that you can learn in current university classes—and much more—with more fun, more confidence, and a greater sense of accomplishment.

Read the warning labels. Make a commitment. Be prepared for frustration and setbacks, hard work, and maybe some heartache. Then go for it. You can experience the intellectual excitement and rewards of student adventures in democratic experiential education on your own!

Overview of the Contents

This book is divided into two parts.

Part One (Chapters One through Three) concerns creating a new educational vision. It redirects the debate over American education—a debate that has lost sight of fundamental goals and has lost touch with the real problems that stand in the way of improving American education.

Here, we present a perspective that is unusual to find in print but that will resonate with most readers: an overview of how American universities appear from the point of view of students and communities. It is a much-needed reality check on politicized debates fueled by national media and by academic infighting—debates that touch on flash points in the society but are out of touch with the questions that those most affected by this paralyzing debate are asking about education.

We follow with a description of a democratic experiential philosophy of education, one that comes out of strong traditions in American culture but represents a distinct intellectual tradition from the prevailing view inside the bureaucracies of modern universities. We show how our philosophy is linked with a concept of rebuilding and revitalizing communities and of greater citizen participation, fulfillment, independence, and self-esteem.

It is not essential to start here. The reader who wishes to jump right to solutions and to avoid picking apart the debate can move to the second half of the book, in which we present our philosophy with real and practical solutions.

Part Two (Chapters Four through Ten) describes ideas for revitalizing American higher education through what we call *student adventures*. These ideas include models that have already been put into practice and can be tried elsewhere, and the ideas that follow from them, as part of an ideal model curriculum.

These ideas not only reflect a set of principles that can restore important values in higher education—a sense of community and moral values, consensus-building and democratic skills, and high standards of scholarship—but they are also easy to implement. They are even less costly than many current educational approaches that have sacrificed educational quality under the justification of cutting costs.

We include detailed descriptions and how-to materials for several different university courses that have already been tested successfully and for an international policy project (which took a group of students to Ecuador in its initial trial), and other detailed ideas for experiential courses at all levels of the university curriculum, including graduate and professional schools and complementing courses in several disciplines.

We also provide useful tips on setting up university projects, in the form of courses and of innovations that supplement the curriculum but are extracurricular, along with suggestions for coordinating them within existing universities.

Finally, we carry the ideas of earlier chapters even further, pointing the direction to go from here in order to remake the structure of higher education—its funding, its links to the community, and its view of its role and of the roles of faculty and students. It is here that we propose a fundamental change that we hope will start at the university level and permeate the educational system in the United States as well as in other countries seeking successful educational models for healthy and productive societies.

To make this book even easier to use, readers are welcome to copy parts of our syllabi without obtaining our written permission, since we are placing the syllabi in the public domain. Feel free to call us for any additional help you need in getting started.

Overall, the aim of this book is to share ideas for rekindling the spirit of America's young people for productive and fulfilling lives. It is a quest to reopen the American mind in every sense of the word.

Acknowledgments

As young scholars and professors now entering the teaching and consulting ranks and putting our newfound knowledge into practice to improve communities here and abroad, we owe a debt to a number of educators and friends who supported the efforts we began as students in designing new models of education.

Several faculty members in various departments at Stanford University and the University of California at Berkeley encouraged, inspired, and sustained us. Were it not for their energies, interest, and spirit of listening to students and trying new ideas, our curricular experiments and educational models would never have had the chance to be tested or to survive. Besides giving us their intellectual enthusiasm and support, these special educators helped us negotiate university bureaucracies and taught us the strategies for institutionalizing positive reforms within existing university structures. These are skills in which formal education does not yet prepare students and that we share in this book as integral to the model of education we present. We thank Kennell Jackson, a professor in the Department of History at Stanford and a legendary resident fellow at Stanford's Branner Hall, William Muir of the Department of Political Science at University of California at Berkeley, Jack Potter of the Department of Anthropology at Berkeley, Robert Brentano of the Department of History at Berkeley, and Claudia Carr of the Department of Peace and Conflict Studies at Berkeley.

We also owe our thanks to those educators, administrators, and students who came before us and who continue to advocate for fresh approaches in education and to incorporate the best of the country's traditions of scholarship, service, and adventure. As founders of clinical programs, workshops, and forms of experiential and democratic education, they are too many to name beyond the few whom we cite directly in this book. Many of them—from whose dedication we benefit—we do not even know. But we owe them all our gratitude.

In developing our own programs under the rubric of Unseen America Projects, Inc., we owe a special thanks to those who stood by us as we crossed uncharted territory and who helped steady our course—in particular Steve Long, Debby Toomey, Randy Riley, and Marci Lempert-Riley. As board members and administrators of a new nonprofit organization, they helped us keep our dream alive through its first decade.

Much harder in America today than developing new ideas—or even overcoming the obstacles to testing them—is getting a chance to be heard. For too long, those who are seeking solutions have often been relegated to the "unseen." For helping us to amplify our voices so that others can learn from and apply our experience, we thank Steve Rutter, who generously directed us to Jossey-Bass after taking an interest in this book, and Gale Erlandson, who tirelessly helped us to strengthen our message and to reach those to whom that message is most useful.

Finally, we owe our thanks to our students—whose sense of adventure, thirst for knowledge, and willingness to experiment inspired us to design even more effective and interesting models of learning—and to the many different people and communities who shared their experiences and time with us. Not only did members of local and foreign communities join with us as part of a shared adventure of learning but they also opened themselves to new ideas and probing questions from students who pushed them to reconsider and improve their ways of doing things. They are the real heroes and beneficiaries of democratic experiential education.

Washington, D.C.　　　　　　David H. Lempert and contributors
September 1995

The Authors

David H. Lempert professor, educational and international development consultant, and attorney, is the founder of Unseen America Projects, Inc., and an associate professor (adjunct) at George Washington University. He first taught The Unseen America at Stanford University in 1985 and Adventure in International Development Planning (the Ecuador Project) in 1988. With a student team, he produced a report for the president of Ecuador, published in English as *A Model Development Plan: New Strategies and Perspectives*.

Lempert earned his B.A. degree in economics and political science from Yale University (1980), his J.D. and M.B.A. degrees from Stanford University (1985), and his M.A. and Ph.D. degrees in social anthropology from the University of California at Berkeley (1992).

Escape from the Ivory Tower completes his trilogy of works on social revitalization, covering social and economic development (*A Model Development Plan*), legal and political structural reform (*A Return to Democracy: The Modern Democracy Amendments*), and educational reform. These works complement his interdisciplinary theoretical models of complex societies and processes of change (*Daily Life in a Crumbling Empire: The Absorption of Russia into the World Economy*, three books in two volumes) and his works of fiction and poetry.

Lempert has worked as a development consultant in the Philippines, Costa Rica, Russia, and Ukraine and on projects for Kazakhstan and Lithuania. He has taught at George Washington University, Leningrad/St. Petersburg State University, the University of California at Berkeley, and Stanford University, and he has designed curricula for universities in Vietnam and Bulgaria.

Along with Jim Pitofsky and Wendy Whitehill, **Xavier N. de Souza Briggs** taught The Unseen America at Stanford in spring 1989. Briggs holds a B.S. degree in engineering from Stanford (1989) and an M.P.A. degree in public administration from the John F. Kennedy School of Government at Harvard University (1973). Currently a planning consultant and researcher based in New York City, Briggs is also a candidate for the Ph.D. degree in sociology and education at Columbia University. He has written on poverty issues and public participation in planning and has been a guest lecturer at Harvard University.

Escape from the Ivory Tower

PART ONE

Creating a New Educational Vision

Picture these two different scenes.

Scenario one: a familiar scene in higher education in the United States and throughout the world. A group of students files into a large room with bare walls and rows of seats facing the front. A professor walks in, stands at the front of the room, opens up a notebook and begins speaking and writing on a board. The professor moves from one category of information to another, presenting material from a predetermined syllabus and from a preplanned curriculum, and administers a series of prearranged assignments, exercises, and standards. For an hour, students sit copying in their notebooks.

Following this, the students go home or to the library, where they sit quietly, read texts, answer questions that have been posed to them, memorize what is in their notebooks, or look for materials on library shelves. At the end of several weeks, they come back to the same room and answer more questions, routinely following the instructions given to them by their professor.

In some cases, the routine will be relieved by an unusual class that follows the same pattern but has a bit more discussion and where the chairs might face in a circle, or by cookbook laboratory exercises, or by interaction with a computer screen or audio- or videotapes. In other cases, students may be able to supplement this daily routine with uncompensated "gofer" work in an organization near campus—with the obligation that they keep a diary or turn in a paper with their observations and research.

At the end of the term, the professor will have the authority to subjectively "grade" student performance on abstract measures like "participation" and conformity with predetermined standards. If students are successful at responding with what the professor wants to hear, they will be rewarded with opportunities to sit at a desk and pursue similar tasks for the rest of their lives.

Sound familiar?

Scenario two: a model of education now being tried at a small number of universities. Several undergraduate students are working as a team collecting information in mountain and jungle villages, in farmers' fields, and on factory floors; presenting ideas to a newly inaugurated president in a presidential palace; and defending their work at a press conference in a foreign language in front of television cameras. Here, students are not working on a single discipline or preparing for the final exam. Instead, they are preparing recommendations for the future of a country, recommendations that will present the concerns of ten million people and draw on new conclusions about their lives. These students are testing theories and improving their skills in economics, political science, foreign language, communications, and development studies in a developing country. They are setting their own objectives, designing their own experiments, and establishing their own research library and taking responsibility for their housing and the management of an administrative center.

The students arrange meetings and set up interviews in a second language with ministers, governors, peasant farmers, factory workers, prisoners, missionaries, indigenous peoples, multinational executives, officials of various embassies, writers, clerics, health workers, smugglers, soldiers, and local scholars. They visit fish farms, oil wells, mines, prisons, hospitals, factories, and archaeological sites, where they learn about different production processes as well as the country's history and its political, economic, and social systems. They collect field data through observation and experimentation in order to test World Bank models and social science theories, and they question the practitioners applying those theories. They perfect their statistical skills by running the data they have collected on computers and developing their own models. They learn to publicize their work through the local media. They learn to prepare a development plan by doing it. They learn politics by seeking and arranging a meeting with the country's president and trying to impress their conclusions upon him. They learn communications skills and see what gets reported, and why, by participating in a press conference with national media. And then they learn about academic publishing by producing their work as a book in the United States.

Rather than sitting in judgment of them, their teacher—an older peer with previous training in such projects—serves as a backstop when problems arise. The teacher also acts as a member of the team, provoking discussions and encouraging students to develop to their potential and teach each other, to cooperate and compromise, and to maintain high ethical standards in their work.

If you had to make a choice for maximizing your own learning and sense of accomplishment—and you had the blueprint to do it—which form of education would you choose?

To many professors and administrators in universities today, the second scenario is unthinkable and impossible; it goes well beyond their view of what a university is, of what students are capable of doing, of what their chosen political constituencies would want, and of what they have the energy to pursue. They view it as unrealistic—a fantasy. They claim that it sounds like an aspiration that could never be tested, and would likely fail if it were. The odds that they would give on such a program succeeding on a first try are probably infinitesimal. Rather than discussing it, they write it off as a pipe dream and turn the conversation to budgets and standards and traditions and shift into the contours of the current debate in higher education as the "real" and "important" area of concern.

We know, because that was the response we faced when we first suggested putting that scenario into practice along with several similar ideas at other levels in the university setting. When we designed our program in South America six years ago—as Harvard, Brown, and University of California students acting on our own to do what our universities would not do for us—we not only had to implement it but we also had to finance it ourselves.

Now, after ten years of student-initiated educational experiments that have proven successful and that we have convinced faculty and administrators to accredit and support, we know that programs like these are not only possible but are less expensive than traditional programs, are a more effective form of learning, are more exciting to students, are of more benefit to the community, and are more rewarding for those faculty members and administrators who are involved.

We answered many of the challenges facing higher education without taking sides in what is perceived as the critical debate in higher education but that barely touched on our concerns as students or on the concerns of our communities. Rather than seeing the debate as enlightening, we saw it as paralyzing—distracting attention away from real improvements in education and from most of the contemporary problems for which we sought solutions and role models in the university. We felt that we had little to gain in the battle over whose dogma would be read, what color our professors would be or what ethnic group they would belong to, and what would be on exams.

The kind of educational model we put into practice—and seek to expand to its full potential—is one in which students test reality and theory directly and hear all sides on an issue, including the views of those most directly affected and involved; in which they develop real skills and measure their progress objectively; in which they work on real problems; and in which, in the spirit of democracy, they do as much as possible by themselves, with universities as their guides instead of their taskmasters.

Part One presents our new educational vision. We begin with an attempt to clear the air by focusing on the poverty of current debates over higher education, debates that distract all concerned from the real issues rather than illuminate solutions. We describe the path we took in developing an alternative, our journey of intellectual discovery that led to something new. Then we lay out our philosophy and the key components of democratic-experiential education, comparing and contrasting it directly with the prevailing model.

- *Chapter One: The Battle for the Soul of the University.* We begin our discussion of higher education by examining the current dispute being waged between professors and administrators in the mass media and comparing it with the reality as observed by students and the public. Given society's needs and the reality of how students learn, we refocus the debate on the real issues.

- *Chapter Two: The Birth of Student Adventures.* In this chapter, David Lempert draws upon his diary entries from the 1980s to describe how a vision of education as it should be emerged in the context of one of this country's most renowned universities, Stanford. He describes how he turned his experience of dissatisfaction with higher education and his feelings of alienation and powerlessness into a series of courses that he and other students were able to accredit and teach. It is a story that will likely resonate with students, faculty, and administrators elsewhere and that should provide hope and inspiration for others to take education into their own hands and rebuild the universities from within.

- *Chapter Three: Experiencing Democracy: A New Approach to Education.* In this chapter, we describe the particular vision of democratic experiential education that we have developed as an educational philosophy quite separate from that found in most universities today. We present that philosophy in its ideal form and show how it fits into a new concept of democracy for modern society, as well as into a new vision of a model society. We describe its overall goals and its tenets about the nature of students, citizens, and learning, as well as its practical components.

Following these three chapters, Part Two of this book lays out our model of a new form of education, from introductory undergraduate courses all the way up through graduate and professional levels. While we do not believe that there is any one standard curriculum to recommend—since all education must start with community and student needs—the chapters in Part Two present an outline of a variety of courses and suggest how these courses fit together. They also contain sample curricula, materials, and advice on designing and implementing courses and projects.

1

The Battle for the Soul of the University

In sentencing a White House felon, a federal judge recently required the type of activity that might have prevented the criminal behavior in the first place had it been part of university education. The presidential adviser's punishment was to work in the community near the White House to help devise solutions to problems faced by those whose interests he had ignored. Ironically, this punishment was in sharp contrast to most contemporary university education: it was something closer to the institutional confines and behavior modification of prison life.

When White House felons can be sentenced to seeking solutions to the drug problem in the slums of the nation's capital while students who sit in a classroom reading and being evaluated on reciting the views of the same officials and their teachers are told that this form of education is a privilege, something is amiss in American higher education and American society. Only recently has the idea of linking education to community needs and creating a real partnership between the university and society even had a hearing.

For the past decade, the touchstone for national debate on American higher education has been Allan Bloom's assault on universities as the sources of a national "moral" and "intellectual" crisis (*The Closing of the American Mind*, 1987). At the basis of Bloom's attack is the singular unchallenged premise that "book learning is most of what a teacher can give" and that universities' main flaw is in hiring the wrong teachers to assign the wrong books. In making this argument, Bloom cleverly hides several unexplored assumptions and creates a general insecurity in which everyone is a potential target and must respond, merely as a form of self-protection (Bloom, 1987, p. 27). In a sense, the responses to Bloom's book have proven him absolutely right in one respect: in seeking to protect their own vulnerabilities by attacking others, few in higher education on either side of the debate have taken the high moral or intellectual ground or have had the open-mindedness to challenge or test Bloom's premise and explore its assumptions.

Bloom's critique, a contemporary restatement of William F. Buckley, Jr.'s *God and Man at Yale* (1951), has been followed by a slew of similar works criticizing universities for straying from the canons of what could be called a national secular theology, upon which many of these institutions were founded and in which (wealthy) American Protestants were long raised (Baltzell, 1964; Domhoff, 1970; Oren, 1985).

Taking cues from his predecessors, a more recent Ivy League graduate, Dinesh D'Souza, has gained notoriety with his broadsides against "illiberal education" and the politics of "political correctness." In a sense, D'Souza has updated Buckley's implicit attack against Jews and other minorities who had managed to enter the ranks of Ivy League teachers in the 1950s and stand in the place of the schools' original Protestant minister founders. By expanding the targets to include the new entrants—people of color, other previously underrepresented groups, and women—he demonstrated his own devotion to the founding theology (D'Souza, 1991).

Joining in the chorus are those blaming this country's latest ills on "imposters in the temple" (Anderson, 1992) or on "tenured radicals," described as "corrupting" higher education (Kimball, 1990) and perpetrating a "profscam" (Sykes, 1988). Kimball goes so far as to describe the struggle waged by the previously excluded as a kind of holy "war against Western culture," seeking the "destruction of the values, methods and goals of traditional humanistic study" (Brooks, 1991).

It is hard to counter these statements—or the responses of those who are being attacked—directly because to do so would subject the debate to certain rules and standards. That would create the need for evidence about the effectiveness of different kinds of learning and the perspectives of those whom an educational system is supposed to benefit: its students and the community. It would require a challenge to the premise that education for adults is limited to indoctrination by book learning administered by professors, administrators, or those who have amassed political power over disempowered students and a disconnected community.

To take sides for or against Bloom or Buckley or D'Souza, or those arguing with them, would be to accept that what is most important in higher education today is which set of ideologies, political beliefs, or physical attributes of faculty members should dominate in the existing structure. At the same time, taking sides would divert attention from whether the existing structure actually serves to educate, whether it reflects democratic values, and whether it is geared toward meeting the needs of society as defined by the citizens who support these institutions.

In place of a real debate over how to improve education, the exchange has degenerated into an exercise in name-calling over the strength of one or another culture, ideology, myth, and god, the number and power of the believers, and whose symbols and sacred books will prevail. As Nat Hentoff has described the battle, its underlying theme is "free speech for me but not for thee"; the tenets of democracy and the goals of the institution lost in the process (Hentoff, 1992).

Meanwhile, as the gods fight it out among themselves, mortals might instead turn their attention to the process of learning. It is best to refocus the debate on the motivation, methods, and objectives of the educational system rather than on the power of doctrine. Some of the country's leading educators have tried to do that, and we echo their call and go further (Bok, 1982; Boyer, 1981).

We are in complete agreement with Dr. Benjamin Spock, who said that "[youths] are motivated best when they feel loved and appreciated by a parent or teacher, when they want to grow up to follow strong role models, when they feel a sense of achievement every day—and when they can learn about new ideas and concepts in an active hands-on way. [It is a shame that despite knowing all this], schools have relied on the lecture method, a tendency that contradicts everything we know about [learning]" (Spock, 1993, pp. 115–116).

Voices Left Out of the Debate

Within the university, the climate is one in which administrators and faculty understandably view themselves as vulnerable to attacks on their reputations, on their positions, and on their department budgets, and in which they seem to have no choice but to align in factions and snipe at each other in doctrinal and tribal gang wars in hopes of self-preservation.

The unfortunate reality is that these drive-by attacks in academia have taken another set of victims and scorched the ground of battle: the communities in which they are waged. Academia's resources are shrinking, in part because of the victimization of students (who are potential supporters or opponents of educational institutions) and the abandonment of communities in or near the university landscape. The leading voices in the universities and in the national political debate over academia have sealed their own fate by alienating those who need these institutions the most and who react understandably to the indifference that the universities seem to offer. The cycle is self-reinforcing. The public's skepticism and withdrawal of resources serves only to intensify the rage with which academics attack each other, justifying further hostility toward the university and further calls for answering its self-imposed isolation with greater indifference.

Rather than point fingers, we believe that all of these reactions are understandable and that everyone needs to be heard. A fully open debate is the first step toward ending the madness. We do not blame academics and administrators for being fearful of change and for defending themselves, but at the same time, we recognize that the public and students are absolutely right to challenge the universities' indifference and irrelevance to their needs.

Why should the public pay for theories that do not help them solve the problems they face in their daily lives? Why should citizens pay for the support of faculty and the training of graduates who blindly and arrogantly seek to solve community problems without consulting community members or who scapegoat and stereotype those who live at the feet of the ivory towers while the faculty and graduates seek simple textbook solutions to their interpretation of others' problems? Why should communities support institutions whose endowments are never invested in those communities and that provide students with skills that are taken elsewhere or seemingly employed against local interests? Why should parents contribute to institutions that seem to take their children away to replace their identities and loyalties with sets of alien symbols and beliefs while draining the best intellectual talent from their communities?

With the university limiting its attention to book learning and repetition, why should employers want to hire graduates who lack real skills and are not prepared for work in the areas in which they have been educated—a deficit employers find in one-fifth or more of recent graduates (Applebome, 1995)?

The problem is not just that students are bored and learn to feel alienated from themselves and their communities—seemingly held captive to face a system of regimentation and indoctrination that saps their energy and their initiative while failing to teach them the skills that they need. The problem is that universities have contributed to a profound cynicism among the young and to resentment among its graduates outside the ivory tower. Administrators, teachers, and political leaders have failed to fulfill their calling and obligation to serve, not because they have selected the wrong texts and dogmas with which to indoctrinate the young but for a reason that is more profound. Their abdication is in their inability to inspire values by modeling them in their own behavior through commitment to intellectual life, to democratic values, to human connectedness, to service, to spontaneity, to creativity and courage, and to leadership by example rather than through mere words. Whatever their reasons, they have let down the community and the students who look to them for guidance. Rather than advocating for the young and for the community, and working with them on common aims, they have generated mistrust and disconnection rather than feelings of respect and a common bond.

Facts Missing from the Debate

Merely shifting the perspective of the debate to that of students and the community suggests that Marshall McLuhan was right—that "the medium [and not its content] is the message" (McLuhan, 1964). Educational methods and the structure of the educational system are the key areas for regeneration and reform, but they have almost entirely been excluded from the debate.

The recent focus on *service learning*—even if only in the limited form of adding voluntary community work to classroom learning—has begun to address one of the missing pieces of the equation: how higher education can begin to serve the public in a democratic society. That leaves another set of questions regarding the quality of skills training and how educational methods and student-teacher or student-administrator relationships shape students' attitudes toward democratic values and students' sense of self and community. To see what is missing merely requires applying standards that were developed within the academic community through empirical research.

This is nothing new. Generally accepted means of educational evaluation and appraisal date back at least twenty years, with new discoveries continually adding to an understanding of the complexity of learning and its many dimensions (McCoy, 1971; Dressel, 1971).

Among the most current and widely acknowledged findings of modes of learning and the need for more variety and creativity in the structure of the educational system, for example, is Howard Gardner's discovery of "multiple intelligences." Gardner identifies seven different types of intelligence, each suited to a different educational approach: linguistic, mathematical logic, spatial, musical, bodily kinesthetic, intrapersonal, and interpersonal (self-knowledge). He also finds that educators have been selected on the basis of—and continue to restrict their teaching to—only the first two types of intelligence (Gardner, 1993).

In other studies of cognition, it has long been recognized that certain strategies improve the process of learning in any field. In describing "the thinking curriculum," psychologist Lauren Resnick confirms what most students know intuitively but what university educators ignore. Learning is indivisible from motivation, is enhanced by cooperative methods, and is far more effective through problem solving and participation rather than through rote or abstraction (Resnick and Klopfer, 1989). Students learn best when they enjoy what they are doing—when learning is an adventure rather than a repetitive chore, when they are motivated by positive incentives rather than through fear, when they work together cooperatively as a team, and when their learning is oriented toward solving problems.

As much as there has been a strong base of work to draw from in the theories of developing particular skills, so too has there been a line of theory and empirical testing of how to teach the skills and concepts for civic participation and for being an adult member of a healthy community. From Jean Piaget's work on stages of moral development in children to sociological studies of deviance, from applied research on reintegrating criminals back into society to responding to the needs of troubled children, there has been a century of experience on how to prepare citizens for a role in a democratic society (Piaget, 1977).

Furthermore, citizens cannot practice what they do not learn. They cannot reach consensus or negotiation or be expected to show tolerance if they have only been taught to compete with or ignore whole groups of people unlike themselves—groups with whom they never have contact from within the confines of university walls. They cannot participate actively in government or institutional oversight or in exercise of their legal rights if they have not had firsthand and regular exposure to how those institutions work; to what the laws are; and to using the courts, the media, or the governmental process. They cannot make complex policy decisions about international or domestic concerns if the evidence they receive is all secondary and held tightly by experts.

By claiming that citizens are not ready for democracy and that they need to be indoctrinated with a particular ethic, those who perpetuate the debates over America's moral and spiritual decline have made it a self-fulfilling philosophy. They have shut off access to the knowledge and skills that would allow participation and prevent the "chaos" they seem to fear when citizens demand to take the concept of democracy seriously (see, for example, Whyte, 1991; Fals-Borda and Rahman, 1991; Mason, 1982; Freire, 1970; Illich, 1971; and Phelan, Link, Stueve, and Moore, 1995).

Who Closed the American Mind?

If the American mind is closed, and no one person or group is really responsible, how did it become closed?

How is it that America retains an educational system in which one ideological faction or another can simply use the existing structure to indoctrinate—to reward adherence to or punish disagreement with the views of whatever authority takes control? How is it that in a country whose economic growth is a result of practical skill and ingenuity so little is really open for debate and challenge? How is it that institutions in which students are unable to hold their teachers' points of view up to the light of empirical reality and in which rewards are allocated on subjective grounds are cut off from community scrutiny and accountability?

To understand the contemporary shortcomings of higher education means standing back for an overview of the kinds of changes that have occurred in America in the last century, particularly as a result of the economic technological revolution, the rise of large industry, and the ascendance of the United States to a world power.

Prior to the industrial revolution, families provided much in the way of early education, and much of the rest came through apprenticeships—on-the-job training in small businesses. The United States was a country in which half of the workforce owned its own means of production—land or small businesses. Technology was simple. The basic unit of economic and social life was the family, and individual families were a part of small and stable communities. Democratic participation and moral values were parts of community life. Marriages and families were more stable because people were tied to their land, families, and businesses as part of their economic life.

The universities did not change that. Starting out as the equivalent of seminaries, universities mostly served a religious and bonding function for elite families, only slowly responding to the changes that came about with industrialization.

Today, less than 10 percent of Americans own their own means of production (Lempert, 1993); most Americans work for large corporations that buy and sell their labor. In such an economy, incomes are as unsteady as communities because laborers follow the movement of jobs in and out of communities—and now in and out of the country—something noticed by sociologists several decades ago (Lynd and Lynd, 1929, 1937; Warner, 1947). Corporations buy and sell labor rather than promote families or communities. In fact, corporations tear people out of these relationships (Harris, 1982). Although different public policies or educational models could have changed this, the public seems to have had too little power over the past century to have made a difference, and has less power now with the rise of global firms.

With the coming of more-specialized means of production, the teaching of specialized skills was placed in national institutions rather than communities. Individuals were uprooted from their communities and homogenized in these institutions located in or near urban centers. Through the nationalizing institutions of public schools and television, families were replaced by corporations and the state in their role as educators.

While it would have been possible to create different educational curricula oriented more toward community, toward the needs of the individual, or toward public policies centered more on family and morals, such a change did not occur. It is a modern fable to blame the social ills of modern life on the powerless minorities who were then immigrating to the country's shores to find work in the factories.

In the 1930s, a Senate commission laid out for the public record many facts of the workings of the country's institutions, indicating that industrial associations had begun a long and sophisticated campaign of "propaganda," including the sponsoring of public school curricula by rewriting the texts, and co-opting university professors through special dealings (U.S. Senate, 1935). Ultimately, it became an accepted fact of modern life that universities, through their boards of trustees and their funding structures, were tied to industry and the state rather than to the larger community (Tyack, 1974; Feldman, 1989).

The result is what one author describes as a paradigm in which education is now viewed as little more than the production of "human capital" for "competition" rather than the development of citizens in a productive society with a high quality of life. The "official ideology" of higher education is one that has become corporatist and bureaucratic (Slaughter, 1991).

Some popular sociologists, such as Alvin Toffler, view the current paradigm of education as representative of the social shift that occurred as the United States was transformed into an industrial administrative state—perhaps an appropriate role in the early years of industrialization but one that is now out of synchronization with the changing national and international economy and with individual and community needs. Two old ideas still remain in the minds of traditional educators: that the factory serves as the model for most modern institutions, including those in education, and that the university remains, in part, a religious institution that transmits dogma for elites and those recruited into elite positions (Toffler, 1980).

The political effects of the factory model of society and its educational institutions have been dramatized in startlingly descriptive terms even more poignant than its portrayal by early sociologists (Durkheim, 1893; Weber, 1947). William H. Whyte wrote of "the organization man" and the educational system that produces people as components (Whyte, 1956), or, as another critic put it, "personnel" (Goodman, 1967). Yablonsky has described the psychology of modern universities as "robot pathology" and its graduates as "robopaths" (1972). In other critiques, Ivan Illich (1971) gained notoriety for addressing the paternalistic effects of modern educational methods, while Stanley Milgram (1974), in his classic studies of obedience, pointed most directly to the dangers that could result from such training, even in a democratic society.

Educators in the traditional classroom, even those at top universities, often agree in private that the description of the problem and its potential consequences ring true. They see that students are adept in symbol manipulation: memorizing key words and facts with little understanding of the concepts and reality that they describe (Roszak, 1979). Many professors say it has even become a chore to teach for this reason.

To really understand the failure of the current paradigm is to see where it has already been successfully rejected in the university and where it is recognized as inadequate. At the heart of teaching the natural sciences, fields that fuel the technological growth demanded by an industrial society, is and remains laboratory experimentation and problem solving, though even science education is often narrowly directed toward specific types of exercises, approaches, and problems that support a particular pattern of scientific and technological development. Often with corporate funding and direction, schools purchase larger and more expensive equipment for faculty and student use in the sciences. By contrast, in the social sciences it is rare to find experiential laboratory work, just as practical exercises and skills development are unlikely to be found in many of the humanities or in professional training.

In addition to the sciences, a number of disciplines have long recognized the need for experiential education as well as student-generated objectives, projects, and forays into the community—

including drama, art, architecture, foreign languages, and communications. These are subjects that combine theory with participatory work as the best methods for teaching skills and concepts and holding student interest. Yet some of these subjects have also often fallen back on the simulated, mass-produced lecture or textbook approach to learning.

More than just arranging to meet industry's own needs, the industrial transformation of America has occasioned a cultural change as well—one in which disciplines that actually pose questions and address community issues have been silenced. To understand this is to see the cultural logic of modern industrial societies at work.

Re-creating the sense of community, overseeing large economic and public bureaucracies, and strengthening the sense of integrity and creativity in each individual would restore the democracy and initiative celebrated in this country's rhetoric as core values. But doing so would conflict with the need of the larger industries and dominant social groups to take the lion's share of resources out of communities—their best minds as well as their natural resources—and to weaken those bonds and identities that are seen as the greatest challenge to mass consumption, nationalism, and replaceability of individuals in the labor force (Galbraith, 1967; Lempert, forthcoming).

In a sense, critics like Allan Bloom and Dinesh D'Souza are examples of the products of such a society and its institutions of higher education; they have been raised to take their identities from these national institutions. The subconscious mission of their schools has been to train a new elite by taking people from family and community, reducing their community and family ties as a way of making them more effective as symbol manipulators and managers of the global bureaucracies.

Creating a mass culture—which is one of the goals of the university in industrial society—has entailed a process of standardizing behavior and removing differences other than those of social class and professional role. That is why the debate occurring today in academia and in the mass media is not over giving individuals the right to develop themselves—which is what one would expect to hear from those who believe in America's traditional (Revolutionary-era) values or from those who support the "multicultural" view—but over which groups will control (or win a slice of control over) the standardization process. In most disciplines, the church model of the university as a place for guarding sacred texts and dogmas behind a mystique of university teachings as "truths" survives today as it prepares its adherents to cite the right ancestors, repeat back the accepted dogmas, and uphold particular traditions.

At the same time, the preparation of workers for factories and hierarchies by mimicking those workplaces in the university has also meant substituting uniformity and conformity for creativity and experimentation. A great deal of the hidden curriculum in the university is about learning how to sit at a desk, please a superior, compete for rewards, and produce a little piece of a product without looking at the whole or questioning its implications. This is not about training citizens for democracy, for the values of family and community, or for a competitive market society; it is about training people to be obedient workers and to function as inert masses. It is essentially about social control (Illich, 1971; Roszak, 1979).

By recruiting certain groups for different levels in society and by creating networks and an esprit de corps among them, the university hierarchy maintains its role of segregating and perpetuating social classes and the barriers between them. The top universities continue to take the best young minds out of their home communities and bind them to others like themselves, disconnected in their ivory towers from both their home communities and the communities in which they are educated. Were this to change and the top universities were to encourage students to empathize with those whom they will manage, to view the less gifted and the less fortunate with tolerance, and to test the views of elites against the social reality, they would be less likely to enforce policies that deny the liberty and opportunity of those groups. The universities might advocate more-inclusive decision making, more-open media, more institutional oversight, and more participation. They might work to build their home communities rather than to protect the interests of their professional class. That does not seem to be part of their accepted mission.

Overall, to understand the contemporary flight of the social sciences and humanities into myth making rather than exploration of social reality, one must review the tortured history of the American university during the Cold War. This was a time in which the emphasis was on national unity, rapid production, and social control during the earlier years of industrialization and expansion of American influence. Only now is it possible to even begin writing about the impact of the Cold War on the university. In the debate from Buckley to Bloom, this critique can be found only in a few little-publicized responses, often by those who were domestic victims of the policy and were "rehabilitated" or began speaking out years later (see, for example, Kamin, 1993).

The impact of the Cold War on American education is an unfortunate one from the standpoint of scholarship, tolerance, academic freedom, and democratic values, though it could be seen to fit the objectives of an industrial society at war. Dozens of tenured professors lost their jobs at public and private universities in the 1950s—despite the rules guarding academic freedom and despite their not having been convicted of a crime—while others were harrassed or frightened. There were no forums to which they could appeal, because hiring decisions then, as today, were mostly private, closed-door affairs and were not publicly accountable. That history is only now being revealed (Keen, 1992; Robins, 1992; Diamond 1992; Schrecker, 1986).

Purges in America's academic institutions date back at least as far as the 1920s, as described in victims' reports collected in the book It Did Happen Here (Shultz and Shultz, 1989). When the purges occurred, those who were most likely to deviate and to face the wrath of the state for invoking the paper protections of the Bill of Rights were, not surprisingly, minorities. By 1950, for example, 8 percent of university faculty members were Jewish, and they were well overrepresented in the purges' roster of victims (Lewis, 1988, p. 39).

In *Cold War on Campus*, Lionel Lewis noted that the McCarthy-era purges were based less on nationalistic fervor and willingness to condemn an ideology (which in itself was not very well defined) than on administrative control (Lewis, 1988, p. 197). "Communism" was only a secondary and symbolic issue. The goal of university officials was to make sure they had a faculty that did not bring unwanted attention to the university through the non-conformity of any of its members. In describing one of the purges in a small college and its impact more than thirty years later, McCormick described the American university as a "nest of vipers" (1989). Retreating from the community was a form of self-protection, though it was ultimately self-defeating.

Then, as today, there was no objective standard for measuring the performance of faculty members, and what standard did exist was based on politics rather than on competence in transmitting skills or in discovering new knowledge. Only over time did other factions emerge to exert their own political control over particular departments or faculties in a ghettoization and fragmentation of the university (Meisler, 1984; Lewis, 1975).

In measuring the preliminary effect of the McCarthy-era purges on intellectual life in the university around 1958, two social scientists, Lazarsfeld and Thielens (with the help of pollster Lou Harris), found widespread self-censorship in the personal activities of university teachers and in their formation of the curriculum during these "difficult years" (Lazarsfeld and Thielens, 1958).

While those effects may have disappeared over time, they may also just have taken other forms. The effect of 1960s politics on universities has yet to be fully documented yet rumors abound within the university community of politically active professors never receiving tenure during that period and of universities seeking better methods of attaining social control over potential challenges from students following the student revolts and demonstrations. The most recent in the series of stories, for example, is the notice that while the State of California has cut faculty hiring in its public universities, it has nonetheless increased funding for S.W.A.T. teams on campuses where low crime rates little justify them (Lee, 1994).

In the 1990s, university faculties are still the self-selected disciples of those who survived the purges of the 1950s and those who were socialized in the 1970s and 1980s, eras of more subtle mechanisms of fear and conformity that were only reinforced by declining resources for those who would seek the room to experiment.

The reality of American universities in the 1990s is not that they are battlegrounds between a mainstream culture and a pluralistic potpourri of competing intellectual traditions and approaches to education. Most of the competing traditions have been removed. The newest members of the academy's upper ranks may have different pigments to their skin and a second X chromosome instead of a Y, but they rose within the same structures and were rewarded and selected directly by their predecessors (and competitors). The battle, instead, is between two types of understandably cautious and warring camps facing dwindling resources and seeking to protect themselves in whatever coalitions they can find.

One group, long rewarded for conforming to the large institutions of the industrial state, seeks to maintain the universities as the equivalents of theological enclaves. This group sees any knowledge gained through social science or humanities as a means of controlling resources or people and as a way to maintain security and stability and to replicate American culture in places it has yet to spread.

The other group seeks to control the same levers and to gain positions for its members and those like them who have previously been excluded, but members of this group are afraid—perhaps in response to backlashes following attempts to rethink education in the 1960s—or lack any current models for introducing competing educational approaches. Rather than revel in knowledge, openness, and democracy, many in this group have sought to make the mind an escape into itself, to use humanities and social sciences as a tool for writing their own histories and for sponsoring new sets of myths. Their action is a reaction, a kind of game unto itself (Gross and Levitt, 1994).

Together, both groups really represent an anachronism: a university structure geared toward a war that is over and toward an age of uniform mass production that has long passed (Toffler, 1980). Because the penalties for educational innovation during those eras were so strong, it is understandable why both groups would be afraid and unwilling to ask their students and their communities how they can work together to design an educational system that deals with reality and incorporates everyone's interests and needs, one that treats everyone with equal dignity and objective standards and seeks to benefit all.

In a sense, the past has poisoned the mission of the university and made it difficult to restore it to its educational ends. There is no one group to "blame," and no group with authority has the answer. This is the reality; the solution depends on working together to establish a more objective standard and a different set of rules that meet current needs and incorporate this country's best traditions.

Building on Past Traditions to Remake the University

The educational models described in this book represent a different intellectual tradition from what has become the dominant model of American education in the past decades. Yet at the same time, these models spring from American traditions and a long history of experimentation, pragmatism, participation, and community. That is where the debate over higher education must shift: back to these principles.

The success of the projects described in this book, and their potential for being applied with equal success elsewhere, is the result of several decades of innovations—successes and failures— that have kept alive a countertradition of promise and renewal. We cannot name all of these successes or document the work of all of those who are now quietly and courageously innovating in higher education. However, we can try to shift the debate in order to help open a forum for discussing their ideas as we compliment them by incorporating and repeating the best aspects of their work as we make these ideas accessible to others through the models that we present.

Students and educators can only take inspiration and delight, as we do, in the successes and the increasing demand for clinical education (that is, learning acquired by students as they provide professional services in clinics of numerous kinds) and service learning. For example, we incorporate some of the best attributes of the work of law schools when they create educational experiences combining theory, acquisition of professional skills, and community service through the establishment of legal clinics in which student attorneys are supervised by faculty and professionals, projects that are often initiated by students. We build on the idea of clinical course work by applying it on a broader and deeper level, expanding from specific professional skills to policymaking and community development.

The goal of service—the basis of President Clinton's Americorps initiative, for example—draws heavily from the successful experience of universities like Rutgers (using theories developed by leading educators such as Benjamin Barber, 1992) and represents some of the same traditions. We applaud the history of internships and voluntarism in education, and we also use these models to go further. We take a broader view of what constitutes a participatory experience and service and place it firmly in the context of the educational mission of developing skills, insight, awareness, and "multicultural literacy" (LaGuardia and Guth, 1993). Beyond placing students in existing institutions as observers or apprentices, we have designed and tested programs and model curricula in which students study particular institutions and critique them as objective observers, in which they work as teams to develop larger solutions of which those institutions may just be a part.

The tradition and approach of field trips also runs parallel with the solutions offered in this book, as do student-initiated courses, peer learning, and seminars. We incorporate their best features and go beyond them to establish a new partnership between students and the community—a partnership in which students are not tourists but active participants in seeking solutions to public problems in all spheres, from sciences to the arts, and in which students offer their contributions in public forums.

Many of our ideas have some of their roots in experiments made during the 1960s and 1970s at some of the top universities in this country. Without those experiments, the student adventures described in this book would never have been possible. In a few cases, we have found not only that such adventures did exist at one time in America's most prominent universities but that they continue to exist in different forms at scattered places throughout the United States. We only wish that the successes, failures, and disappearance of some of the past programs had been documented, as we seek to document our work, since those experiences would be invaluable guides to achieving greater effectiveness in educational reform today.

In studying that legacy both in the universities with which we have been affiliated and elsewhere, we have sought to learn from past mistakes. We believe that we have been able to incorporate many valid criticisms in order to strengthen our projects and educational models and to widen their bases of support. We recognize that many past criticisms address important issues, as well as, perhaps, serving as unfortunate and unavoidable realities of American life. It is this legacy that has led us to seek not only an academically stronger and more grounded approach but also one that is more inclusive, pragmatic, cost effective, and community oriented than several previous models, including those that are expanding today in the form of internships and service learning.

First, the strength of our approach has been to avoid formal politics or bias and to seek incorporation wherever possible; to build coalitions with, for example, a former Reagan speechwriter (a professor who sponsored and institutionalized one of the student-taught courses described in this work) as well as with teachers considered to be on the political "left." The materials presented and the people and places visited in curricula that we support cut across the whole political and cultural spectrum—by design and by the demands of intellectual rigor and objectivity. We seek to work directly with the community and to build into the approaches a sense of cooperation and exchange as well as an openness to all views and approaches.

Second, the educational programs that we have designed are more than just "exposure" to new experiences or attempts to develop survival skills in the wild, and they are more than partisan efforts to involve students in service. The academic, theoretical, and skills components of our model curricula and courses are strong. We have worked alongside established faculty to complement existing courses and approaches in order to reinforce learning, to test theory, and to build skills.

Furthermore, the key differences between the student adventures described here and the student-initiated seminars and field projects offered elsewhere are our programs' broader reach and attention to skills and democracy. The guiding philosophy of student adventures is to incorporate students in the educational process and to treat them as partners alongside their teachers, encouraging their independent thought and measuring their skills rather than their conformity to particular teachers or texts.

The programs that we have designed are not make-work or regimented exercises, nor are they offerings of inexpensive labor to existing institutions in which students serve in subordinate roles. The vision that we have implemented is one designed by and led by students, empowering them in a democratic and participatory atmosphere to take an active role in designing their own education, in teaching others, and in contractually setting objective standards by which to measure their progress.

Finally, we have designed student adventures not only for basic university courses and exploration but also for development of qualitative and professional skills at advanced and interdisciplinary levels. Our programs provide not only challenges to and tests of current theories, but also sophisticated exercises in building theoretical models and encouraging student participation in public policy and the building of institutions at state-of-the-art levels.

Our Experience with a New Model

Overall, we have created an "escape" from the shackling confines of the ivory tower. We have sought to recreate education as an adventure in learning, based on books and theory as well as experience, starting with students' intellectual curiosity and interests in a democratic format and combining the best features of education and scholarship with the best American traditions of community and participation.

The adventures described in this book began with an experiment in a single course and expanded to several courses and projects. They now constitute a full university social science curriculum with models for humanities and natural science courses at the university level as well as for professional and graduate school programs and for secondary schools.

An Introductory Political Science/ Public Policy Laboratory Course

Our first experiment, in 1985, was a quiet one: an introductory course taught by a graduate/professional student at Stanford University through field work and visits to the "unseen" aspects of American life. The idea behind The Unseen America was to introduce democratic education in the context of an introductory political science and policy course that would challenge and supplement the political science department's traditional course, Major Issues in American Public Policy. Rather than merely reading about political issues of poverty and homelessness, immigration, defense, crime, and economic stagnation, our course offered field trips in which students could test the theories with their own observations and research.

An Introductory Social Science Theory and Philosophy Course

Two years later, The Unseen America was followed by a bolder experiment under the same course title. Three undergraduates at the University of California at Berkeley chose to apply the course's basic principles and concepts and teach their own version, demonstrating its broader appeal and its ability to incorporate peer learning. That course was sponsored by five departments in the social sciences and humanities—political science, anthropology, history, conservation and resource studies, and peace and conflict studies. In a sense, the course was really an introduction to philosophy and social science theory. Following its well-publicized initial success, the course is now a permanent feature of the political science curriculum. It has now been taught for eight years and is in its fourth generation of student instructors at Berkeley.

An Intermediate Sociology Course on Marginal Groups

One year later, in 1989, three Stanford undergraduates applied the same set of concepts to designing their own version of The Unseen America, turning the attention of the course to particular policy issues and expanding its approach. That course, also called The Unseen America, has continued off and on at Stanford, with different foci, through two more generations of students.

An Introductory Anthropology Laboratory Course

Also in 1989, on the strength of a proposal written on behalf of a faculty member, and on a suggestion to a graduate student—the Department of Anthropology at the University of California at Berkeley used the techniques sharpened in the first three courses to implement a laboratory social science course alongside its existing introductory theory course and as a supplement to it. Concentrating on applying the methodologies of anthropological field work in the community surrounding the university, this course entered the curriculum as the introduction to anthropology through laboratory work.

Following the success of the first two courses at the introductory and intermediate levels, we tested the idea one step further, with advanced undergraduates.

An Interdisciplinary Project in Economic Development in Latin America

In 1988, students from Harvard and Brown accepted the challenge to travel to a developing country (Ecuador) to write their own development plan for the country. This was a test of our educational techniques in an upper-level accredited overseas project. The students presented a plan—written in a foreign language and prepared in three months—to the president of the country and defended the plan on national television and in the press. They have now gone on to publish their plan in a book for both scholars and practitioners in the development field (Lempert, Mitchell, and McCarty, 1995).

In addition to these particular courses and projects under the rubric of The Unseen America (which we turned into a California nonprofit corporation in hopes of making our materials and expertise more widely available to students and faculty), we have also experimented with model curricula at a variety of levels—for example, a sociology of law course for advanced undergraduates—and with experiential methods and grading options.

We have proposed a variety of courses and clinical projects in the United States and in Eastern Europe and Southeast Asia, and we have participated in and observed the efforts of others. We pull all of these experiences together to discuss the possibilities in this book.

Overall, our ideas stem from very simple concepts about the individual, about education, and about democracy. They are simple, but when they are put together—which is the secret of this book—they are powerful. They are self-activating and replicating. They build on themselves and grow.

2

The Birth of Student Adventures

This chapter tells the story of the birth of student adventures largely as David Lempert described it in his diary at the time. He has updated some of the material, but it still captures the flavor and energy that lay behind the creation of a new educational model at Stanford University.

The year was 1984. I was in my last year of an expensive professional program for combined degrees in business and law at Stanford University. I was returning from a year overseas, and I wasn't looking forward to going back to an educational system that seemed uninspired and oblivious to much of what I had seen in the world and to the needs of real people. I particularly didn't like the feeling of being on a conveyor belt, trained to be an automaton in a big corporate law firm, investment bank, or consulting firm or for a military contractor. That is what most of my classmates (and now, my former students) were and are doing, and that is the role for which Stanford was preparing its graduates.

I wasn't eager to fill one of those slots, though I tried them for several summers and knew that the material rewards were good. Such positions financed much of my Stanford education, and I filled them well when I had to. I was wined and dined and flown across the country by recruiters seducing me to fill one of these roles for my career. Nevertheless, I didn't really see how putting my energies and talent to work on behalf of institutional entities would contribute to solving America's domestic and international problems and to helping those who were being left behind in America. It seemed that I would become part of the problem if I just filled a slot.

I had worked around the clock just to earn the money for expenses and to pass my courses. I didn't want to hear a constant sales pitch for fitting mindlessly into an institution and finding myself on a conveyor to an unhappy future. I wanted to feel that I was developing real skills, that I could make a difference in the world, and that I would not have to sacrifice my identity in the process.

Over the course of that year, however, I managed to learn a great deal more than I had ever expected—a lesson that went far beyond what was in the formal curriculum and that was well worth its price. If a university is designed as a place to help students pull confusing ideas together, even if to come up with a troubling picture, for me, Stanford did just that. My return to Stanford showed me something terrifying that I had never expected to see. Mostly, I owed my new perspective to my travels, but returning to the university helped me to process my experiences. For me, Stanford opened a window into aspects of America that I wouldn't have seen if I hadn't worked during a year away from the university. My year abroad held up the reality of the university and American society for me in a way I had never noticed before. It provided me with both the inspiration and the sense of urgency to change it. It also showed me how.

There is nothing like travel to help one come back with a refreshing perspective. I had had the fortunate experience to find some of the most interesting internships in the world—those that I designed myself. They were not accredited but were funded with a special grant from my Stanford Graduate School of Business classmates and a percentage of their earnings from the corporate world. In general, internships take people from subservience in one institution to insignificance in another. But my internships deepened my perspective on how different institutions work.

I spent part of the year in the Philippines as part of the U.S. Agency for International Development (USAID), the U.S. government's foreign "aid" program. I was assigned to use my business and legal skills to look at the effect a recent constitutional provision in President Ferdinand Marcos's personally designed constitution would have on the country's development. At the time, American tax money was being spent to prop up Marcos's regime—a government that had just assassinated a political rival, Benigno Aquino, on his return from exile in America. Within the U.S. diplomatic community, as well as among officials in the Marcos government, were graduates of the same schools I had attended or was attending. I discovered that few of these officials seemed to care about what was happening in the Philippines, but they designed elaborate mythologies and defenses to shield themselves from what they didn't want to see. The actual institutional structures and the psychological mechanisms were as complex and fascinating as they were tragic.

In addition to my time in the Philippines, I also spent part of the year inside the U.S. Embassy in Costa Rica, at a time when the U.S. government was funding a secret war in Nicaragua and when government officials were lying to Congress and the American people about it. It was an eye-opening experience for an American citizen—one that few citizens had.

Overseas, I learned how dictators maintained their authority and how U.S.-backed illegal wars happened even when they contradicted basic American beliefs. In my final year at Stanford, I realized where the system needed to be—and could be—changed to stop the pattern from repeating ad infinitum.

Overall, by the time I returned, these experiences had given me an entirely new perspective on the university about the values it was instilling in its elite graduates and what they did with their education. What I saw quite clearly, after my eyes had been opened overseas, was how the elite universities worked as places that:

- Create isolation and promote the building of networks and an esprit de corps among elites, with a reverence for property and status.

- Prepare their graduates for segregated living environments.
- Teach the upwardly mobile how to fit into the upper class and shed their ties to the communities from which they came.
- Teach a very subtle disrespect for democratic freedoms while promoting the universities' own "intellectual" culture to the disparagement of others.
- Keep world events out of the classroom other than in "acceptable" ways.
- Discourage dissent outside of certain preset boundaries.
- Protect and insulate themselves.
- Distort American democracy and the perception of it while demonstrating the lesson of social control through force.
- Train the leaders of foreign dictatorships.

And they do all of this within the form of the curriculum and the university structure itself, regardless of the content of specific courses.

All throughout my Stanford experiences, in the classroom and without, I heard the echoes of subtle forms of control in a variety of ways.

University Preparation for Stratification and Separation

The one thing that I looked forward to most in returning to Stanford was being able to interact with the diverse group of students that entered the university as undergraduates, before they became assimilated into the institution. In many ways, I had found a coziness among the undergraduates at Stanford that I had not found elsewhere. Not only were they full of energy, but in the Stanford residences, there was a real effort to create community through group activities, recreation, and supportive counselors. Being among undergraduates as a teacher or resident adviser or older friend didn't require me to hide my own identity and blend in or to discard my interests and the things that made me unique, as I felt I had to do with my own cohorts.

As a professional student among undergraduates, it was easy to accept the belief that the university was a place of equal opportunity and meritocracy and that it provided a way up the social ladder while leading to a society of greater tolerance and understanding. Indeed, Stanford and other elite schools pride themselves on their numbers of minority students and scholarship students from poor families.

What I began to see for the first time, however, was how this new Stanford "community," this blending and melding, actually did just the opposite of what it was supposed to. Rather than create tolerance, it forged its own identity among students in a way that reinforced professional and class divisiveness between its graduates and everyone else. By raising a few people up the economic ladder and erasing their pasts and connections to their places of origin in the creation of a new identity, it impoverished communities. It was, overall, a process that created feelings in students of separation from most Americans, a set of elite bonds, and a disdain for the democratic process. But it all occurred under the comfortable pretext of harmony and a veneer of unity. I had bought the myth at first because I was one of the excluded—a middle-class kid whose grandparents were immigrants and who wanted to believe all of the American Dream.

In fact, at elite institutions like Stanford, families of almost *all* students earn more than the median income for American families (Katchadourian and Boli, 1985; "Equality to Me, Bias to You," 1995). While scholarships may continue to bring in some minority students, the separation of students by ethnicity and class, the difficulties the less privileged face, and their high attrition rate continue.

Many believe that class divisions between public and private universities have worsened in recent years, just as they have between inner-city schools and suburban or private schools. At private universities, for example, increasing tuition has meant that fewer and fewer students have parents who work in education or in the public interest (fields of decreasing salaries and status in the West), a phenomenon that may be resegregating schools and opportunities on the basis of political outlook of families as well as their economic status. But I had to be hit by the reality before I could come to this realization and to see how it all worked.

The first shock hit me when I was looking for a place to live. The year before I left Stanford, I had lived in Branner Hall, the university's biggest and liveliest freshman dormitory. It was cozy and squeaky clean, filled with cherubic faces and healthy bodies and laughter. Harsh realities intruded only in minor ways, and because Branner was a place that felt like home, it didn't matter. Branner was comfortable and warm. It was a big family of hugs and eyes filled with wonder and energy, chocolate-chip cookie nights and talent shows and a dorm newspaper and a grand living room and a courtyard with magnolia trees.

Branner Hall was one of the few places I have ever thought of as home. I could have gone back there to work as a resident assistant, but I didn't. That kind of transition and mobility—having to meet a whole new stream of people every year and spend less time with old friends—may be part of modern American life, but it is hard. I wanted to be in touch with something familiar for just a little while before I would have to move again at the end of the year and maybe again soon after that.

Instead, I applied to change my position to a different residence, where some of the 180 students I had known in Branner, who were then juniors, would be living.

That ordinarily wouldn't be a problem, and for me, it shouldn't have been. But, while having been part of efforts to create cohesion and good feeling, I had also acted independently and had encouraged students to value their heritages, to think for themselves, and to ask questions. As a political science teaching assistant, before I ever was a resident assistant (RA), I had sometimes worn costumes to class to add excitement to the material. As an RA in Branner, I put together a speaker series. As president of the Stanford Law

Forum, I brought a number of celebrities and experts to speak at the Law School, and I set up several new programs to improve alumni-student and faculty-student relations. In Branner, I wrote poems and stories for the dorm newspaper and participated in skits and plays. People also knew me by my articles in the student newspaper, the *Stanford Daily*, with suggestions for exhibiting student art, protecting student history (achievements, mentions, artwork, and political legacies that too often disappeared or were whitewashed out of university memory), and stimulating intellectual life.

That is why I couldn't understand it when the Office of Residential Education told me it didn't want me in the upper-class residences. I was too "East Coast," one administrator explained —something that someone many years later told me might have meant "too Jewish." I was too energetic, they said; I had "too many" ideas and didn't "fit in" with the "Stanford concept of education in the residences."

"It's not that they don't like you," one administrator explained. "It's that you make them start to question what they're doing. They just want people who do things the way they've always been doing them, and who will enforce their policies." As a professional student who hadn't been an undergraduate at Stanford, I was told that I didn't have a strong enough "Stanford ethic." I didn't quite understand what being like everyone else had to do with my ability to educate, which I thought meant challenging students to think while gaining their respect, friendship, and trust. But I slowly began to realize that the Stanford commitment to diversity was only skin deep and that it didn't extend to approaches or ideas.

Stanford's administrators claimed that what they wanted were educators and innovators in the dorms: people who cared about students and the university and who would help minimize drinking and encourage academic and intellectual life. But the actual priorities, revealed in their pronouncements and where they placed their advertising and resources, were very different. As RAs, my peers and I did our best to create new speaker programs and dorm newspapers and intellectual discussions, which is what we were hired to do. But these were begrudgingly funded and rarely praised. It seemed that the university wanted something else.

Stanford encouraged RAs to help sell football tickets and to bring students out to sponsored sporting events and tailgate parties, which is where some of the heaviest drinking occurred and where entering students learned that it was an acceptable part of the university culture. The administrators wanted us to help provide information about fraternities and sororities but balked at suggestions that we sponsor discussions about whether the university should have such organizations and whether they were appropriate in an institution that claimed it promoted students on merit and abhorred discrimination and special privilege of any kind.

The administrators encouraged us to sponsor events on academic majors and other requirements that were designed to force students into a structure of rules, but they didn't like it when we asked for help in setting up discussions on the concept of majors itself as a means of tracking and narrowing that interfered with intellectual life and with democratic free choice.

They encouraged events such as Viennese Balls and formal parties, where students learned how to dress in tuxedos and suits; happy hours, cocktail parties, and "sherry hours" with professors, where students learned the arts of small talk and social drinking; and casino nights, where administrators staffed the roulette tables and where students dressed up in pearls and diamonds or as mobsters.

We were encouraged to bring new students out to band rallies, bonfires (where they now burn effigies), official ceremonies, and speeches by the university president and other key officials, even if the students weren't interested and wanted to spend time reading or thinking on their own.

It seemed that they wanted us to instill in students an uncritical loyalty to the institution and the Stanford name rather than a spirit of discovery and learning. The mission seemed to be one of protecting the institution itself and its prominence and funding, instead of fulfilling an educational mission. The mission went beyond socializing students into certain values. Some of the "education" and "counseling" turned out to mean that students were even policing other students. Administrators were in control of the living environment and channels of expression and art and space and all growing things on the campus.

As I had found out a year earlier, anything that interfered with administrative control—including something as insignificant as students' leaving their names or designs in wet cement—was termed "structural damage" and fined. Student educators were supposed to enforce those policies and name names. As a law student, I refused to enforce policies that violated students' rights to due process. I informed administrators that they might be in breach of their contract with students. Since I had earned students' confidence in privileged relationships and was hired to protect them, I felt that it was ethically, morally, and professionally wrong to turn in students for actions that weren't clearly offenses. This belief cost me my job.

It was then that I saw something else as well: how administrators viewed students. I heard administrators refer to students in general, in our presence, as "hoodlums" and by other derogatory names. They seemed afraid of the young people they had admitted, and it was difficult or impossible for students even to have access to the people who were supposed to provide them with services.

Overall, there seemed to be much less interest in education than in building a group identity and achieving social control.

I was startled by flashbacks from the year I had spent abroad. Life at Stanford seemed to parallel what was part of a strategy of community control in dictatorships like China and Marcos's Philippines—control that started at the top and worked its way down. At Stanford, the control was so subtle, and so accepted, that it never even came up for debate.

The Segregated Living Environment

Because I had not been invited back to work as a resident educator at Stanford, I needed to find a place to live. Since I wanted to be part of the university community, I looked for something near campus. At Stanford, one has three choices: suburban housing on campus, suburban housing off campus, and housing for poor students in the slums of East Palo Alto, more than three miles away.

A fourth option was to put myself more heavily in debt and live like other professional students, in expensive homes or apartments off campus. But then I would have had to put on what my law and business school classmates were calling "golden handcuffs" and mortgage my freedoms. The debt would have ensured that I would start out in life at the same corporate law firms or investment banks or consulting firms as my classmates, just to pay it off. This was how the system seemed to work: closing off choices a little at a time.

I wanted to be on campus to mix with people and to be surrounded by ideas—interactions that I wouldn't find in Stanford's suburbs or East Palo Alto's slums. Being off campus in a suburban home or apartment reminded me of the life of the American diplomatic community overseas: cut off from everything and living alone in luxury, removed from ideas and people and therefore choosing policies that ignored the public interest. Professional students were supposed to make that choice.

Law school started a month before everything else, so I decided to wait for the arrival of my undergraduate friends and see if I could find a common household of people in different disciplines and backgrounds. But my friends weren't the same as they had been more than a year before, when they were curious, energetic freshmen. As juniors, they were busy packaging themselves for jobs and weaving their way through organizational structures, without having time to think about what they were doing. "Why don't you live with your own kind?" some of them told me. "You're a professional student. Why don't you do what they do?"

They were reflecting the reality that we don't really mix people in American society. Ties to family and community have been replaced with ties to professional roles and disciplines and specific institutions. As I came to realize later, this separation reinforces itself. Once you fall out of a defined group and social role, you lose many of the measures of your existence.

I started to see, then, why it was so important for students to identify strongly with Stanford—or when they left Stanford, with the organization they worked for or the degree they held. The way they were defined, and how they saw themselves, was by organizational affiliation. That was their identity. It gave them a role to play and afforded them a certain degree of comfort and belonging in a society in which there was little real community.

Stanford didn't train its graduates to set up their own organizations or to be economically independent. They were trained to earn their livelihood from large institutions. In a society of millions of people with tremendous mobility, without an institutional affiliation they would be out of place and unknown. As Stanford graduates, they were scared of being alone and without an affiliation. I learned from the experience not only about segregation among professions but also about how Stanford groomed its graduates for upper-class life—removing themselves economically from most Americans in a life-style in which they became surrounded by possessions and by others who had the same things. It was something that no longer had any meaning for me, if it ever had.

Rationalizing Entry into the Upper Class

In the course of my year overseas, I couldn't easily carry property with me, and I really didn't need it. And when I did have possessions, I felt guilty precisely because of what I had seen there that I never would see on the Stanford campus.

Throughout my year at Stanford following my return from the Philippines, I had recurring waking nightmares of hungry kids begging and sleeping in the streets of Manila where I had worked. I could see their faces and their imploring eyes and hear their stomachs growling and their shrill cries asking me for just one piso (about five cents) because they were hungry.

No ten-year-old Filipino child asks to live in the Manila streets, spending his life selling newspapers in traffic and begging for pennies and picking through garbage dumps, while his older sister prostitutes herself so that maybe he can buy clothes. Similarly, no American child asks to grow up malnourished in our slums.

The reality of America, and of most college campuses, is that we never have to see those kids living on the streets or think about them in any real way—not in college or afterward, when graduates can afford to move to the suburbs. If you start to think you need to explain it, you might be told, as I was, that thinking about it isn't normal. Conformity is enforced with a simple but double-edged phrase: "You need professional help, because you aren't like us."

I couldn't justify paying $400 a month for an apartment; that was the equivalent of taking ten Filipino kids off the streets and giving them at least the chance for something better in life. I didn't want to mortgage my future choices by taking on an additional $5,000 in debt, nor did I want to surround myself with possessions. I made personal choices that were comfortable to me and had come out of my experiences overseas, and these choices made me realize how differently everyone else was being socialized within the traditional campus environment.

Everyone who had known me before I went overseas was complaining and trying to interfere in my personal choice. While my unusual choice of life-style was not unhealthy for me or harmful to anyone else, the strength of my belief seemed to shatter the images on which my peers had been raised of how they were supposed to lead their lives and how people like me were supposed to live. The disapproval caught me by surprise.

My undergraduate friends told me how they couldn't understand how I could be happy without surrounding myself with material possessions and without fitting into what was a stereotyped professional role. My sense of self and attempt to be a caring human being upset them as they were making up their minds about their own lives and heard other messages everywhere around them.

Their reaction was confusing to me, because most of these friends were people I had always thought were much more considerate and understanding than I was. I had always been afraid to demonstrate for my political beliefs because, even though I read that I had political rights, I knew that campus police took pictures at university demonstrations, and I thought it would ruin my career in some unexplained way if the campus police or classmates saw me there. Since I had been raised to believe in hard work and competition, I had always felt that most of the undergraduates I knew spent more time making friends or seeing their families or demonstrating for a cause—more than I ever allowed myself to do—and that I was the one who was afraid. I had been raised to be politically afraid and to value achievement and success. In my experiences abroad, however, I was suddenly confronted with the implications of my own behavior, and I found the voice to recognize my fears more openly and to act with much more confidence in my own choices. It was this confidence that seemed to scare everyone around me, perhaps making them feel uneasy about themselves.

I didn't even begin to understand, until an acquaintance took me aside and told me, "Dave, you have the American Dream. You don't have just one—you have the two best degrees in the country. You have everything. Everybody here wants what you have. That's what we're all supposed to be striving for and what we're slaving over. But you're not happy with it. You're showing us it's all wrong. How are we supposed to react to you? What happens to me if I say that you're right? What will happen to me if I start asking questions and trying to change things? You can do these things, but we can't."

It was a troublesome echo of something I had heard in the Philippines under Marcos: Filipinos who said that they were scared and just too paralyzed to do anything, even though they disagreed with the policies of the regime they lived under. For years, they had done nothing.

Somehow, the dream that Stanford students had programmed into their consciousness was one of private accumulation far beyond the point of simple comfort and good health. It was a dream of wearing the clothes that someone else has told them to wear, of conforming their bodies and grooming in certain ways, of being confined in cubicles and tall buildings, and of being isolated from whole groups of "undesirable" people. It was a regimen of following organizational rules and believing in (or at least not challenging) the benevolence of business or government, and of seeking escape without posing a challenge.

It was a dream of private wealth and public squalor, of intricate rationalizations that would take away responsibility and guilt while allowing Stanford students to take for granted all the luxuries and privileges they had—or were being prepared to receive—and to convince themselves that they deserved it. For me, that was somebody else's dream. I had seen too much suffering and indifference from those who were privileged and well educated to be able to close my eyes and walk away without trying to make a difference.

At Stanford, there were no alternative philosophies or core communities to help me reinforce my views. The pressures there to accept a different standard and one way of viewing the world were enormous. It was a community in isolation; that was why people around me accepted the roles that Stanford gave them and tossed away what they had been before if it didn't "fit."

Ideology in the Classroom

I soon returned to my old job as a teaching assistant in the political science department, and in no time, I was conducting class demonstrations—for example, dressing as Alexis de Tocqueville for discussions of *Democracy in America,* a book that grew on me the more I read it.

However, I began to notice something different in the Stanford classrooms that frightened me, that I hadn't seen before. I first noticed it on exam answers when I graded essays. They contained such jarring statements as "the proper balance between liberty and equality is a fifty-fifty split," as if, in the view of the student, liberty and equality were little different from commodities on a stock exchange. "The proper balance is the one we have now because everyone has equality," another student wrote. "Our biggest mistake in Vietnam was not bombing more heavily," wrote a student who had never been to an Asian village. "All the poor in America are lazy bums," wrote yet another student who had never been poor or met anyone who was.

It seemed that, to Stanford students, education was just a meaningless stream of words. What students were being taught, even about democracy, was something they could memorize out of a book or lecture. The process of university education seemed to be premised on the belief that students could demonstrate their understanding of something as fundamental as American democracy merely by reciting some sort of a pledge, repeating a slogan, or waving the American flag.

The good answers disturbed me as much as the bad ones. In the lectures, the best students just repeated back the facts the same way they had gotten them. The concepts were just words. The best students just knew how to use the words more skillfully.

When I thought about it, I realized that as an undergraduate, I had done the same thing, and had done it better than almost anyone. Conformity was the key to success as an undergraduate at Yale, where I had taken several honors. In law school, too, conformity was the name of the game. In undergraduate classes, I would usually say exactly what professors wanted to hear. Even though I knew that on paper I had a right to free speech, the truth was that the more I agreed with the professor, the higher the grades I was awarded, and the higher the grades, the better chance I had for professional advancement, scholarships, and high salaries. Cynically, I censored myself and played the game, and it worked just as it was supposed to, opening the door to material wealth and status.

Reading those exam answers was disillusioning and an unpleasant awakening for me. Every time I saw an answer that mentioned something new and thoughtful or that tried to stress ideals or moral values, I realized that those were the answers I was supposed to penalize as incorrect.

The message I was receiving and enforcing was that the universities were more concerned with teaching a very specific and limited set of technical skills—particularly paper skills devoid of content—than they were with helping students to develop an intrinsic and gut appreciation of how those skills might be used.

What I saw was that university "social science" was being conducted and taught in a vacuum. Certain work was defined as rigorous because the way in which the symbols were manipulated was the way things had always been done in the discipline.

There is never true value neutrality in the social sciences, but since students weren't being asked to solve problems or make measurements, what was left was just presentation of predetermined "facts" or "concepts" that they were supposed to write down from lectures or find in textbooks, and on which they were to be graded as if all they had been given was objective and neutral.

In my role as a teaching assistant (the apprenticeship for the job of professor), I ranked students on how well they could take their human emotion and understanding out of political issues and replace them with whatever biases the professors gave them through preselection of facts and approaches. Sometimes the professors used mathematics instead of esoteric polysyllabic words, but there was little in these approaches that was "objective" or "neutral" or grounded in observations of real phenomena. The only thing objective was that the political or ideological line was being enforced by a group of like-minded people. As teachers, our job was to mark how well students could deal with concepts as abstract words, could memorize facts, and could psych out the professors.

If we didn't give the best marks to the students who regurgitated the best and whose values were the most malleable, the students would come up afterward and fight for points. "How could you mark me wrong?" they would ask. After all, they were just following orders. They were just doing their job—and so was I. The defense that had not worked at the Nuremberg trials seemed to be the rationalization that buttressed the intellectual order in American social science.

The pressure for conformity and the elements of control are worse the higher up in the hierarchy one rises, both in academia and in the professions. The difference is that the higher one rises, the more skill one requires to figure out what the rewarded perspective is, and the more there is at stake. For a minority, it means having to learn to mimic an entire new culture and way of thinking. That was what I was experiencing at one level, as a middle-class New York–born Jew whose grandparents had been immigrants. For my friends of color, the process was even more difficult.

I soon came to realize what the debate about strengthening the teaching of humanities and "great books" courses was really about, too, buried beneath the fancy argument. It was about finding a way to require students from diverse backgrounds to play a game they couldn't win; where their "success" would be judged on how well and how quickly they could erase their previous identities and substitute a new one. It was a game in which they would be asked to write papers and would be graded on whether or not they could come up with "valid" interpretations (from the perspective of whomever is deciding what those interpretations are) and phrase them in a culturally predetermined way.

Some people think that having a few professors of different perspectives, or professors who claim that they give students better grades for original thought, would help even things out. But it can't because the game is always the same. At best, all it does is create little ghettos in the universities, where those who feel they would be discriminated against take more courses while sacrificing greater learning. I recognize it as the same game that was taught to me from the very beginning of my education, going back to primary school, back to "Simon Says" and "Follow the Leader."

Democratic Freedoms and the University's "Intellectual" Culture

What this sort of education is doing to America—as a culture and as a world power—suddenly began to link itself in my mind to what I had observed during my year overseas, which seemed so far away in time and place. Slowly, a number of once unrelated pieces began to fall together.

When I returned to Stanford, I started asking new and better questions in my law school classes. I wrote an article in the law school newspaper comparing the Philippine legal system under Marcos with the American system. In the Philippines, the written laws were in place, imported from the American legal system. But at the same time, the politics and objectives behind the laws and the way the system was structured were more important than the specific rules. The written laws, which law schools spent almost all of their time focusing on, really had no meaning apart from the reality of how the system worked, with its inequalities in legal representation and in prosecution, enforcement, definition of crime, and legislation of the laws. But in class, we were supposed to pretend that the reality was irrelevant. I was a little frightened by some of the parallels I was seeing in the United States.

For years I had been silent in my classes, believing—quite correctly, as it turned out—that the best way for me to succeed was to censor my own point of view and remain silent, to avoid the risk of my beliefs singling me out and hurting my grades, and simply to mimic the views of my teachers (once I knew what their views were). But when I returned from the Philippines, I chose to exercise my freedoms and to risk the consequences. I raised issues from anthropology and sociobiology in law classes, and I asked about dispute resolution mechanisms and why the courts were being asked to decide questions that didn't belong there at all. Whether I was right or wrong, I was told invariably that such topics were "outside of the scope of the courses."

The more questions I asked, the more I realized that every intellectual issue was placed outside the curriculum. The issues weren't touched on in any courses in the curriculum, and eventually I got the message that I had internalized years before: that I wasn't supposed to raise such issues and that few who had reached my level ever did.

Everything that seemed to me to have a practical bearing was assumed irrelevant in my classes. The noble assumptions built into the law curriculum, for example— equal access to legal representation, informed and objective judges and juries, and a penal system that rehabilitated, to name a few—were myths. Everything we were taught was based on these assumptions, and everyone agreed that they didn't exist, but no one was interested in the practical aspects of how to achieve them or how to change the system to meet the reality.

As a professional student, I didn't see all of the implications then. I only knew that there was something distorted about our legal system and our educational system, and I wanted to change it.

Once I started trying to hold the Stanford Law School to its principles, though—asking deans and professors to help students think about ways to improve the system—the Stanford faculty members became quickly defensive and said there was very little they could do. They told me that curriculum change toward improving the legal system was "impractical" because it would offend the people who paid their salaries and supported the school. Sometimes, I heard this view from them in the strangest ways—in a short note in my mailbox from one professor who thanked me for speaking out but said he was personally afraid, and from others who would speak to me in whispers in hallways or behind closed doors.

I tried to voice the issue in subtle ways, but even that was risky. The law school's alumni magazine, the *Stanford Lawyer,* let me write a story about the school's class of 1952, and about how life in the law school between 1949 and 1952 compared with life in the school three decades later. I flew to Washington, D.C., to interview the two Supreme Court justices in the class (Sandra Day O'Connor and William Rehnquist), the late Senator Frank Church, and a number of others. An interesting and not entirely flattering picture of the school emerged in the alumni's own words, which suggested constructive ideas for improving the school. Stanford's dean wouldn't print the story.

What I had noticed in the law school seemed to be happening elsewhere on the campus as well. At first, almost every idea I had for improving the university and the community around it seemed to run into a wall, though the obstacles seemed to have nothing to do with the feasibility of the ideas.

I tried, for example, to increase recognition of student art, achievement, and interests, not expecting to find that a particularly radical notion. I had ideas ranging from lending the university's art collection to the dorms, to recognizing and protecting student wall murals (Stanford prefers to paint them over, and thousands of works of art have been lost), to installing commemorative plaques, to establishing the first student-history museum. The reaction stunned me.

I began to implement one idea that would have cost about $200; I even found some alumni to put up the money. My idea was to put up a small plaque in honor of President John F. Kennedy, who had been a student at Stanford, taking courses at the business school for a few months in 1940 before he enlisted in the Navy in World War II. In fact, when Kennedy was president, Stanford praised him as an alumnus and worked very hard to enlist his help in their fund-raising campaigns. It was inspiring to know that some Stanford students—especially from the business school—had gone on to public service. Kennedy represented a different set of beliefs from those that Stanford had already chosen to commemorate with its buildings honoring Herbert Hoover, an alumnus, and its then-approved library named for Ronald Reagan, a president who had no connection to the university.

Pursuit of this idea took weeks and provided me with an inside tour of Stanford's bureaucracy and insight into how the administrators made decisions. I had countless conversations with people who were sure that a plaque already existed, though they were not sure where, and who suddenly became afraid of supporting the idea when they found out that there was none.

I started my efforts at the business school, where John F. Kennedy had taken courses. The development people loved the idea, because they wanted to use the Kennedy name to make money—which wasn't my intention. Eventually, though, some of the deans vetoed the idea. I never knew exactly why.

The historical society, composed of elderly alumni who record the history of the Stanford family and of campus buildings and gardens, wouldn't touch the idea. The history of Stanford students and workers, educational philosophies, and community relations was packed away into musty corners of the archives or—like student art—destroyed. It rarely if ever entered into the type of history that the historical society presented.

For weeks, I discussed this simple idea with department heads, groundskeepers, historians, and campus planners. Nobody would take any responsibility for implementing the plan. Nobody would move until hearing from the top university officials. Donald Kennedy, then Stanford's president, said no, claiming that symbolic actions were inappropriate means of celebrating the university's commitment to diversity on a campus already filled with symbols.

Local newspapers picked up the story on the J.F.K. plaque, but they had little interest in the real issues of student initiative, public service, and diversity of opinions at Stanford on any range of subjects. They packaged the dispute in a way that missed the point—liberal versus conservative, Democrat versus Republican, the Hoover and Reagan influences versus J.F.K.'s legacy.

The reaction that followed showed me something that went even deeper, something I never expected. My friends were upset with me over this issue, especially when it appeared on the front page of the student paper. They told me that it was wrong for a student to disagree with the president of the university. They felt that I was being "disloyal" to Stanford because I disagreed with a man who administered its policies.

World Events and the Classroom

An event that occurred a week after the November 1984 elections in the Philippines—timed too closely after the election for comfort—told me a great deal more about what wasn't happening in the classroom. The news carried an announcement of the assassination of Cesar Climaco, mayor of Zamboanga City.

Climaco was a gentle and committed old man with a terrific sense of humor with whom I had spent a day in the Philippines while interviewing officials at the grass roots. He was one of the few Philippine politicians who continued to speak out against President Marcos. Speaking out finally caught up with him.

Climaco's death put the realities of foreign events closer to me than anything else could have. I had identified with him in a way, and I understood the dangers he faced. A year later, he was gone: a bullet in his brain.

I was upset when I walked into my political science discussion section, and I decided to tell a story to my class about politics in the Philippines. I was scared for the Philippines and wanted to bring world events to life for my students. I faced a wall of silence. In the silence and stares, I detected an impatience and an inability among the students to understand my feelings. I could almost hear them saying, "That's not my problem. That's five thousand miles away. It's only one person. Thousands of people die every day." I could almost hear them asking, "How is this going to help me on the exam? Why doesn't he just tell us what's in the readings? We're going to be disadvantaged compared with students in other teaching sections. Why doesn't he tell us how to get jobs in the Foreign Service instead?" Those were the questions they were prepared to ask, as I had been when I was an undergraduate.

I wrote about Climaco's assassination in the *Stanford Daily*. I made it relevant to the university by pointing out the Stanford-educated officials who held high positions in the Marcos government—some who had chosen to work for Marcos well after he began to assume dictatorial powers. I don't know if anyone read the story other than some of my friends who described themselves as politically liberal. They told me they agreed with the article but hoped that what I was writing didn't go any further than the campus. They didn't want the story to "lessen the value" of their Stanford degrees. It didn't. The major newspaper in the area was staffed and managed by Stanford graduates.

Dissent Within the University

I felt that something was wrong with the intellectual culture at Stanford that people would want to change if they only knew and understood. I decided to write about it, in one long, twenty-six-page open letter to the Stanford community, raising questions about Stanford's commitment to intellectual life and commenting on everything from life in the dormitories to the courting of symbols—the Queen of England, the Super Bowl, the Olympics, the Reagan Library, overseas campuses that were like villas—that seemed to be turning the university into a corporate theme park.

The reaction frightened me. Members of Stanford's board of trustees (at the time headed by Warren Christopher, now secretary of state) and administration pretended that they hadn't read it. But they had. Many pages into the letter, I observed how the law school library's bulletin board (an open forum) censored any critical articles published by students, exemplifying what I referred to in the letter as "the death of ideas" at Stanford. Within days, the law school librarian called me into his office, told me how he had come upon my letter, and informed me of the library's new policy not to post *any* student letters at all, to avoid charges of bias and censorship. This is how the Stanford administration dealt with my open letter.

The *Stanford Daily* dealt with my letter by not printing any of it. The reason the editors gave was that they agreed with the points I was making, that ideas had died at Stanford and that the university culture would not support them. They agreed that people weren't interested in ideas at Stanford. And, since a newspaper was only supposed to print what people were interested in, they explained that my article didn't have a place in the paper.

One of the ideas I presented in the article was heard—three thousand miles away, quoted in the *Boston Globe*. I found that bit of information extraordinary.

Unfortunately, I learned that there was no public forum besides the *Stanford Daily* for an idea at the university. It was and is a one-newspaper campus, just as Soviet universities were. There was a magazine at the time, and the editor had agreed to print my letter, but she was busy arranging a sorority formal and let the magazine die. A freshman who had been selected as a columnist for the *Stanford Daily* did write about the letter, calling (unsuccessfully) for the paper to print it but only alluding to its contents.

One might think that there were other ways for students to be heard on the Stanford campus, but they were extremely few. There were no student speakers at Stanford graduations—there haven't been for the past ninety years—though every year one could listen to the university president talk about the virtues of diversity and democracy. Parents' Weekend had a student speaker until 1969, when the students started disagreeing with the view that the administration wanted to present. So Stanford eliminated Parents' Weekend altogether for sixteen years, until everyone forgot about the dispute. It was revived in 1985, but this time without the student speaker.

The concept of rights of any kind at Stanford was laughable. The university was still a place where a student could sit in an auditorium and be talked at for an hour by someone on a stage about the American civil rights movement, then watch the speaker run off at the end of the lecture to use a key to enter a separate and unequal bathroom or lounge.

For me, early spring of 1985 marked the end of my opportunity for speech at Stanford. The *Stanford Daily* would no longer print articles under my byline or any ideas it could identify with me. Aside from the *Boston Globe* and the *New York Times*, which had printed some of my comments on Stanford that year, there was nowhere else to go. "We don't understand why someone like you should be interested in undergraduate education," the *Stanford Daily* editors said. "We figure you must have some ulterior motives."

Stanford student journalists felt a loyalty to the university that prevented them from challenging anything more than minor matters. Probably correctly, they viewed their own personal success as tied to their cordial relations with the Stanford administration.

Their most critical stories that year were not exposés of university policy but rather attacks on fellow students.

Birth of The Unseen America

The concept of rights at Stanford went beyond the university culture and could be found right in the curriculum itself. That was when I decided to test whether or not it could be changed. I decided to undertake an educational experiment to see if I could share the new perspective I had gained, by devising educational adventures for other students in which they could develop their own confidence, skills, and independence.

Professors had answered criticism about Stanford's educational philosophy by saying there was no alternative. The only way to find out whether that was true was to do what should have been done in the classes themselves: test the theory by experience—try it by myself to see what would happen. So I did.

In the spring of 1985, I designed a new course called The Unseen America, accredited as "Undergraduate Specials 38." I finally saw clearly what had been giving me an uneasy feeling for years, and I began to understand how to do something about it.

Kennell Jackson, a professor of Afro-American studies and history, who was also a resident fellow in Branner Hall and my friend and former boss, challenged me to develop the new course for Branner freshmen; he agreed to sponsor it. I designed The Unseen America to respond to what I thought was missing in Stanford education.

In the course of one term, I brought students to an Indian reservation, a federal prison, a farm labor camp, an inner-city high school, a soup kitchen, a mansion, a homeless shelter, a mental hospital, and other locations. In addition to the visits, students read from a wide spectrum—from Tolstoy to Toffler—and saw classic films and documentaries (see Chapter Four).

It worked. In fact, five of the eight students came back a year later, *on their own time*, for more field work.

What I realized in structuring the course was that at almost every step—assignments, grading, use of classrooms, student-teacher relations, discussion topics, and so on—there was a completely different approach from the one universally found in the Stanford curriculum. Not only did the alternative result in students learning more but it gave them more confidence in themselves, a greater hand in their own education, and a sense of individual responsibility.

It wasn't until I researched the literature on the philosophy of education that I realized the educational approach I was introducing was not new. It had just disappeared at Stanford, by design.

Stanford's approach and the one I had chosen experimentally were two directly competing philosophies of education: one based on the concept of paternalism and obedience—something to be administered *to* students in hierarchical structures, programming people into specialized slots; and one based on the concepts of democracy, equality, participation, and firsthand experience.

A society produces exactly the type of people it chooses to create. Stanford chose the more paternalistic and rigid model, with little or no room for an alternative. Everything was to be arranged *for* the students "in their interest," placing them in a dependent relationship. Students were never consulted, and after a while, they didn't even feel that they ought to be. They were placed in a system in which they learned to trust authority and to have little faith in themselves and their own judgment.

Although universities are supposed to be among the freest places in our society, Stanford administered the campus like a company town. The university owned all of the property and controlled all of the freedom of expression in public places—murals, outdoor art, places for political posters. Administrators decided how the buildings were used and by whom, including all dormitories, student group houses, and individual homes on university property. They had to approve of all construction, repairs, and renovation, despite the concerns of the people using these facilities. They ran the food services and authorized the bookstores, the cafés, and all the shops.

Stanford even owned the nearest shopping mall. The administrators authorized (or didn't authorize) the funds for student press. They controlled communications to alumni, presenting one view of events on campus and soliciting money for their programs. They used student tuition to buy legal counsel to defend themselves. They spent student tuition to prepare pamphlets for students that showed only the administration's side of campus issues. They controlled the police department. They could even ban individuals from campus, at will.

When students entered the university, they contracted away their power of decision over many of the features of their education and life-style, including their exercise of rights that would otherwise be constitutionally guaranteed. This situation isn't unique to Stanford. Students can choose to sign away their rights to one fiefdom or another, where the rules may differ slightly but decision-making structure is almost always the same.

The potential for abuse resulting from such concentration of power is enormous, and it was clearly demonstrated on campuses during the McCarthy era. Somehow, Stanford's expression of democracy and the "free market" seemed like an enormous contradiction that made me question every other aspect of society as well. If there is any one fundamental belief in a democratic society, it is this: prevent concentration of power. The message that students received at Stanford, however, was the opposite one. Concentration of power was something we were taught to trust.

My experiences with The Unseen America began to dismantle all of the assumptions that I had taken on faith. The Unseen America not only challenged the ideology of the established curriculum, it also posed a challenge to Stanford's historical separation into an isolated enclave apart from the rest of society—an ivory tower.

Most Stanford students were encouraged and rewarded for writing essays on subjects they had never seen firsthand. They might have been encouraged, for example, to write about U.S.-Philippine foreign policy without ever meeting a hungry Filipino. They might write about the American legal system without ever seeing the inside of a prison. They might write about social issues without ever contrasting, firsthand, life in a mansion with life in a slum. The students learned to say that they didn't need any firsthand or empirical knowledge and that approved secondary sources, filtered through the approved observers, were enough. They learned to believe that the reality was irrelevant to the authority they would assume as decision makers and that only the statistics and the abstracted conclusions mattered. They would never see where the numbers or authorities they cited as fact came from or how reliable such sources were. Yet these students, who would later be graduates in high places, spoke out with authority about their knowledge, and continue to do so.

Elite private universities such as Stanford are proud of their curricula and the results. Stanford's provost, an economist, explained to me that courses like The Unseen America, which tried to break down the walls between Stanford and the larger society, were not part of the "educational mission" of the university. It was for this reason that teaching assistants in political science were paid six hundred times the salary of instructors who designed their own courses. (The "salary" for designing and teaching The Unseen America in 1985 was $2.50 per week, or about 10 cents per hour.)

In the Stanford value system, administering information about issues in American society from books and telling students what to think was six hundred times more valuable than offering them both books and shared experiences and helping them think on their own. Stanford even funded a students' gourmet cooking project more enthusiastically than it did The Unseen America. These were the university's priorities.

American Democracy and the University

Beyond its educational success and its challenge to the excuses about why the educational system was the way it was, what The Unseen America revealed at Stanford was, in the words of the provost, the "political mission" of the university. What that mission was doing to American society also became clear.

One could measure the results of a Stanford education on democratic values by talking to freshmen and then finding them a year or two later and asking the same questions, or just by taking samples of freshmen and upperclassmen to see the differences. Freshmen exposed to what they had always considered "unseen"— but that was part of the reality of America outside their isolated campuses—would point to injustice or excuses and say: "That looks unfair." "That sounds like a contradiction." "Show me how I can do something about it."

But after a year or two of the traditional approach in higher education, most students quickly learned not to ask those questions or even to think about them. By their sophomore or junior years, the typical Stanford students I taught or knew as friends had little smiles plastered on their faces, and they told me: "That's the way things are. You can't change them. Be happy. Don't fight it." They would decide that they weren't interested in making improvements in their surroundings or off campus, unless the projects were for show and earned them status points while keeping things as they were. They would look the other way, not realizing that democracies could be lost.

I asked a number of Stanford students, for example, how they felt about some of the basic concepts of democracy such as citizen review of government decision making (through juries, for example), a concept that would give students the responsibility in political decision making that they had had in the 1800s.

They answered that citizen participation didn't sound very much to them like an important goal of American democracy. They told me, "You can't trust the people."

The higher up in the Stanford educational track they were (law students versus undergraduates, for example), the stronger this belief. They didn't believe in democracy because they had been prepared not to. Undergraduates didn't even believe in themselves: they told me they wouldn't trust themselves to make decisions about American policy. They preferred to put their trust in experts to carry out technical tasks and to handle all the moral and political decisions, too. They had absolute faith. They didn't want to question.

At the same time, Stanford students felt that they were more important than other citizens because they were chosen in a "democratic way"—in a meritocratic way—to receive a fine education, and that anything they chose to do was democratic because they were part of this meritocracy. They felt that people had already invested faith in them as an elite and that their mere presence in the corridors of power signified that all was well.

It was an ethic I had encountered among graduates of elite schools, including Stanford, who were serving as political leaders in developing countries and as foreign-service officers working for the United States. They had chosen to forgive the sins of dictators simply because the dictators were among the best and the brightest. They perceived as legitimate those dictators, generals, and advisers who had murdered their opponents and siphoned off their countries' resources, because they were brighter and better educated than their countrymen and often had attended American universities. Their virtue of professional competence, of being part of the same elite club, was what allowed students to forgive them for indifference or ruthlessness.

At the same time, I began to notice that the elite curriculum and the hidden curriculum had deeper effects on attitudes. I truly believed then, and I still believe, that Stanford students and graduates want to use their skills and the fruits of their labor to help others if they can. But after isolation in a place like Stanford, the students never meet the people with whom they would otherwise share their resources and luxuries. The standard of comparison of what one needs to be "comfortable" with what one needs for a little status and recognition slowly becomes a comparison among *themselves* rather than to any outside group. When such a narrow spectrum of people is used as a basis for comparisons, the result is to keep ratcheting up the acceptable standard.

Slowly, the students learned to rationalize everything away. They developed a value system in which even attempts at constructive reform within the system were impermissible. This is what I heard from my students after they got a heavy dose of Stanford's curriculum: "You don't have the right to innovate. You don't belong." "You have no right to enter systems with the goal of changing them. Systems have the right to continue without being changed. You have no right to criticize an institution. If you disagree, you should leave. Go somewhere else." If I persisted, their cry became more shrill and personalized against anyone who was different. "They don't want you," they would say, pointing the finger. "Don't expect to do what you want or make the system adapt to your needs. You have to fit into the system."

Stanford goes on, busily preparing its students for life in organizations—sitting at desks, following orders, defining themselves by their skills and roles and organizational affiliations. Graduates are trained to carry out specialized, assigned technical tasks without ever seeing the results of their work or questioning the political reasons for any of their actions. The value choices are not theirs to make, and never have been. They believe that everything will work out all right if they just achieve the highest technical competence. This was a viewpoint that I had heard or read before at other times, in deluded references to "body counts" by former Harvard professors who were destroying villages throughout Southeast Asia in the 1960s and 1970s and in the words of the German technicians in the 1940s who had built new kinds of factories and efficient transport systems to them.

The Lesson of Social Control Through Force

There was a darker side to all of this that explains what was happening and what was being learned. It is part of the message that administrators of America's top universities make sure that students receive. It is rare to see it in print or to hear people talk about it openly, but it is always there, beneath the surface.

I saw it in the late 1980s, after I left Stanford for one of this country's great public universities, the University of California at Berkeley. There, hard-working students from minority and poor families who can't afford Stanford often ask questions about the doors they thought were open in America, and that now seem closed, and about the injustice that confronts them every day because they can't avoid seeing it on the streets. They ask about the irrelevance of their education and their packaging as a product and the indifference they see from the government and from their public servants, be they teachers or administrators or the powers behind the university. Sometimes, when the students' questions are met with silence or with name-calling or with lies, they get angry. And when they get angry, they also get hurt.

At institutions like the University of California, the message isn't given only in words. It is backed up with force—not just with police informers who have infiltrated student organizations or with the Supreme Court decision allowing the police to break into newspapers such as the *Stanford Daily* (as a result of a landmark court case involving that paper: *Zurcher v. Stanford Daily*, 98 S. Ct. 197, 1978), or with FBI wiretaps conducted against students—even in places like Iowa, reported in the 1980s (*Wall Street Journal*, March 8, 1982, p. 1)—but with the use of police and military power, which has now become commonplace. When administrators decide to shut down communications with those who are being affected by their decisions, they have riot squads ready and trained (Churchill and VanderWall, 1988).

In the late 1980s, one could walk through the Berkeley campus or up Telegraph Avenue leading to it and see helicopters circling overhead and police clubbing students and beating up newspaper photographers. The university would sweep the blood off the streets as if nothing happened. I saw it with my own eyes. Yet to most people, it never happened because the major media almost never reported it.

On the day after President Bush's election, on the fiftieth anniversary of Kristalnacht (the day when Nazi storm troopers killed hundreds of Jews in Germany), someone sent out the riot-geared Berkeley police in full force. It didn't make the evening news because it wasn't considered news—it was all too common. But the incident sent a very clear message to young Americans about expression and trying to be heard. Most of them well understood the message and took it to heart just as I did as a student, hoping to make my way in America.

Professors got the message, as well. When students came to class late because they were delayed by riot police, professors could call up the Berkeley chancellor's office and hear his secretaries say, "He's out," or, "He doesn't know anything about it." Many Berkeley professors had learned to keep their mouths shut long before the incident. They had learned that talking about these things in class was foolish because they could be denounced in the California legislature—and some were. They kept their office doors closed because they didn't like or trust their colleagues. Even now, they won't say much on the telephone because they believe that faculty telephones are still tapped at Berkeley. They're scared.

The preparation for institutional life has itself become institutionalized, with force as well as with an ideology that makes it resistant to change.

It is not only that the practice of democratic education has been almost entirely excluded from college campuses. It goes deeper than that. A purge has taken place, more subtle than the loyalty oaths and blacklists of the 1950s but a direct continuation of that era by the handpicked successors of those faculty who remained in their positions during the McCarthy era.

The professors who taught by a different philosophy and methods are mostly gone. Readings and curricular materials that provided the intellectual basis for such philosophies are largely gone, too. Most of the key works that teach alternative values are gone from the curricula.

You can conduct your own test merely by counting how many basic courses now teach classics by authors such as G.D.H. Cole or Ivan Illich, or milder literary views of the workplace and organization, to lend some perspective. The works of the last thirty years that ask serious questions about industrial society—William H. Whyte's *The Organization Man*, Alvin Toffler's *The Third Wave*, Lloyd Warner's *Democracy in Jonesville: A Study of Quality and Inequality*, Theodore Roszak's *Person/Planet*, and Paul Goodman's *Growing Up Absurd*—are rarely found, nor are earlier classics, like Berle and Means's *The Modern Corporation and Private Property*, or the U.S. Senate studies in the 1930s of propaganda techniques used by utility companies to gain control of curricula in ways that are here to stay (U.S. Senate, 1935).

If you proposed to include these works alongside the traditional texts, you likely would not be hired, since screening of syllabi is a major function of review committees. If you were hired and you did teach these works, you would probably have trouble with tenure. More likely, new faculty members would not even learn about alternative classics: they would have to either stumble upon them or find a rare professor who is teaching them.

There is another kind of university purge at work in the marketplace. Bookstores (many of them managed or owned by the universities) stock up on books that are in the curricula, and so do libraries. Publishers also follow suit, deciding not to publish a book unless they already know that professors will assign it in large lecture courses or until demand exists. (It took seven years, for example, before publishers would even consider this work, because at the earlier time, its authors were still students, and no major institutional leaders had announced a commitment yet to what is now called "service learning.") Overall in libraries and bookstores, when shelf space becomes crowded, librarians and booksellers just pull the "old" books with "old" ideas that aren't being taught anymore, to make room for the "new" books.

The Moral of the Story

It is easy to fall into the trap of thinking that university education results in something benign and that campuses should be isolated havens where students and scholars can "think" undisturbed about great problems, and in which unmarried, energetic young people can be locked away from the rest of society as a way of creating social harmony. It is easy to assume that what is taught in the university can be easily unlearned.

But the imperatives for change, and the real moral of this story, can be found in places like the Philippines or Latin America, where graduates of schools such as Stanford put their new skills to work against weak democracies, in many cases plundering and destroying them and leaving them ill equipped to redevelop when the populace rises up and tries to build democracy again.

In the Philippines, those who set out to destroy a fledgling democracy and impoverished their country were not all people who were ruthless and bloodthirsty. Many of them were trained technocrats who just followed orders and rose to power by doing their jobs. And that is exactly the problem. One need only look at where they were trained.

In the Philippines, Ferdinand Marcos and his wife, Imelda, were both educated in the Philippines, but they hired the best people they could find—people with American educations. Imelda Marcos's right-hand man, Deputy Minister Jolly Benitez, held a Ph.D. in education and a master's degree in economics from Stanford. He joined up with the regime after martial law was imposed, after attending Stanford for at least six years. Benitez was among the ninety people who fled the Philippines with Marcos in 1986; some Filipinos still say that Benitez may have helped Imelda Marcos plan the Aquino assassination. The press reported that more than $1 million in cash was found in Benitez's home after he left the Philippines.

In choosing a director of the Philippine Central Bank, Marcos turned to the Stanford Graduate School of Business and hired Jaime Laya, who holds a doctorate from the school. Laya was around when almost $1 billion disappeared from the accounts of the bank in 1984.

General Fabian Ver, the head of Marcos's military forces, was educated in the Philippines, but Defense Minister Juan Ponce

Enrile, who implemented and enforced martial law, earned a law degree from Harvard. Enrile was a last-minute defector from the Marcos regime who was later accused of trying to lead coups against President Corazón Aquino and attempting to destabilize the government in a coalition with Salvador Laurel (a Yale Law School graduate).

Those were the key players, and there were others with elite American degrees. In training their children for succession, the Marcoses sent their daughter Imee to Princeton, and their son Bong Bong—who now holds public office in the Philippines—to Wharton. It was Tony Peña, the minister of natural resources and holder of a master of laws degree from Yale, who explained to me that elections were too costly for developing countries like the Philippines but that martial law wasn't.

This is more than just a coincidence. It may help explain why America's leaders seemed so willing to rationalize Marcos's dictatorship in the Philippines and to overlook dictatorships for so long elsewhere—in places like Mexico, where it is believed that President Carlos Salinas won his country's election by massive fraud and set in motion Mexico's economic destabilization and need for U.S. loans and controls. Salinas is a Harvard graduate. Salinas's handpicked successor, President Ernesto Zedillo Ponce de Leon holds a doctorate in economics from Yale. The pipeline is still full, too. There are young government servants like Robert Owen, who testified in the Iran-Contra hearings in the late 1980s that he was just doing his job running guns and money to South America for Oliver North, his hero, and that he did not ask any questions about the legality of what he was doing. Owen is a recent Stanford product.

In the Philippines, Aquino and Climaco—and so many others whom we usually do not hear about but who met with the same fate of political assassination—were not radicals. They were well educated people. They were respectable. They tried to work within the system. They held elected positions in the government. They were quoted in the newspapers. They knew influential people. They were not coarse or mean-spirited. They spoke simple words and stood for simple values and appealed for protection of human dignity.

They knew the weaknesses and the contradictions inside the system. They understood their opponents' thought processes. They knew how the game worked, and they played it very well.

Marcos's dictatorship seemed more understandable to me when I was at Stanford—too much for comfort. It became clear to me how a Stanford education was not having a positive impact in transmitting some of the values of democracy. It was, in fact, doing quite the opposite. It was training leaders in the arts of rationalizing, public relations, and creating connections between elites. That was the most devastating realization of all, and it hit me unexpectedly in one of my business classes when I opened up the curricular materials, written by Stanford business school professors for a course called Business and the Changing Environment—ironically, once the school's course on ethics.

In a chapter about balancing individual rights with society's interest was a paragraph criticizing students who would ever think of suing a university. According to the text, the student would be acting immorally because exercising one's constitutional rights would force the university to spend money, and that would directly reduce scholarship monies for needy students who would never think of disagreeing with a large organization such as a university.

It was the type of argument that goes unnoticed or pushed aside every day, but to me, it was more than that. It had a chillingly familiar ring to it because it was that same argument Tony Peña had used to explain to me why the Marcos government did not hold elections: elections cost money, he told me, and that meant that less money would be available for the Filipino poor. Unfortunately, the money saved was never distributed for development purposes, and the government probably never intended that it would be. Without elections, there was no way to hold the government accountable for actions that violated the law. But Peña assumed I would accept that answer. It was among the repertoire of rationalizations that I was being encouraged to learn.

When I thought more about the curriculum, other parallels became clear as well. The leaders in the Philippines who commissioned assassinations and the impoverishment of their nation were not savages running around in the jungle. The Layas and Benitezes, the Enriles and the Peñas, as well as the second generation of Marcoses, had all gone to those same American universities. The new president of the Philippines, Fidel Ramos, a graduate of West Point is also a member of the club.

The powers that be in the United States did not really care about the Marcos dictatorship until Marcos had pushed the system to its breaking point, and they still seem to dislike drawing attention to the actions of their classmates and friends elsewhere.

Marcos loyalists were very proud of their American educations, and they told me so often, in justifying their abuses. I can never forget the words of Minister Peña when I asked him about political corruption and martial law and the government's brutalities in the Philippines. I thought of his words over and over again, every time I sat in the classroom, watched a lecture, sat for a graded exam, listened to the doublespeak of university administrators, or heard of the decisions of faculty at closed meetings. I still hear Peña's words, each time with a new sense of horror and panic. They make the clearest statement I have heard anywhere for reform of American university education and the compelling need for a new approach.

"We learned all this from you."

3

Experiencing Democracy

A New Approach to Education

The vision that we have of democratic experiential education is more than one of methodological innovations for rapid learning combined with adventure. The lodestar of student adventures is an ideal of democracy and development in modern industrial societies. The educational approach that we describe here is part of a philosophy of an ideal democratic society and takes into account the specific skills and personal qualities needed by those who participate as citizens in such a society.

Our vision is a comprehensive and unified one deeply rooted in American and Western traditions. It builds on the concepts of social contract and active citizen participation dating back to the eighteenth century and the birth of Western democracy. In designing student adventures, we began by imagining a system in which the goals of a healthy and productive society and a thriving democratic order could be fulfilled in the context of modern industrial society.

This book is but one piece of a larger vision of modern societies—of productive and vibrant communities and of a political system that reflects the ideals of the social contract in which individuals have the opportunity and rights to develop themselves and to participate as equals in negotiating their own interests with others and in which they can oversee and participate in the decision making of all the institutions that affect their lives.

In a sense, this book fits naturally into a three-part scheme of revitalization—one in which education plays a major role in creating a new awareness and preparing citizens for a restoration of their historically important role. We see democratic experiential education as part of a sustainable development strategy and of community renewal, linked to an alternative model of growth that some of us have already envisioned in a companion book, A *Model Development Plan* (Lempert, Mitchell, and McCarty, 1995), in which we present new solutions to social problems and environmental and spiritual decay. At the same time, we see democratic experiential education as intimately linked with a renewal of political institutions and forms, preparing citizens for an active and fulfilling role in a democratic society based on social contract democracy—one that is modeled in another companion book, A *Return to Democracy* (Lempert, 1993).

This vision of social revitalization builds on our philosophy of intellectual life—that knowledge, exciting teaching, effective learning, and intellectual advancement are based on empiricism. In this chapter, we build on our conception of effective teaching methodologies and true intellectual advancement that we presented in Chapter One, and then we move on to a description of a philosophy of democracy and democratic culture.

We present our philosophy of education and intellectual life in its ideal form and show how it fits into a new concept of democracy for modern society as well as a new vision of a model society. We describe the key characteristics of democratic experiential education and its particular democratic components in theory and in application to citizen needs, and we compare our vision to the prevailing view of education and of the individual's role in modern society. We also provide an overview of how to apply our vision in a variety of disciplines.

Characteristics of Democratic Experiential Education

The key components of democratic experiential education fall into three categories: democratic characteristics and the two sides of experiential work—the combination of theory with empirical work and the combination of theory with practical application for social betterment.

These are the key attributes of a successful program and are the features we have sought to include in the design of all of the courses and projects we have created. While these features apply to all disciplines, they do not necessarily apply to all courses or subjects within them. Some forms of learning require drilling. Others require more theory, the use of thought experiments, and more reliance on experts. But where the three sets of characteristics can be incorporated, they represent our ideal. The following sections list the characteristics and describe them briefly.

Democratic Features of Student Adventures

- *Student-initiated learning.* Democracy starts with the individual, at the grass roots, and so does democratic education. This is the core of the social contract. Students can participate in their own learning by designing their own curricula and running their own classes with general guidelines. Given the chance, their best instincts will emerge to drive them to intellectual achievement.

- *Teachers serving as facilitators.* Leaders in democracies are not authority figures but guides. In democratic education, teachers are participants and guides, not lecturers or taskmasters.

- *Contractual methods of evaluation.* In democracies, advancement is on merit, with objective and nondiscriminatory criteria. Democratic education measures skills acquisition through contractual rather than subjective measures.

- *Responsiveness and accountability to the community.* Democratic institutions are directly responsive and accountable to the community. For many subjects, not only is the community the best laboratory but greater community involvement means greater direct accountability of the educational process.

- *Multiculturalism*. A strong democracy recognizes and affirms individual difference and takes it into account in the process of consensus. Democratic education embeds multiculturalism in its methods, incorporating it directly through exposure of students to a variety of peoples as part of comprehensive and inclusive research, rather than giving students a token acknowledgment through select books or contact with professors of minority status who are ghettoized in particular departments and courses.

- *Traditional community values and ethics*. Democracies perpetuate community values through participation and consensus, as well as through pride of ownership. Democracies are often affiliated with capitalism because of the opportunity for individual activity and control over resources that enable participation and lead to a stake in consensus. Democratic education creates a student stake in education and the community through giving students access to resources and responsibility for the educational process as well as through student interaction with the community.

- *Self-activating potential*. Democracies outlive individuals, because they are independent of any one charismatic or particularly skilled leader. Democratic education must also be able to survive particular professors and to continue through the activities of interested students.

Experiential Features of Student Adventures

Combination of Theory with Empiricism (the Concept of Field Work)

- *Testing of theory through direct observation*. Theory without the chance to test it is merely dogma. Experiential education accelerates theoretical learning by enabling students to test and build models directly. It is theoretically rigorous in that it encourages students to derive theory directly from practice and to understand the methods of developing and expanding knowledge.

- *Learning by doing.* The most effective learning is through experience rather than through the passive acquisition of facts or the study of symbols. The testing of theory not only reinforces abstract learning but develops all the skills of collecting the different kinds of information about the world that are unique to each discipline, with the chance for students to work with the various technologies for acquiring and testing that information.

Combination of Theory with Practice (Making Education Useful)

- *Skills orientation.* Experiential education measures its success on the basis of skills acquisition rather than fact acquisition or familiarity with particular texts or theories. It measures knowledge by the ability of students to perform tasks rather than recite them.

- *Community and service orientation.* University projects can make students active participants in the democratic process, as policy makers on real issues and as contributors to the social and cultural life of their communities, allowing them to select and participate in constructive tasks for society (not necessarily tasks that are bought in the marketplace with dollars). From engineering and construction to small business planning and policy making, students can combine education with contributing in a meaningful, direct, and empowering way to better society.

The Democratic Experiential Vision: Empowering Citizens with Civic and Sufficiency Skills

In a society in which the educational system has come to mimic institutional life in the workplace and elsewhere, and in which the view of the individual citizen is often defined by the needs of large institutions, it is important to reflect back on the earlier meaning of democracy and the value of the individual in society.

Basic Principles of Social-Contract Democracy

Implicit in the concept of democratic education and social contract—and distinct from the prevailing view of education as a means to serve the needs of institutions—is a view of a society (1) in which citizens can best meet their own individual preferences and needs while being tolerant of the different needs of others, (2) in which they are active and informed participants, and (3) in which they possess the skills to negotiate and compromise with others.

These three basic principles are at the heart of the Western ideal of social-contract democracy. They serve as a guide to the particular skills that ought to be an integral part of the educational process in a modern democracy and that are central features of democratic experiential education programs.

- *Citizens as individuals negotiating their own needs*. Inherent in democratic education is the idea that every individual is unique and learns in his or her own way and that society and its institutions must be shaped to serve the preferences of those individuals in a compromise between citizens. The definition of social-contract democracy is one in which individuals charter and have oversight over the institutions around them, making decisions about their activities by mutual agreement rather than by conforming to institutional needs. Democratic education exists to prepare citizens not for roles as personnel in large institutions but to be strong and independent individuals with the skills to create their own organizations and to carry out their own initiatives, with the knowledge and savvy to use the political system to meet their own needs while understanding the rights of others.

- *Citizens as active participants in the political process and in civic activities*. Democratic experiential education prepares citizens to communicate their values directly in a fully informed manner to the experts who have been chosen to implement those values. While there is no substitute for experts, there is also no substitute in a democracy for citizen participation in all decisions of government and of organizations that play public roles. It is essential that citizens be able to express values and preferences if those institutions are to work. Citizens in democracies should be generalists in their political participation and specialists in their careers, with a liberal education that enables them to ask questions and to contribute on all important topics. The philosophy of democratic experiential education is that citizens must be trained to participate in evaluating real policy issues and to use the political process.

- *Citizens as consensus builders*. Policy makers and ordinary citizens must be able to communicate, empathize with, and understand the perspectives and needs of others who are different from themselves—be they geographically removed, from another racial or religious background, of a different socioeconomic class (rich or poor), or in a different institutional setting (managers or workers). Students who develop the skills to understand and appreciate others who are different, as well as to compromise with their peers, can interact in a meaningful way in public life with other individuals and groups while working toward mutual objectives. This is what experiential education does.

Basic Education for Social-Contract Democracy

The three principles of social-contract democracy serve as clear guides to the kinds of skills that are incorporated in democratic experiential education, and they are also an effective means of evaluating the success of any educational program in preparing citizens for democracy. They translate into specific applications.

- *Education for independence and self-sufficiency*. The social contract harks back to a time when citizens could not only specialize in certain tasks but were also self-sufficient and entrepreneurial, participating in a market economy through proprietorship and ability to manage complex affairs. Democratic experiential education is education for empowerment. This means that the goal of education must not be disconnected service in large organizations but the skills essential for production and for managing public and private organizations.

Thus, the success of an economics course is not measured in one's ability to draw a graph but one's ability to manage a small business or farm successfully and to understand the workings of the economy through experience. The success of a chemistry course is measured in one's ability to use the course's principles in applying chemical processes. The success of a literature course is measured in one's ability to communicate effectively through different media while developing sensitivity to human relations and emotions.

- *Education for institutional oversight and civic participation.* At the foundation of Western social-contract democracy are ideals of equality of opportunity and institutional accountability to citizens. The ideal of democracy is that all institutions that affect citizens are subject to citizens' oversight and come into being only with their agreement. To be effective in their roles—as jurors, voters, and potential officeholders and decision makers; as communicators using available media; as consumers, workers, and members of organizations and social groups—citizens need to be prepared with a variety of skills (Lempert, 1993).

In modern society, effective participation and the ability to oversee institutions and hold them accountable require that citizens have a full and complete understanding of how those institutions work and that they have direct experience with military and foreign policy apparatuses; with national security state apparatus and law-enforcement bodies; with financial institutions and transactions (including a thorough knowledge of white-collar and organized crime); with government bureaucracy; with business enterprises and the power they exert over communities, resources, labor, and consumption; and with educational institutions, the media, and unions.

To participate actively and effectively in their legitimate roles as citizens, individuals need to not only *directly* understand the workings of institutions by visiting them and learning of their operations and structures, but they must also be empowered to enforce their rights and to be heard. In particular, they must be prepared to use:

The legal system—not only as passive jurors but in roles of independent prosecution when government fails and through independent investigation of institutions and their activities, as well as through class-action suits, private attorney general mechanisms, and other citizen-initiated processes

The mass media—not only as consumers evaluating the information they receive and its correlation with reality but as active and equal participants in presenting their own views and communications using available technologies and techniques

- *Education for consensus and community.* Finally, the ability of citizens to contract with others and to negotiate preferences as part of a community requires that they have a set of important skills in communications and human relations. Education for democracy requires the ability to communicate across cultures, to understand and accept others' emotions and values, to empathize with those in different circumstances, and to negotiate and reach compromise.

Comparison of Two Intellectual Cultures

Table 3.1 outlines the specific differences between two philosophies of teaching and of political and social life—the prevailing view of education and the democratic experiential approach of student adventures—in their larger context. Comparing the political and social implications of the two approaches side by side, seeing how the approaches fit into different conceptions of political decision making and of the citizen in society, is one way to understand these implications more fully.

TABLE 3.1. Two Educational Philosophies.

Prevailing View *(Paternal/Authoritarian)*	*Student Adventures View* *(Democratic/Humanistic)*
Functional Purpose Education for obedience (Social control in the administrative industrial state)	**Functional Purpose** Education for democracy (Social contract view— citizens are equal participants)
Student View Education for androids	**Student View** Education for world citizens
Motto "There is no substitute for a professor and a textbook (or a computer package)"	**Motto** "There is no substitute for firsthand experience"
How Students Are Viewed **1. *Lazy*** Students must be disciplined regularly. Most are unable to deal with a lack of structure and need firm direction to protect them from their own (bad) instincts.	**How Students Are Viewed** **1. *Need Adventure*** Students are bored and cynical with the routinization of meaningless tasks and are frustrated by regimentation. Too much time is wasted dealing with bureaucratic rules.
Solution. Impose strict grading standards and a series of differential, externally imposed rewards and punishments. Maintain strong requirements.	*Solution.* Encourage student initiative and intellectual freedom through self-paced learning. Provide guidance and positive incentives but few requirements.
2. *Ignorant* Students are blank slates. Faculty members have all the answers and even know the right questions. (This is what Tolstoy	**2. *Curious and Intelligent*** Students are equal (and perhaps superior in potential) to their professors, but they are not as advanced in skills.

called the professorial notion of "papal infallibility.")

Students should be treated as partners in a cooperative adventure of learning.

Professors do not have a monopoly on truth. Old answers could be wrong. The young can help find the answers.

Solution. The professor's role is to disseminate knowledge while the role of the student is to memorize and regurgitate it in the manner that the professor chooses.

Solution. Respect the intelligence of students by sharing more unprocessed data and by allowing students to try to solve problems and draw their own conclusions. Teach students how to ask questions and build models.

3. Irrational and Closed-Minded

Students are incapable of informed decision making. They do not know their own best interests.

3. Alienated and Scared

Students have been forced to specialize early and are fearful of an economy in which opportunity has become more and more limited and where generalists and thinkers are feared. Risk taking in the university is not protected but is punitively sanctioned in such a way that it has severe economic consequences.

If students do not know their own interests—and are not given the space and direction to find them—what does "democracy" mean?

Too much time is expended trying to meet procedural requirements and satisfy conflicting institutional demands. Students feel manipulated, processed, and prevented from thinking and experimenting.

Solution. Strong distribution requirements, tracking (majors requirement), requirements in the major.

Solution. Provide more guidelines instead of arbitrary rules. Provide more consultation, advice, and encouragement.

Reduce requirements and penalties while offering more freedom to experiment in course selection, as well as in materials within courses.

4. Incidental to the University

Students are merely an input.

Research is the most important university function.

4. Lifeblood of the University

What is research for, if not for the future? Discoveries are useless unless they can be translated into benefits for mankind. Any researcher should have to convince not only the public but also students of the value of research. Such is the role of the "philosopher-king" in society.

Research cannot and should not proceed in a vacuum. Among the best stimuli are the sincere and curious minds of students.

5. Destructive and Untrustworthy

Students will destroy property unless strictly controlled. If given responsibility and control over

5. Frustrated and Turned Off

Destructive behavior is an escape valve and a message of alienation.

resources, they are likely to make mistakes at the public expense.

Student ideas threaten the status quo and must be restricted to minute and incremental changes.

Students will not destroy property unless their creative energies are being thwarted.

When given responsibility, students will make mistakes, but they will also make major innovations and produce useful and successful work. Mistakes are part of learning. Most good doctors have had to bury their first mistakes, but that is the price of training a good doctor to care for and save lives.

If students are given the opportunity to do something useful and can see the results of their labors on projects in which they have a sense of personal worth and accomplishment, they will make a meaningful contribution and will respect the property for which they are given responsibility.

Solution. Tighten controls. Establish stiff penalties and fines for property damage or academic failure. Restrict access to resources. Ensure that any student involvement with the world outside the campus is subject to strict clearance.

Solution. Treat students with trust and respect. Students will respond with respect for property and will use their energies in positive ways.

Recognize that exploration is the key to education.

Purpose of Education
Train students for specialized and established roles in society.

Purpose of Education
Develop the individual human being capable of fulfilling multiple roles; teach values as well as skills.

Prepare students for entry-level positions in large organizations, with the ability to follow orders on narrow tasks without asking questions. Prepare them to adapt by conforming to new situations quickly.

Students must always be ready to shape themselves to fit into society's needs.

Education is a backward process. Students should consider what jobs are available and then fit themselves to the job.

Implications. Create tracks into specific social roles by stressing majors, preprofessional counseling, job fairs, and the placement office.

Train students to work within society to shape it to their needs.

Train students to develop and run their own organizations and to be independent.

Students should try to develop all their talents so they can appreciate more facets of the human experience.

Education is a process that works forward. Society is a social contract to benefit individuals and allow them to best meet their needs—even if that means re-creating society.

Implications. Teach students how to open private practices in the professions, how to take pride in their craft, how to find funding for independent work, how to sell writings and other work products, how to open businesses, and how to live frugally and be self-sufficient.

Train future citizens in consumerism, use of the legal system, and political access.

Teach students how to hold political and economic organizations accountable and how to provide greater opportunity and more human environments for those served by or working within them.

Reward students for following rules and determining what authority figures want.

Negotiate standards and methods of evaluation with students. (Encourage students to meet high standards, work aggressively, and live up to their potential, but do not set arbitrary standards.)

Prepare students to remain in unpleasant environments for long periods of time, doing tasks that someone else has determined for them, and on which they have little power to negotiate.

Help students design independent projects and courses of study that will enable them to establish themselves independently.

Teach technical and specialized skills in segmented categories (disciplines) while removing discussion of values or any connection to larger concepts. Claim that discussion of values is unnecessary (since skills are value-neutral) and that values cannot be taught to adults. Assert that competence in a skill is the most legitimate source of authority.

Teaching only skills is itself an ideology and a value judgment. It is best to introduce and allow students to discuss values and conflicts when they acquire skills.

The problem in a nuclear age is not inadequate technology but inadequate communication and understanding between peoples. Systems must be responsive to individual needs.

Information is less important than the way in which it is used. Students should learn to question and to seek solutions to problems rather than just to document problems or past solutions.

No skill is legitimate unless the people affected by its use have a say in that use.

Teach democratic values through experience, while also teaching students to solve practical problems that cross disciplinary boundaries.

Education Is a Business

Private universities must "expand" to be viewed as successful. Profits and expansion are the ends, not the means to the ends.

Education Is an Ideal

Universities exit to serve society. Society is served by the dissemination of skills that can be used to solve problems, and by providing individuals with the means of meeting their own needs. Ideas and ideals are central parts of this mission.

Profits are a means and not an end. Without consultation, resources are often misallocated.

Funding implications. Football and other sports programs, the courting of popular symbols, and spinoff programs—be they partisan or anti-intellectual—are valid parts of a university if they attract attention and resources.

Student needs are less important than faculty research because they generate little in direct prestige and income. Students are both a source of revenue and advertised products, and they can provide important input of labor for use in fundraising, income generation through athletics, and other services (such as research).

Funding implications. When students work on community problems and provide services to the community, they show the public directly how educational funding results in social gain. Thus, education and funding become linked in a socially positive way, without interest groups or budgetary decisions by administrators distorting the activities of the university.

Students can devise low-cost and high-quality methods of education when they are consulted.

Further, students can help generate funding for the

university in new types of educational projects (for example, student-run small credit institutions).

Governance implications. Institutional control should be placed in the hands of those with strong ties to the financial and corporate communities. Boards should not include intellectuals, artists, authors, academics, researchers, or any other thinkers or do-gooders apt to question the profit ethic.

Governance implications. A university must maintain its integrity and act in accordance with the highest moral concern, uphold the public trust, be open and responsible in its communication of values and its relation to the community. Governance must include all affected members of the community.

Methods
Administered Education
Format. Lectures from professor to student.

Methods
Interactive Education
Format. Discussion and exchange of ideas between students and faculty.

A school is not a factory. Students must be consulted and share in the responsibility of education.

Materials. Packaged materials with abstract conclusions and sterile exercises chosen by faculty or publishers.

Materials. Where possible, lead students to data and help them apply newly learned tools to the data.

Education should be empirical. Students should see the world for themselves and draw their own conclusions. Skills should be tested in the field when possible so that students understand their uses and limitations.

Faculty-Student Contact

Contact should be distant, limited, and controlled by lecture format, office hours, and residential setup. Student-faculty contact is often viewed as a professional service in which the only real get-togethers are "faculty dinners" and "sherry hours."

Contact with the Community

The public is separate. The university is an enclave.

Content

Teach symbol-manipulation skills only.

Implications. Teach democracy by assigning books by selected authors and lecturing about the subject.

Faculty-Student Contact

Close student-faculty contact in research settings. Intellectual and social interaction and mutual respect are emphasized.

Contact with the Community

The only way to teach concern for the community is to bring students out into the community. Otherwise, students will be out of touch and afraid of those unlike themselves.

Content

Develop communication, teamwork, participation, responsibility, initiative, and skills.

Implications. Democracy is not a spectator sport. It must be taught through practice and participation and demonstrated in respectful relations between people in different social roles. The student and university press must also be free and accessible; students must be involved in governance issues, and there must be wide opportunities for student speech and expression.

Teach American political values by assigning eighteenth- and nineteenth-century novels and other works in which students discuss hypothetical situations in oral or written exercises.

Teach American democracy by exploring current political issues and by engaging in the political process to bring about reforms. Train students to be active and aware in the protection of democratic values and to recognize the myths and limitations of the system.

Bring students directly into institutions to see how decisions are made.

Teach aesthetics by requiring humanities courses.

Teach artistic values through shared interpretation and expression.

The humanities should be recognized as valuable in their ability to bring meaning and understanding to students' own experiences and in communicating and sharing directly the experience of other living beings.

Humanities education should be brought alive, not treated as abstract, separate, and isolable.

Students must see the aesthetics in and bring compassion to the physical and social sciences, recognizing the science in art and the art in science.

Require education in "Western Culture" or "Western Civilization."

American culture includes bits and pieces of all cultures. Its heritage and its future are multicultural. It is not "Western" culture.

Procedure

Create well-rounded students by requiring an array of courses in several disciplines.

Teach material in segments—discrete units—disciplines, courses, terms, and fifty-minute lectures.

Impose rules to "strengthen character." The absence of formal rules and requirements may lead to laxity and chaos in which students' instincts may produce negative results.

Socialize students to view their personal experiences as unimportant by not encouraging discussion of personal experience and by not developing their skills in self-awareness and interpersonal exchange.

Measures

The quality of education can be measured by quantitative inputs (number of buildings, size of faculty and renown, size of endowment, alumni salaries).

Procedure

Develop well-rounded students by requiring that the courses themselves are well-rounded and relevant.

Disciplinary boundaries are artificial and arbitrary and promote closed-minded thinking in rigid, anachronistic paradigms.

The more courses and rules required, the more manipulated, programmed, and frustrated students feel.

Treat interdisciplinary problems with interdisciplinary approaches.
Teach the whole person.
Allot the time to fit the problem, not the problem to fit the time.

Measures

The most valid educational measures either are qualitative or are measures of results, not inputs.
The life skills that graduates take away with them, as well as the ability of individuals to

fulfill national and personal dreams and ideals, are what is important.

The test is: Have graduates been innovative and creative? Have they discovered new knowledge? Have they created a safer and more livable world?

Implications. Rank students competitively through grading systems. Allow professors to work as gatekeepers and to aid organizations in their selection of employees.

Implications. Measure performance by measuring achievement of certain stated contractual objectives and by measuring competence in specific skill areas (such as language competence at a measurable level).

Individuals have the right on consent to mutually negotiated standards.

Use contractual grading systems with more objective and less competitive measures of skills. The focus must be on the ability to perform certain tasks or to have participated in certain experiences, rather than on competitive position or the ability to fulfill subjective expectations that are subject to distortion and individual bias.

Result
Dependency
Students develop blind faith in institutions and learn to believe that institutions make better judgments for their

Result
The Dream: Independence
Students develop strength in and commitment to their sense of values and to the individual rights of others.

interests than they can make for themselves.

Students learn that their role is to serve the values and meet the needs of the institutions of which they are a part and to keep the institutions going, without feedback from the public on whether the institution is still effectively serving society and without considering whether certain university functions have become anachronistic or out of touch with reality.

Students learn to expect everything to be prepared and packaged for them.

They recognize that institutions that do not meet the needs of individuals should be made to do so, and students are empowered with the skills to attempt it.

Moral Irresponsibility

The message students learn is that if they only follow orders, they are not responsible for the outcome—the "system" is responsible. They learn to feel powerless and accept lack of control over their destiny.

By being taught to focus on the tasks directly at hand, students get the message that citizens are competent to act and speak out only about their area of technical expertise.

Since tasks are separated from the values and goals behind them, students learn to accept performing without questioning the overall results.

Individual Responsibility

Individuals bear responsibility for their acts. Any act and its effects are a reflection of values. No act is value-neutral or unimportant.

Recognizing their responsibility and ability to control their environments, individuals will take pride in themselves and in their work.

Students define themselves by their social role and by the status of the organization (e.g., the university's national ranking) in which they are working.

Limited Individual Economic Choice

Without learning the set of skills required for going out on their own, graduates are at the mercy of organizations and locked into a kind of industrial feudalism. Their only real economic choice is to move to another organization in which they can use a particular set of technical skills.

Self-Reliance

Individuals will apply and reapply their skills in different ways and will shape their work to individual areas of interest.

Net Social Loss

The energy spent on conforming to an organization and meeting the demands of superiors interferes with citizens' innovation and adaptability to changing markets and socioeconomic conditions.

A lack of confidence in their abilities restricts the likelihood of their acting to improve the efficiency of slow or dangerous systems.

Ingrained fear, paranoia, and apathy about their competitive position and relation to superiors and institutions stifles the dialogue of innovation and cooperation, making social problems seem all the more overwhelming and insoluble.

Net Social Gain

Citizens will discover practical solutions to problems and will build a more adaptable and productive society.

Individuals will be happier, given their greater skills in pursuing and fulfilling their own needs.

Applying Democratic Experiential Education to Various Disciplines

In moving from the goals and ideals of democratic experiential education to specific applications in the university setting, we have added a final test: a test of results to measure what values and skills students learn.

In addition to measuring educational quality through its methods and structure—the skills taught, the methods used, the relationship of teachers to students, the processes of evaluation—it is equally important to test the outcome of an educational system to see whether it meets its objectives and measures up to its ideal. In the university setting, we ask not only whether the process of education is democratic and meets the highest standards of quality but also whether each discipline is serving important democratic and social objectives and its stated mission.

In evaluating the results of the educational system in different disciplines, we pose the following questions.

Social Sciences

Do social scientists train students to do their own experimentation, to apply and test their ideas, to work and plan with the community to save decaying cities and disappearing rural areas, and to improve the productivity and safety of workplaces and products—or do they just talk about these issues in their courses, lecturing from texts and assigning abstract exercises? Are professors and graduates interacting with foreign cultures and understanding their fundamental principles, as well as applying these principles to their own reality—or are they discussing them only abstractly and claiming that this discussion will have had greater positive long- and short-term effects on the students and on the communities with which they interact?

Humanities

Do humanities courses provide students with an appreciation for the world that translates into true understanding and empathy for real and living people, and for real and uncomfortable differences, rather than just giving students the abstract book versions that do not cry, do not shout, and do not make a scene? Does the contemplative life in the library translate later into greater advocacy for protecting the environment, for building up museums and libraries, for holding institutions accountable, and for protecting parks? Does it teach real communications skills for presenting ideas and critically interpreting them? Are professors appropriate role models in these areas, interacting with those who are different and seeking to give them a voice and help them be understood, or have the professors retreated into ivory towers?

Science and Technology

Do the sciences train students to develop innovative and appropriate technologies within their communities, to convert economic production away from armaments and toward peaceful and productive uses, and to ensure that these benefits are widely available? Are professors helping students understand how the technology in their daily environments and from which they benefit works? Are professors helping to teach experimental thinking and the ability to apply principles to construction and design to meet particular needs? Or are professors off in laboratories, working on specialized projects and appearing only to present abstractions and cookbook exercises?

Professional Schools

Do professional students develop their skills through helping to build small businesses, to rebuild financial institutions, to create meaningful opportunity, to provide services for those who need them, and to address larger needs of the public for services currently inadequately distributed—or are these students being prepared to deal only with the abstract, to work for whichever clients pay for their labor, and to look away? What types of role models do their professors provide in putting their own skills into practice?

Overall, are educators themselves concerned with being proper role models for students? Are they applying what they teach to do more than produce articles and books, make media appearances, attend conferences, and generate consulting fees? Can they show real, meaningful, and tangible results that have benefited the lives of people unlike themselves? Do they include students in community-development activities that have improved the quality of life both at home and overseas? Have they given a voice to those who otherwise would have been voiceless?

The rest of this book (Part Two) moves from ideal to practice. It not only describes our model programs and praises the successes of others working along similar lines but also discusses how to institutionalize an educational model that seems at odds with the prevailing view of education. This new model seeks to remedy many of the problems that the prevailing one has caused by depleting the university community, the student population, and the larger community of many of the basic skills and assumptions of civic participation, critical thinking, and democracy.

PART TWO

Student Adventures

Practical Ideas for Remaking Higher Education

Part Two is about student adventures great and small. It is about putting the joy of learning into practice. Each of the following chapters is part how-to, part success story, and part outline of a larger curriculum.

The following seven chapters present a vision of a new curriculum in the social sciences and humanities, showing how democratic and experiential courses can build on one another to form the basis of university education from freshman year all the way through graduate and professional school. We start with small projects—individual courses at the introductory level that can be taught alongside or as replacements for existing introductory courses—and move up to larger, more complex interdisciplinary field projects with implications for national and international policy.

Along with course ideas and successful proposals are syllabi for courses and projects, as well as reports from students and instructors outlining democratic experiential courses and projects that have been successfully tested. All share the essence of creative adventure and imagination at the university level.

Just as there is more to a university or a secondary school than lectures and classes, there is more to educational change than redesigning the formal curriculum or putting a new blueprint on paper. Education takes place in an institutional and social context. Therefore, beyond courses and course projects, we present ideas for coordinating a democratic experiential approach with other aspects of education in a typical student's life and meeting the demands of educational institutions. Finally, we turn our attention to the future with a vision of a new kind of university at all levels. Achieving educational reform ultimately requires transforming existing structures to reflect a different philosophy.

Part Two consists of the following seven chapters:

- *Chapter Four: Reaching Beyond the Classroom: Introductory Level Course Adventures*. This chapter offers a description of new types of courses that can be taught along with existing university courses in existing departments at the introductory level and discusses three different social science applications, at Stanford, the University of California, and Harvard.

- *Chapter Five: Building Skills for the Real World: Intermediate Level Course Adventures*. Building on introductory-level courses are those at more advanced levels for upper-division students. In this chapter, David Lempert and Xavier Briggs outline several possibilities and describe applications at the University of California and at Stanford.

- *Chapter Six: Connecting the Disciplines: National and International Adventures for Advanced Students*. Next, we jump to applications of our techniques in advanced projects at the national and international level, through interdisciplinary projects in which students at advanced levels can work on teams to solve real problems in the community. Here, we not only describe our dreams for new advanced projects that are in the planning stages but we also present a report on a successful project for undergraduates of Harvard and Brown universities in international development planning in a developing country—a project that shocked and amazed those who said it could never be done. We follow that report with a description of a second project in the making: a nationwide student research project across the continental United States.

- *Chapter Seven: Applying Professional Expertise: Adventures at Graduate and Professional Levels*. In this chapter, we describe potential democratic experiential projects for students at the graduate and professional levels that we have participated in, designed, or observed successfully elsewhere. These include the establishment of a small student-operated credit institution in an inner city, community studies and student-written community plans, and other adventures to give professionals a renewed sense of commitment to their communities as well as stronger bases for decision making and better preparation in their chosen fields.

- *Chapter Eight: Back to the Campus: Making Adventures Part of Residential Life*. This chapter presents a vision of adventures that bring new approaches to learning right into student homes. We describe adventures for students to wake up to. This approach to educating the whole person coordinates the "formal" coursework portion of democratic experiential learning with exciting changes in the less formal portions, through the healthy spontaneity of life in the dorms.

- *Chapter Nine: Coordinating Adventures: Questions, Answers, and Practical Tips*. In this chapter, we get down to the nitty-gritty of educational reform to answer the question, How does one go about setting up student adventures that work within the existing parameters of university structures? Ideas for student adventures have to fit into the institutional frameworks that already exist if they are to gain acceptance and to spread. They have to have practical means of implementation. We use a question-and-answer format to offer a few tips for setting up student adventures and to give answers to the most commonly asked questions that designers of such programs face.

- *Chapter Ten: Remaking the University Through Democratic Experiential Education*. In the final chapter, we go one step further. We describe how to wage the two important battles of reform: first, convincing educational ideologues that the ideas behind student adventures are not that different from the kinds of changes the ideologues have been advocating all along without knowing how to implement them and, second, demonstrating how democratic experiential education actually meets administrative goals more efficiently than current approaches.

4

Reaching Beyond the Classroom

Introductory Level Course Adventures

The best place to start with adventures in learning is at the place where learning begins. For university students, that place is in introductory classes. It is in freshman courses that we began to test our models for supplements and alternatives to classroom education to prepare students for ever more challenging, sophisticated, and exciting projects and programs and to give them a chance to have a positive and important impact on the community.

It is in the freshman and sophomore years of the university curriculum that democratic experiential education offers the opportunity not only for the most rapid and creative acquisition of skills but also for hands-on work on real problems, for contributions to the community, for active student participation, and for peer learning.

If there is one almost magic word in academia today that sparks adventure and opens the floodgates of administrative support, particularly at introductory levels, we think we have found it. By appealing to what is holy in industrial society—science and technology—and applying its mantra to the social sciences and humanities without compromising them, we think we can spread an intellectual aura around subjects that hardly would have been noticed before. The magic word is "laboratory."

In places one might think would be the most averse to any borrowing at all from science or technology, there are examples of the exciting effects of laboratory approaches at introductory levels.

- In history courses, simply adding laboratories encourages students to conduct their own investigations and to "do" history while learning its methods and theories, making that discipline more exciting and vital.

- In philosophy classes, adding laboratory work to a subject that many think can be pursued only in a remote or dusty space pushes students to conduct thought experiments (that is, to use the scientific method to think through a problem, often applied when it is not possible to collect other kinds of data) and to pursue investigations in areas in which philosophical issues are not abstract but are components of real decisions. It opens students to the possibility of "doing" philosophy and experiencing it.

- In literature classes, adding a laboratory dimension turns study into a chance to observe behavior, to use communications techniques, to experiment in dissecting language, and to produce new work and literary patterns and techniques.

- In social sciences classes, it is even easier to see that pursuing laboratory work is what turns the discipline into a "science" and restores it to its original aims of detecting patterns in human behavior and being better able to work with that behavior.

We recognize, at the same time, that lower-division courses require slightly different adaptations of democratic experiential education from more advanced courses. Our concept of democratic education and student-initiated work at introductory levels is not that professors abandon teaching these courses and merely approve of students' syllabi and commitment (as they could do with upper-division classes and professional courses, in which the professor's role is more one of innovator, quality controller, and backstop). As part of gradually empowering students and preparing them for classes and projects that they can initiate on their own as they learn a discipline's basic material and become familiar with its approaches, we suggest that the courses follow student interests and deviate from the texts into particular types of problems for exploration of their full dimensions. There is also a role here for peer learning, for graduate and upper-division students who understand the role of a facilitator and of democratic education and who can lead and design the courses.

Furthermore, we are not experts in every field, and we can only apply the same energy and curiosity that we had as incoming freshman to suggesting ideas for improving classes in disciplines in which we remain only intellectual hobbyists. Nevertheless, we present the ideas we have brainstormed across disciplines as a means of inspiring students and experts in those areas. We place them alongside the more-detailed recommendations and descriptions of successful implementation in our own fields, in which we were also once viewed as hobbyists and not experts.

Take, for example, a typical list of freshman and sophomore courses:

Humanities

English and Literature

History

Philosophy

Arts

Foreign Languages

Social Sciences

Economics

Political Science

Anthropology

Psychology

Natural Sciences

Biology

Chemistry

Physics

Mathematics

In almost every one of these areas there are possibilities for opening up entirely new dimensions of learning by applying the concepts of democratic experiential education.

The following, listed by discipline, are a few of these potential additions to or revisions of existing introductory courses and laboratories to accompany existing courses. In addition to these short proposals, we present detailed curricula and results of implementation for specific courses. We have tested two courses using this approach in the social sciences at two universities, and we present a long description and syllabus for a third course. In the first detailed description, we present an account of the first of three courses that we call The Unseen America—a name designed to capture the idea and spirit of student adventures and one that several students have employed in different disciplines, in different ways, to apply to concepts of democratic experiential education and to demonstrate their links with each other.

More-detailed explanations of how one might go about designing, teaching, and implementing courses like these are presented in Chapter Nine.

—⟋⟋⟋—

Course Proposals Across Disciplines

Many faculty have successfully incorporated short laboratory exercises in experimentation into their courses—through required participation in psychology experiments for introductory psychology students, for example, or through archaeological digs, assignments in oral history or journalistic interviews, sociology assignments in conducting surveys, political exercises in visiting legislators and monitoring their activities, or internships. It is important and possible to take these steps much further.

Often such field assignments are just tacked on to a basic introductory course without being integrated into the teaching of theory or taught as a means of developing all the basic skills in the discipline and then developing insight into how the discipline developed and what its limitations and potential are. Within the framework of classroom courses, there isn't nearly enough time for students to learn research skills with adequate instruction, to deal appropriately with ethical and theoretical issues, or to gain the insight and enjoyment that the more open-ended laboratory experience brings.

Here is how we envision the next step.

—◦◊◦—

Humanities

The humanities offer tremendous opportunities for democratic experiential education, for it is here that courses have often forsaken a large array of important skills and adventure for battles with dogma that have buried what is truly exciting.

English and Literature

The study of literature and of past insights into human behavior, the human condition, and the workings of society does not have to be just the dry dissection of books or stories. Literature and written communication are ultimately about connecting with real life and people, understanding the sound and context of language, and being able to use language as one medium for creating pattern and resonance and beauty. Similarly, courses in composition and writing can be much more than exercises in writing creatively about one's personal experience.

At the heart of literature and language courses are specific skills that can be identified and taught—not just through books but through creative and participatory ways of understanding and communicating in the world.

Introduction to English/Western Literature Laboratory. There are no greater texts than the live political and social dramas of modern lives. Such stories are as compelling as those in written work. Moreover, students can even play a role in them after they analyze them. It is a fact that most great writers and artists developed their talent through carefully observing behavior and through practicing their craft, not just by reading and dissecting books. Incorporating laboratory exercises that do this in literature courses is simple. An introductory English or literature laboratory can bring students into the community to work on an array of component skills while gaining an understanding of human behavior and becoming a part of larger community experiences.

Investigative journalism, documentary and dramatic film, radio and stage plays, and other media go well beyond term papers and fiction writing in teaching communications skills, while still moving others and transmitting ideas. Certainly, basic courses can adopt some of the skills taught in communications and journalism schools as part of laboratory exercises in recording and interpreting events. These exercises can involve going on field trips, meeting with individuals in the community, spending a day with different types of people in their routines, and taking part in investigative journalism exercises.

To deepen understanding of human behavior, literature and English courses can be combined with psychology and its applications. Detectives, for example, essentially decode stories and interpret behavior, and they are taught these skills in laboratory settings. If the goal of these courses is to understand the complexity of motivation and the importance of detail in description, students should have the opportunity to learn it directly from those who apply such techniques most directly and to participate in their own investigations through options for investigative detective work and journalistic writing.

Approaches like these actually create a greater appreciation for literary classics than do current courses. As writers of poetry, fiction, humor, and academic books, we know from experience that we can truly appreciate only what we have attempted ourselves. We value the ability in others to see detail and find subtlety and pattern through experiences of seeing, recording, and interpreting.

History

History is more than just a store of written information; it is a means of reconstructing social reality, understanding myth, and putting oneself in a social context. At the same time, history requires applying certain skills, in detective work and data collection, to derive the material necessary to test theory and to apply guiding principles to predict events and interpret behavior.

To bring history alive and revitalize its study is to use actual sites and living "fossils"—groups that preserve traditional ways. To understand the recording of history itself is to see how historians turn the recent past into data and into fable.

American History Laboratory—Recent American and Community History/Oral History. Students currently study American history in books produced by others, but few actually have the chance to discover history as they are living it or to participate in the process of discovering and interpreting history through primary sources. A laboratory class can teach all of the skills of historians while allowing students to investigate the histories of their own communities and institutions, to strengthen the links with older members of the community, to learn about those whose history has been excluded or misrepresented (and why), and to develop a more critical eye for reading and interpreting the history presented in texts and in the media. A model for investigating local history and recognizing its educational value can be seen in the recent German film *The Nasty Girl,* about a young woman who digs into the pre–World War II pasts of her neighbors.

There is good reason to do this, particularly in courses in American history, which almost always end before presenting the history of people who are still alive. Entire areas of recent history are unknown to students because they are not validated in the media or by leaders. Potential areas of study in which students can investigate history through interviews include meeting with Nisei (children of Japanese immigrants—to learn about the period of Japanese-American internment camps), Vietnam veterans, blacklisted writers of the 1950s, civil libertarians of the 1960s, and so on. Topics of local study might include school history, local politics, community archaeology, and institutional history (of corporations, religious organizations, and unions), as well as the study of how local history is kept and who records and presents it.

The various skills to be learned in such a laboratory include digging through archives and records of probate, lawsuits, and property, as well as searching for oral history.

It is easy to combine these exercises with theory of history and historiography (the study of the discipline of history itself). Coursework could include readings of writers such as Tolstoy and Beard, along with postmodern views and more complex understandings of issues of class, race, symbolism, and culture in historical interpretation.

Philosophy

Most of philosophy as it is currently taught is really a history of texts and a secular form of religious scholarship. But it does not have to be lifeless or impenetrably abstract. Key philosophical questions permeate everyday life, whether they are issues of political philosophy—of what constitutes a "good" and "just" society—or situational ethical ones. Philosophy did not develop in a vacuum; it came out of human experience, and its issues and debates remain embedded in those experiences. This is where it can expand. Phenomenological and cognitive questions, or the limitations of symbol systems and other metaphysical issues, are embedded in all of the disciplines. Bringing students to the settings in which these issues arise will make the issues real and allow students to feel better able to address them.

Philosophy Laboratory. Designing a philosophy class that is experiential can be difficult, but creative methods of teaching can adapt the issues raised in classic works to modern settings and bring students to those settings or to meetings with individuals who are addressing the same issues on a daily basis.

To understand situational ethics, students must be in situations that express particular value systems in the context of institutions or individuals. They must be engaged in specific actions where they can express and apply their values.

To consider issues of the human mind—its capabilities and inner workings—is to test the mind, something being done now in computer labs with computer programs and in laboratories where students can directly confront these great issues.

Philosophy is also experimentation through thought experiments—a way of using scientific methods in mental processes that can be practiced and taught.

Foreign Languages

Foreign language courses are often among the most successful because they already apply a variety of methods and media—language laboratories for repetition, films, recent newspapers, and playacting, as well as overseas trips and home stays abroad.

We cannot improve a great deal on techniques we believe in that are already being used. We do, however, support adding to the democratic dimension of language learning as follows.

Language Laboratory in the Community. Even for beginning students, group and individual laboratory exercises can speed learning: pairing students with native speakers in the community who can share their experiences while giving students real practice, assigning students to visit stores where proprietors speak the language, seeking out pen pals, and submitting articles and letters to publications and organizations in which the language is spoken so that students have real feedback. Letting students design the exercises and choose forays into the community also enhances the motivation and democratic content of the courses, thereby enriching learning. These exercises prepare students directly for a more advanced level of study in which they can integrate foreign language into complex projects, such as presenting policy recommendations to foreign leaders and defending the recommendations on national television in the host country language (see Chapter Six).

―◦◦◦―

Social Sciences

Economics, sociology, political science, psychology, and anthropology could all include laboratory courses alongside their introductory theory (mostly lecture) courses to teach research skills and to test the theories. Yet most do not. It is possible to earn a social science degree at many universities today without ever conducting research on societies or actually observing any human behavior. In some cases, it is possible to earn degrees in these fields without any attention to methods or even to simulations using data that have been collected by others and can be processed with statistical or computer techniques.

Computer courses in applied statistics, econometrics, and survey design, for example, have all used laboratory methods, but they have done so in an abstract way, with no attention to collection of primary data or contact with the real subject of social sciences: people.

Taking the idea one step further involves setting up course exercises in the techniques of data collection and observation to spark student interest in qualitative observation, to develop a critical eye in students for looking at data that others have collected, and to allow students to work through the ethical issues of studying other human beings. The study of society can include the adventure of empirical science with democratic and humanistic goals (Malinowski, 1922).

Economics

The use of laboratories involving statistical analysis and econometric modeling in upper-level economics courses is the equivalent of the laboratory write-up phase in natural sciences once the data have been collected and abstracted. Students often have the equipment to process data but do not make their own observations or try to replicate the direct observations of others. That should be built into introductory level courses, to help students understand how macro- and microeconomic theories developed and whether they are useful in describing real behavior.

Introductory Economics Laboratory.   We have already designed a complete economics laboratory course, to teach basic skills and to explore different components of the economy, for use alongside or in place of the standard introductory course in macroeconomics (which we present later in this chapter). However, it is just one possibility for an introductory economics laboratory course. We have also designed a laboratory course in development economics, for example, that can be taught either at the introductory level or at an advanced level to coincide with theory courses that are now considered upper division (see Exhibit 4.3).

Political Science

There are as many potential experiential political science courses as there are political science courses and introductory courses in the discipline's subfields—American government, political theory, comparative government, and so on. Political science laboratories can aid in exposing students to particular institutions and in their understanding of political and institutional behavior.

To teach government and politics through experience is to create a course with field trips to meet with pollsters, lobbyists, citizen groups, fund-raisers, donors, party operatives, speechwriters, media pundits, bureaucrats, and a long line of inside participants to understand what they do, whom they exclude, and how.

To teach issues of constitutionalism and representation is to bring students to visit community groups, Native Americans, jurors, judges, military contractors, FBI agents, and organized crime leaders and to interpret how the Constitution recognizes or fails to recognize the power and influence of each.

Even in introductory courses (such as comparative government) in which it might be difficult to conduct field observations, the reality is that different kinds of governance structures still exist in communities near universities—Native American reservations, companies and company towns, religious cults, and communes. There is also historical evidence of different kinds of political structures, such as the colonial and precolonial governments, that students can visit in restorations and investigate through field historical methods.

Political science courses can take advantage of all of these community laboratories while also encouraging students to participate in all forms of political action—from lobbying to writing letters, filing lawsuits, using the media, supporting or even participating in labor strikes, and organizing—so that they can learn the skills used in each and actually test their efficacy.

The Unseen America: Laboratory—Political Science and Policy. We have already designed and tested one introductory alternative political science course (developed as a supplement to and a replacement for the standard "Introduction to American Government" or "Introduction to Major Issues in American Public Policy" course), which is described in the essay "Political Science and Policy Laboratory" later in this chapter.

The two intermediate political science/policy courses that we describe in Chapter Five contain several components of methodological skills and ways of thinking that could also be part of a single basic introductory course. In disciplines like political science, in which techniques are not hierarchical but lateral, in the form of different subfields and policy areas, there is much greater leeway and no standard set of building blocks for the sequential development of skills.

Anthropology

If any course is a natural for teaching field techniques in the community and learning to study human development, human origins, human behavior, and "the other" directly rather than from books, it is anthropology. Both of the typical introductory anthropology courses offer opportunities for laboratory work to reinforce theory and skills.

Introduction to Social Anthropology Laboratory.   We specifically designed a laboratory course to complement an existing introductory course at the University of California at Berkeley. The laboratory provided opportunities for students to learn all of the discipline's key methods and skills in conducting research into the workings of a community while they tested the theories learned in class and discovered how to see the world from the perspectives of "the other" (see Exhibit 4.2).

Introduction to Physical Anthropology and Archaeology Laboratory.   The same techniques for teaching history also apply to laboratory teaching of archaeology and physical anthropology, since the subject is a particular type of historical analysis combining all of the different natural sciences with social science. While we present one advanced possibility for understanding the technology of primitive peoples in our section on intermediate courses, an introductory course could include one or two weeks of tool construction, a week or two of archaeological soil and site analysis, and other skills development.

Psychology

Introductory psychology courses can be made more experiential by incorporating more experiment and contact with the community. While many introductory psychology courses currently have a laboratory component, it often uses students as guinea pigs in clinical experiments, rather than allowing them to conduct their own experiments and to test principles. Beginning student-initiated laboratory exercises at the introductory level would be an excellent way to raise the ethical implications of human experimentation directly while also increasing contact between students and children (as a method of understanding development psychology as well as of learning parenting and socializing skills) and between students and the mentally ill (as a method of understanding deviance as well as health policy and treatments for mental illness).

Introductory Psychology Laboratory.   While we have brought students out to mental hospitals, psychiatric wards of prisons, and support groups in other courses, there are also settings that are more "natural" in which students can inquire about and test the use of psychological principles—in media, advertising, jury selection, and education, for example, as well as in controlled experiments within university settings.

At the same time, an introductory laboratory course is the place to introduce students to animal behavior studies and to brain imaging and other laboratory work that remains a mystery to beginning students.

Natural Sciences

Some of the most exciting laboratory courses already in university curricula can be found in the sciences—geography expeditions to explore terrain, for example, and environmental biology expeditions to rain forests, wetlands, and the oceans. Other courses, such as computer science, observational astronomy, and engineering design, make use of hands-on experiences. Yet laboratories in introductory physics, biology, and chemistry are often disconnected from student and community interests and from the ideals and challenges of true experimentation.

Introductory natural science laboratories can be improved by applying the concepts of democratic education—hands-on technology, student-initiated projects that benefit communities, and basic science—to replicate some of the real work of scientists in designing their own tools and thinking through projects and hypotheses. Indeed, a key lesson of democratic education is that many of our most prominent citizens, such as Benjamin Franklin and Thomas Jefferson, were themselves scientists and inventors who learned scientific principles by working with them, just as they learned the principles of democracy and behavior.

Biology

Introductory biology laboratories can extend the concepts of laboratories outward to the community by focusing laboratory work on the environment, public health, and agriculture.

Introduction to Biology Laboratory—Focus on Human Biology. As one example of a set of laboratory exercises that goes beyond microscopic observations and dissections, a human biology and "barefoot doctor" laboratory component could include a more applied study of human anatomy, development, and disease in a simplified version of introductory work in a medical school program. Such laboratory work would not only serve as an introduction to medicine for biology students who have an interest in entering one of the medical professions but would also serve as a way of teaching more useful information in basic health practices and in understanding of disease through work with people and patients. Some of us have done this on our own when we could not find it in the curriculum, visiting medical school laboratories and anatomy courses, volunteering in hospital emergency rooms, and taking part in public health activities. Certainly these exercises could be made part of an introductory biology course.

Chemistry and Physics

The irony of current introductory laboratories in the physical sciences of chemistry and physics is that while they are often described as "cookbook" laboratories in which exercises are little more than set recipes, students do not even learn the basic applications that they can apply to familiar activities like cooking or household technology.

Some upper-level courses have encouraged students to use physics in design projects, engineering their own flying objects, boats, toys, and engines. These kinds of projects would certainly make more useful and adventurous laboratory work at the introductory level than do current exercises that are really just routine forms of labor rather than science.

We think students taking introductory laboratory courses would benefit from learning to design buildings, to construct lightbulbs and simple engines, and to make workshops and crafts a part of their experience. The loss in "material" covered in these laboratories would be more than made up in the self-confidence and thought processes that students developed as well as in the energy and motivation gained to go further in scientific study. More experiential and applied work should also be encouraging to students who currently avoid sciences, helping them realize that many different skills come into play in natural science and that solutions come from different angles.

Introductory Physical Science Laboratory—Technology by Ontogeny. Most university courses in the physical sciences focus on abstract principles, sometimes demonstrated in laboratory settings with simple instruments and models. After taking many of these courses, one might ask, "Could students shipwrecked on a desert island or survivors of a nuclear holocaust reconstitute Western civilization's technology?" An experiential course could teach technology through reinvention of the wheel, the battery, the internal combustion engine, and select other technological advances of human civilization.

In a variant of this idea at Yale University, Anthony Massini has already developed a course in mechanical arts in which students build telescopes, sextants, and other scientific equipment, as well as robots and solar-powered cars. Such courses can easily be integrated into the introductory science curricula alongside cookbook laboratories.

Indeed, we do not see why an introductory course to modern science is not available in the use of laboratory equipment and the understanding of its construction, principles, and design.

∽∾∽

Political Science and Policy Laboratory: Exploring The Unseen America at Stanford

By David Lempert

Roger Miller couldn't wait to get back on the road again. I would bet money he was never a trucker.

So many myths and misconceptions surround the world of the trucker that it is difficult to gain true understanding of what his life is actually like. I wanted to see the real world of the trucker; the world you don't see on television and in magazines. I wanted to speak with truckers and get a firsthand glimpse of what life on the road is really like. This is the account of what I have learned. This is the real world of the trucker.

So begins a report by Curt Cortelyou, then a nineteen-year-old Stanford University freshman from Seattle. Curt spent a full day with teamsters out on the loading docks and behind closed doors at a union meeting in Hayward, California, thirty minutes away from the tranquil serenity of the Stanford campus.

Nate Martin, a freshman from San Diego, pretended to be homeless and spent the night at a shelter in San Francisco. Tricia Swartling, from Twin Falls, Idaho, spent an evening in a shelter for teenagers in suburban Palo Alto. Other students looked at hairdressing and health-food businesses, a children's ward in a state mental hospital, and a veteran's hospital.

The individual visits came at the end of a semester-long whirlwind of short adventures, of tears and stomachaches and intellectual debates to all hours that was far removed from any other academic experience the students had encountered at Stanford. I called the series of adventures The Unseen America, to capture its sense of intellectual mystery and adventure. It is a title that students and friends continue to use for related adventures in democratic experiential education in the years that have followed since I first tested it as a laboratory course in political science and issues in American politics.

As the entry point into the unknown through a new kind of student adventure, The Unseen America seemed the perfect title. For students who were attracted to teaching or learning through field work in social science and democratic education, The Unseen America—and the three courses that followed with the same title—were a ticket to academic exploration of the groups and issues that never seemed to touch the curriculum or the campus. To students used to sitting in the classroom, much of their own country and reality was hidden, mysterious, and "unseen." The Unseen America conjured up images of the powers that be who are hidden from scrutiny, the powerless whose stories are rarely heard, the activists and unconventional thinkers who do not appear on the evening news, the institutionalized and the isolated, the myths and symbols that are so familiar they are no longer questioned, the biases that cloud social science thinking and common knowledge, the groups that exist only in stereotypes and clichés in the national media so that their reality is hardly known, the factory floors and fields where our products are produced, and the people who do not appear in statistics or who appear only in statistics. All are parts of The Unseen America: parts of the reality of American life that are not captured in textbooks, classrooms, or media images—pieces often unseen or unquestioned by policy makers. This was the subject matter to be explored in a new course at Stanford in the spring of 1985.

In its initial voyage, The Unseen America was both an experiment and an escape from the university. It was a chance for me, as the professional student teaching it, to learn and teach, in a whirlwind crash course, everything I felt had been left out of my under-graduate and professional school education that I had really wanted to know when I had enrolled. There were so many things I had hoped to learn in expensive courses with fancy names and that I had expected to be able to teach in my first undergraduate social science classes; but few of them were there in the classroom. They were unseen.

Initially, the course was just an experiment in education encouraged by Kennell Jackson, a black professor of African history from Virginia. I was a professional student from suburban New York who felt isolated on the Stanford campus and out of touch with the people whose lives I was being trained to manage as an executive, a lawyer, or a policy maker.

In the rooms where my classmates and I sat to be educated, the reality from which the lessons I had been teaching and learning were abstracted seemed further and further away. I wondered if the abstract theories I was being trained to follow even had validity anymore. I wondered if my students were learning anything other than how to manipulate symbols and measure body counts, some-thing I saw in nightmarish visions of the use of American military power overseas. I wondered if any of the real issues of the world were being discussed and if what was being taught could ever have any real bearing on the world in a way that might make a construc-tive difference.

In almost eight years of higher education at Yale and Stanford, I had read about poor people but had never spoken with them. I read about crime and prison life, but I had never visited a prison or talked with an inmate. I had studied law for three years but had hardly ever seen the inside of a courtroom. Though I was complet-ing a business degree, I had rarely been on a factory floor, and I never had a chance to speak to workers, union leaders, or consumer advocates. I had studied economics before that, but I had never spo-ken with a farmer or spent any time on a production line. I had taken humanities classes in which I had almost no contact with humans.

In fact, most of what I had studied—and most of what went on from day to day in the region where I lived—I had never even seen. No one in the university was bringing students to see anything outside the classroom or bringing slices of reality to the students. So I decided that it was time to go out and see a few of those unseen things.

I wanted to try combining theoretical readings with off-campus visits to such places as a Native American reservation, a prison, a mental hospital, a homeless shelter, a soup kitchen, a mansion, a courtroom, a military installation, a veteran's center, a migrant labor camp, and a factory. I wanted to test contractual grading and democratic education. I wanted to see what would happen if I started teaching students differently from how they had learned to be taught in their introduction to college life.

That is the story of the creation of The Unseen America: Qualitative Analysis in Social Science Research and Policy Formation, offered at Stanford in the spring of 1985, sponsored by Dr. Kennell Jackson in the Department of History and accredited for three quarter units as part of the Undergraduate Specials program (Exhibit 4.1, at the end of this section, presents the syllabus for this course).

The Unseen America was open only to freshmen and sophomores, and it was allocated a budget of $25. The course was based in a seminar room in Branner Hall, the largest freshman dormitory on the Stanford campus and the one with the most colorful history and intellectual life. Transportation was in a light green and rumbling 1958 Ford Fairlane that students nicknamed "The Lemp Mobile" after their instructor and chauffeur; it fit a small class, along with their notebooks and snacks.

Seven students showed up on the first night of this new class, with its strange name, and something unusual happened. The first class, which was scheduled as a two-hour seminar, did not stop after two hours. Students did not look at their watches or fidget or get out of their chairs. They just kept asking questions and talking: about the mission of a university and about the structure of curricula and requirements that channeled their thoughts and frustrated their curiosity by directing them away from things they wanted to see and learn. The class went on for another hour. Some students left at the end of the third hour. Even then, the discussion continued.

The field trips didn't start for a week. The syllabus began with short readings on historical process and social analysis, including the conclusion to Tolstoy's *War and Peace*, an essay that was hard for students to understand. They asked for an extra hour, just to talk about theories of history and Tolstoy. We took the extra hour. The class talked about stories by Lewis Carroll and Mark Twain that satirized book-learned science and social science taken to their extremes, and some of the "new paradigm" pieces, to point out a few of the assumptions contained in the university's required sequence in Western culture.

A section in one of the readings, Theodore Roszak's description of Stanford students as "trained performers" (*Person/Planet*, 1979), became a new reference point for some students on how they and their peers had been educated and as something they were hoping to get away from.

Though the student role in helping to plan topics was not that extensive in the trial run of this course, I encouraged students to help shape the curriculum to their own needs. Some said that this gave them, for the first time, some real sense of control and involvement in their education.

Debates over issues, while orderly, were not restricted and were always lively. A contract grading system on a "licensing" basis (awarding grades on a specified scale of attendance and completion of projects) gave students much freer rein to present and defend their own ideas and to challenge me on mine.

Before taking any trips off campus, the group discussed both the methods and ethical problems of field work and looked at some short ethnographies and commentaries on American culture and rituals. To put this material in context and develop preliminary skills, the class conducted some minor field work in a nearby setting. The first expedition was to the Stanford Graduate School of Business, where students looked at clothing, building architecture, and posters; at behavior in classes and hallways; at the roles of males and females; and even sought to find bathroom graffiti. As they looked, the students started asking questions and generating hypotheses.

Why was it that NO POSTING signs were posted on classroom walls in the business school? Why was it that the students felt looked down upon? Why were most of the adult women employees working in secretarial positions? Why were there no bathroom graffiti? Why were there no men with beards? Why did students speak so authoritatively in classes?

During the second week, two class sessions were set aside in an attempt to place the method and goals of the course in historical context of other observers of the American scene, both in print—from Alexis de Tocqueville to Jack Kerouac, Bill Moyers, and Studs Terkel—and in film—*Easy Rider* and *Sullivan's Travels* (which, some students said, had uncannily captured their instructor's essence as well as that of the class). Then the students were ready for their own escapades.

The class's first trip was a visit to the ancestors of the first Americans. Students read several pieces on current problems faced by Native Americans in the United States as well as on the history and culture of the Wailaki and Yuki tribes, and then the class traveled to the Round Valley Indian Reservation in Northern California. There students stayed overnight with a Wailaki and Yuki family, making Indian fry-bread tacos, looking at the reservation's five lone buffalo, and walking in the woods.

On the first day, ethical questions arose; they were from a student and targeted at the instructor. "Lemp, this is their burial ground. I don't think we should be walking here," Ron Borzekowski challenged. "Why not? We are here to explore the 'unseen,' aren't we?" I answered. "We are guests, and this may be a holy place to them," Ron said. Ron was right, and the class's hosts later explained why. It was one of the key events that made everyone more sensitive then and throughout the term while it also made the class experience a more shared and humbling exercise.

During the same day, as the son of the family with whom the class stayed sat transfixed in the living room in front of a television screen, a member of the class began a long debate about assimilation. "Why should Native Americans have any more rights now than my family?" he asked. "This house is just like mine. The only things different are the decorations on the walls. Where I have pictures of my great-grandparents in the ghettos of Europe, they have pictures of their ancestors in their tribal clothing. Only the faces and the outfits are different. Everything else about us seems the same." A long debate on ethnicity, on rights, and on the meaning and history of American democracy ensued and continued well beyond the course.

The next set of field trips, or visits, were to the workplace. The first was to a potato chip factory where the class spoke with both managers and workers on a visit guided by managers. "Why didn't the executives let the workers talk to us alone?" students said afterward. "That guy seemed frightened to talk to us with the managers around." "They treated the employees like children." "Why did they show us that propaganda film about the company? Do they think we're stupid?" There were questions and more questions.

Later, the group visited the Longshoreman Workers Union and traveled to a coroner's "office" (a morgue) and to a migrant labor camp in Salinas, California. Some students were shocked at what they encountered in the labor camp. "How can six men live together in a tiny room like that?" students asked. They wondered why they had never seen or heard about this before.

Next, the class met with a group of Vietnam veterans and discussed the effects of war on American society. A veteran broke down in tears before us as he talked about the health problems he had suffered from Agent Orange, about the deaf ear the U.S. government had turned to his claims for support, and about all of the homeless veterans on the streets.

In subsequent weeks, students watched trials in the local courts and visited a coed federal prison (the site of a recent helicopter escape), where they debated the merits of the criminal justice system with convicted former Environmental Protection Agency official

Rita Lavelle and several other inmates. "I don't get it," one of the students said. "These people are convicts, and they live better than we do just because they committed white-collar crimes." "Tomorrow I'm going down to East Palo Alto and telling every poor person I know to commit a *federal* crime," joked another student sarcastically. But after visiting this prison—and, a year later on a reunion trip, a state prison—the overall demeanor of the students was grim. They did not want to go their separate ways after the prison trip. They wanted to meet over dinner to talk about being in a place where people were locked up; about how it made them feel; and about who was being locked up in different kinds of prisons in America, who was putting them there, and what it said about American society.

These trips were followed by a visit to a homeless shelter, lunch in a San Francisco soup kitchen, a meeting at a refugee resettlement center, a tour of a military air-naval station, and a visit to the wards of a state mental hospital.

On all of the trips, debate was open on any topic, ranging from the theories in class readings and how they fit the reality to techniques of information collection, to personal feelings, to ethics. My role as instructor was not to lead to a particular point or draw conclusions but only to help the students speculate, to probe and prod, to ask uncomfortable questions of the students (and, in some cases, of the people with whom they met), and to keep raising issues.

At the soup kitchen in San Francisco, for example, the sight and smell of the food turned some of the students' faces pale, and they refused to eat with the homeless as part of an exercise to experience what it is like to be in their place and to try to feel how they view themselves and their opportunities. "What does it mean that you feel too sick to eat this?" I asked the students. "What kinds of signals are you sending our hosts by reacting this way to the food? Are you acting ethically? If you don't participate, have you opted out of your contractual obligation for participating in democratic education and, if so, what is the appropriate way to handle this issue?" These kinds of spontaneous reactions were the settings for new types of insight and learning.

The final trip, an overnight visit, was to the secluded community of Bolinas, California, across the high weeds on the lawn of civil liberties lawyer Tony "True Believer" Serra, along a sandy beach, and in the shops and homes of a small Marin County town. This was contrasted with the site of the last class meeting, the poolside of a Los Altos Hills mansion in Northern California's Silicon Valley.

During the last weeks of the term, for their final projects, students were to prepare and present a short ethnography following field work off campus. Here was a chance for students to be creative on their own, to experiment with new techniques, and to learn more about groups and issues in which they had a particular interest. It was a chance for them to apply skills and see the unseen in ways that were difficult or impossible in a large group.

For student Nate Martin, pretending to be homeless and spending the night in a homeless shelter was a courageous way to understand the lives of the homeless and to become a modern-day Sullivan, the mythical character in the classic film *Sullivan's Travels*. But it was also a way to provoke an even livelier debate. That was my role as the instructor: to provoke, as a means of pushing the intellectual capacities of the students. "Is it right to lie and say that you are homeless when you are not? Is it an ethical form of research? Did you ever think that you might have been taking a bed away from someone who needed it and who might have been forced to spend the night out on the streets?"

For another student, there were other methods to try: walking and riding through wealthy neighborhoods in different kinds of cars and clothing as an experiment to test police and community reaction and to understand how laws and rights and civil liberties really worked in practice.

Overall, students still had not forgotten The Unseen America months or years later. "That class whetted my appetite. It was one of the most intellectual experiences I've had here," said one of the participants who went on to work as a journalist. "It made me hungry for more."

Building on the Experience with The Unseen America

There were a number of lessons that this first Unseen America course taught me and others about developing future courses like it. Certainly, not everything worked perfectly the first time.

Among the difficulties were scheduling—trying to balance the trips with the students' standard classroom curriculum—and time. With a load of four or five other courses, students did not have time to do all of the readings as well as participate in the trips. The hours of the course were not overly extensive, but trying to work around the logistics of the rest of the curriculum was difficult.

Though the readings were an additional burden, almost all the students purchased their own copies of reserved course readings that they had been unable to complete during the year so they could read them during the summer, requested a longer bibliography, and gathered one year after the course was taught—on their own time—for additional field work and discussion.

Besides the logistics of scheduling itself, there was also some concern that the course had too many topics. While the goal was to expose students to as many types of people and perspectives as possible—to introduce them to the great variety of ideas that were covered in the rest of the curriculum and that they might not otherwise have a chance to think about during their undergraduate years—some students said that the course trips, readings, and array of ideas were a bit overwhelming and that they really needed the experience spread out among other courses throughout the curriculum.

In providing ideas for improving the course, students suggested that it contain fewer topics and be followed by a more advanced course focusing on a particular problem in its larger social context—the criminal justice system, for example, or aspects of the economy. If it were geared to a public policy and political science approach, there was a hope that it might focus more on one or two theme issues. One proposal was to allocate three or four weeks in the introductory course itself to a particular policy area. If the course goal was to question methods and philosophy of the social sciences and of Western thought in general, then perhaps a second introductory course could be created with a more theoretical focus, rather than a focus on the full array of field skills or policy issues.

In fact, that is exactly what has happened. New versions of the course, with different approaches, have appeared at both the University of California and at Stanford. The Unseen America that was given life at Stanford in the spring of 1985 has continued to grow—testing different sites and different methods and working its way into different disciplines, many of them still under the name The Unseen America.

A second version of the course is still being taught at the University of California at Berkeley after several consecutive semesters. Taught by and for upper-division students, this version of the class is described in Chapter Five. Three undergraduates originally taught The Unseen America as a student-initiated "Democratic Education at the University of California" (DE-CAL) course. For four semesters, it was sponsored by five departments, more than any other course in the university. It incorporated many themes from the humanities as well as from the social sciences, until it finally became a permanent feature of the political science department curriculum, where it is now in its eighth year.

During the spring of 1989, three years after its beginnings, The Unseen America returned to Stanford, also as an upper-level course. It had a very different focus but the same underlying philosophy of the original courses. It was taught by three undergraduates and loosely coordinated with the students who had taught the other versions, and then was taught again by another generation of students (this course is also described in Chapter Five).

Currently in the works is a national adaptation of The Unseen America called The Unseen America Nationwide (described in Chapter Six). It is a project in which students will travel across the United States, looking at the unseen in up to forty-eight states.

No longer is The Unseen America just the name of a course. Following the success of the course at Stanford, it is now also the name of a nonprofit educational corporation (Unseen America Projects, Inc.) founded by several of the students and current and future professors of The Unseen America courses.

EXHIBIT 4.1. Political Science and Policy Laboratory.

Instructor: David Lempert   Spring 1985
            Sponsor: Kennell Jackson, Dept. of History
            Course Meetings as Noted in Syllabus

STANFORD UNIVERSITY
Undergraduate Specials 38
© David Lempert, 1985

Course Title:
The Unseen America: Qualitative Analysis in Social Science Research and Policy Formation

Short Description:
This course is designed to supplement the traditional quantitative and theoretical social science approach to American public policy problems with an introduction to both qualitative research methods and data. Interdisciplinary readings will be coordinated with field trips to prisons, courts, a mental hospital, an Indian reservation, and so on. Preference given to freshmen.

Course Objectives:
The course has three distinct objectives:
1) To introduce students to the methodology, ethical considerations, and usefulness of ethnographic analysis.
2) To contrast on-site observations and analysis with written source materials in order to better appreciate the strengths and weaknesses of quantitative and qualitative approaches and means of combining the two in policy analysis.
3) To enrich students' understanding of and appreciation for the diversity and richness of American society and culture.

Requirements:
Students will be required to:
• Complete assigned readings (approximately 100 pages per week).
• Attend and participate in weekly discussions.
• Attend weekly field trips. In some weeks, due to scheduling and space limitations on excursions to certain sites, two field trips will be offered and students will have a choice of trips.
• Prepare one ethnographic analysis of a particular site or type of individual in American society. Possible topics of study include fortune

tellers, "punks," the homeless, and executives. Students will present their work at the end of the term to the Instructor and to three or four other students. Students may choose any medium for presentation of their work—movie, slide show, written report, taped interviews, and so on.

Grading:

This course will be offered on the regular grading options. However, in order to promote the free exchange of ideas in discussion and to encourage intellectual experimentation, grading will be on a contractual rather than competitive basis. Grades will be assigned by means of "certification," reflecting attendance at discussions and field trips and completion of the final project.

Course Plan by Week
(Quarter System)

Week	Topics
1	A) Introduction: Rethinking Traditional Social Science Methodologies and Assumptions; Rethinking Traditional Teaching Methods B) Introduction to Qualitative Analysis
2	A) Further Considerations on Ethnographic Field Work (Including Ethics) B) Perceptions of America (Course's Antecedents)
3	Native Americans
4	The Workplace (Industrial)
5	The Justice System
6	War and Its Domestic Repercussions
7	Wealth and Poverty
8	The Institutionalized
9	Agriculture
10	Alternative Futures
11	Conclusion

Field Trips and Readings

Week 1:   A) Introduction: Rethinking Traditional Social Science
B) Introduction to Qualitative Analysis

Class Meetings:

Two class sessions. No field trips this week. Optional supplemental session: a detailed look at Tolstoy's discussion of history in context of past and current attempts to model historical processes, including the Instructor's current work.

Readings: A) *Traditional Social Science:*
Mark Twain, "Corn Pone Options," "Political
   Economy"
Lewis Carroll, "The New Method of Evaluation"
Holistic Approaches:
Leo Tolstoy, *War and Peace* (final two chapters)
Fritjof Capra, *The Tao of Physics* (first 50 pages)
(Recommended: Douglas Hofstader, *Gödel, Escher,*
   Bach)
Ken Wilbur, *The Holographic Paradigm;*
Thomas Kuhn, *The Nature of Scientific Revolutions)*
Educational Approaches:
Ted Roszak, *Person/Planet* (excerpts)
Herbert Hoover, *Autobiography of Herbert Hoover*
   (excerpts)
(Recommended: Paul Goodman, *Growing Up Absurd;*
   Ivan Illich, *Deschooling Society)*

B) *Qualitative Analysis:*
Horace Milner, "Body Ritual Among the Nacirema"
Neil B. Thompson, "The Mysterious Fall of the Nacirema"
James Finley Scott, "Sororities and the Husband Game"
James Spradley, *The Ethnographic Interview* (skim)

Week 2:   **A) Further Considerations on Ethnographic Field Work**
B) Perceptions of America (Course's Antecedents)

Class Meetings (three class sessions):
1) Topic A, discussion. Also, a short visit from the county sheriff's office
   describing how students can participate in the Civilian Ride Along Program
   spending four hours in a county patrol car on-duty.
2) Introduction to Field Work-An Ethnography of the Stanford Graduate
   School of Business; Class Project: the class will conduct one hour of
   on-site observation and will then meet to write a five-page popular
   article on life observed in the Stanford G.S.B.
3) Topic B, films (exploring America: Preston Sturge's *Sullivan's Travels,*
   Easy Rider)

Readings: A) *Ethics of Field Work:*
Michael Rynkiewich and James Spradley, *Ethics and
Anthropology*
J. A. Barnes, *Ethics of Inquiry in Social Science*
B) *Perspectives of America Through the Past Century:*
Class Handout
(Recommended: Alexis de Tocqueville, *Democracy in
America;* Franz Kafka, *America;* Louis-Ferdinand Céline,
Journey to the End of the Night; Jack Kerouac, *On the
Road;* Robert Pirsig, *Zen and the Art of Motorcycle
Maintenance;* Bill Moyers, *Listening to America;* John
Cheever, "Just One More Time," "The Swimmer")

Week 3:   **Native Americans**

Field Trip: Overnight visit to Round Valley Indian Reservation,
Northern California; stay with a Wailaki and Yuki family

Readings: *Policy Issues:*
Stephen L. Pevar, *The Rights of Indians and Tribes*
(Chapter 1)
"America's Indians: Beggars in Our Own Land," *U.S.
News & World Report*
The Indian Perspective:
Carlos Castaneda, *Journey to Ixtlan* (first 50 pages)
(Recommended: John Neihardt, *Black Elk Speaks;*
Richard Luxton, *The Mystery of Mayan Hieroglyphs)*
Cross-Cultural Issues:
"The Governor of All the Tribes"
"Thinking in Two Tongues"
"The Guilt Is in Our Blood"
"Where Are We Going?"
"Navajos Resist Forced Relocation"
Field Trip Briefing:
Handbook of North American Indians (excerpts)
Handout

Week 4:   **The Workplace (Industrial)**

Field Trips: Frito-Lay Factory, San Jose-meetings with management
and workers; International Longshoreman Workers
Union, loading docks, northern piers, San Francisco

Readings: *Workplace Issues:*
John Kenneth Galbraith, *The Affluent Society* (excerpts)
David Riesman, *Abundance for What?* (excerpt)
Ted Roszak, *Person/Planet* (excerpt)
Studs Terkel, *Working* (excerpts)
Alvin Toffler, *The Third Wave* (excerpt)
Karl Marx (excerpt on "alienation")
Ways of Thinking About Industrial Societies:
Andrei Sakharov, *Peaceful Competition* (excerpts)
John Kenneth Galbraith, *The New Industrial State* (excerpts)
G.D.H. Cole, *Guild Socialism* (excerpts)
History of the Industrial Workplace:
(Recommended: Upton Sinclair, *The Jungle;* Émile Zola,
Germinal)

Week 5:   **The Justice System**

Field Trips: Federal Correctional Institute in Pleasanton
Duell Vocational Institute (State Prison)
State Medical Facility in Vacaville
Santa Clara County Municipal Courts
Coroner's Office, City of San Francisco

Readings: Various Handouts on the Legal System and Briefings
on Field Sites
Jessica Mitford, *Kind and Unusual Punishment*
Erving Goffman, *Asylums*

Week 6:   **War and Its Domestic Repercussions**

Field Trips: Swords to Plowshares Veterans Organization, San
Francisco
Southeast Asian Refugee Resettlement Center,
San Francisco
Moffett Field, U.S. Air-Naval Military Installation

Films
(in-class):   *Toys*
The Nisei (CBS Documentary with Daniel Inouye)
(Recommended: *From Here to Eternity, Coming Home*)

Readings: *Theories of Aggression:*
(Recommended: Konrad Lorenz, *On Aggression;* Ashley
Montague, *Man and Aggression;* Desmond Morris,
The Human Zoo)

Effects at Home:
U.S. Supreme Court, *Korematsu v. United States*
I. F. Stone, *Kent State*
Report on Blacklisting in *Radio/Television, Motion Pictures*
Gene Oishi article on Japanese Americans, *New York Times Magazine*
War Stories:
"Why Men Love War," *Esquire*
William Calley, *My Lai: My Story*

Week 7: **Wealth and Poverty in America**

Field Trips: St. Anthony's Soup Kitchen, San Francisco (lunch)
Canon Kip Homeless Shelter, San Francisco
Mansion, Los Altos Hills
Mission High School, San Francisco

Readings: *Theory:*
John B. Calhoun, "Population Density and Social Pathology," *Scientific American*
John Kenneth Galbraith, "The Heartless Society," *New York Times Magazine*
"Elites":
Ron Rosenbaum, "The Secrets of Skull and Bones"
"Public School or Private," *Yale Alumni Magazine*
Marriage Announcements, *Sunday New York Times*
(Recommended: Peter Meyer, *The Yale Murder)*
The "Poor":
Claude Brown, "Manchild in Harlem," *New York Times Magazine*
Susan Sheehan, *A Welfare Mother*
"Night's Journey with New York's Homeless," *The Village Voice*
"Armed Schoolchildren," *San Francisco Chronicle*
(Recommended: Michael Harrington, *The Other America)*

Week 8: **The Institutionalized**

Field Trip: Napa State Mental Hospital

Readings: (See also readings on justice system dealing with prisons)
The "Insane":
David Rosenhan, "On Being Sane in Insane Places"
"Shared Illusions in Modern America"
Charles Manson (excerpts from interviews)

Sue Estroff, "Making It Crazy: An Ethnography of
Psychotic Clients"
General Policy Issues:
"Human Warehouse," *Time* (institutions for the retarded)
"Exploiting the Aged," *Time*
"Wheels of Misfortune," *Harpers*
(Recommended: William Nolen, *The Making of a*
Surgeon)

Week 9:   Agriculture

Field Trips: Family Farm, Hayward
Green Gulch Communal Farm, Marin County
Migrant Labor Camps, Gilroy

Readings: Leo Tolstoy, *Anna Karenina* (excerpt)
Ted Roszak, *Person/Planet* (excerpt)
Paul Goodman, *Like a Conquered Province* (excerpt)
People or Personnel (excerpt)
Packet of Articles-"Real Trouble on the Farm," *Time*
"Pot Called Nation's Biggest Cash Crop" Tobacco
Industry, etc.

Week 10:   Alternative Futures

Field Trip: Overnight in Bolinas

Readings: *Briefing:*
Charles Reich, *The Sorceror of Bolinas Reef* (excerpts)
"On the Edge," *Esquire*
"Santa Cruz Struggling with Vestige of Its '60's," *New York*
Times
Utopias:
(Recommended: Henry Thoreau, *Walden;* Eugene
Zamiatin, *We;* B. F. Skinner, *Walden Two)*
Predictions:
Alvin Toffler, *The Third Wave* (excerpts)

Week 11:   Conclusion

Class Meetings:

Final projects,   Party

Final assignment: Place in two sealed envelopes predictions for America, for yourself, and for the futures of the members of the class and the Instructor for ten years from the current date and twenty-five years from the current date. Envelopes will be opened at a class reunion at that time.

Readings: Plato, "Parable of the Cave," *The Republic*
Honoré de Balzac, *The Wild Ass's Skin* (excerpts)

=⚬⁄⚬⁄⚬=

An Introductory Anthropology Laboratory Course

In addition to designing new interdisciplinary courses focusing on unseen issues, instructors can incorporate similar concepts directly and easily into existing disciplines through laboratories taught in conjunction with particular courses, as described in the first part of this chapter. While ultimately such laboratory courses have the long-term potential for replacing outmoded and uninspired lecture approaches and the regurgitation of theories with little application to real human problems, in the short term they can supplement existing courses without making the faculty uneasy. In fact, they can bring resources and recognition to existing departments.

This is what we discovered in experimenting with one such course at the University of California at Berkeley, finding ways to fund it and incorporate it into the curriculum as a complement to an existing course.

All it took in 1988 was simply one graduate student to write a proposal and find a faculty sponsor. Within a few weeks, the sponsor's department had been awarded $5,000—enough to hire a graduate student to teach the course. (Of course, the proposal writer and the teacher might be one and the same, but they could also be two different people.)

In this section, we present the key components of our successfully funded proposal, along with evidence of its special success (in the form of excerpts from student projects and student evaluations), followed by a sample course proposal (Exhibit 4.2) as a basis for designing similar courses.

Implementing Berkeley's First Introductory Anthropology Laboratory Course

Although introductory laboratory courses are possible in all the social sciences—as are the intermediate and advanced laboratory courses that could follow in sequence—we believed that a department of anthropology was the perfect place to find out how readily such an introductory course could be adopted and how it could succeed. We believed this course would be a natural methodological fit and that the department would be receptive because anthropology is one of the disciplines most often on the defensive in universities.

At most universities today, anthropology, both social and cultural, is among the most poorly funded and marginalized disciplines and is often viewed by other social scientists as on the fringes of social science. At the same time, it is a discipline that has much to say about solving social problems and about helping people understand each other and work together, a discipline with great potential for social and economic renewal if only it had the right advocate.

One reason to experiment with a laboratory course in anthropology was to see if combining the ideas of "laboratory," "community," and "practical tools" could attract more students into such a struggling discipline. Our goal was to enable students and faculty to see how their ideas could be applied immediately in their communities, rather than in a remote part of the world, and on problems on which they chose to focus. Working within the discipline of anthropology rather than another social science also provided a way to test the view held by many students not only of the social sciences in general but of the discipline of anthropology itself: that anthropology is merely a highbrow form of escape, where one learns about other (exotic) people, and where the information learned in class makes for engaging talk at cocktail parties but is not really useful for anything more.

At the same time, anthropology as a discipline was a natural setting for testing an introductory laboratory course since many of the most important issues about studying humans in groups have been raised by anthropologists. Some see the discipline itself as inseparable from the methodology of field work by a "participant observer" (an initial step toward collecting and improving upon the collection of quantitative data) and that the methodology dovetails with an experiential approach.

What follows is an excerpt from the proposal used to "sell" the idea for this course at the University of California at Berkeley. It is presented in a format that is a sample of what can be used elsewhere. What is written in the proposal about Berkeley and about the discipline of anthropology can easily be replaced with examples and similar appeals from other universities and disciplines that can be used to win support for new laboratory approaches that can be implemented in those universities and disciplines. Indeed, Alexis de Tocqueville, one of the founders of American political science, was a field researcher. Economics and the other social sciences similarly have drawn from the practical experiences and travels of their founders. Proposals that hark back to the founders of these disciplines can make a strong case for funding and accreditation of introductory laboratory courses in these fields.

Anthropology 3 Laboratory (Introduction to Field Methods in Social and Cultural Anthropology)

Why an Introductory Laboratory Course Is Needed and How It Fits into the Academic Program

In the early part of this century and the early years of anthropology at the University of California, Alfred Kroeber—one of the great American anthropologists and a member of the Berkeley faculty—and his colleagues took students out with them on their own research in Native American communities during the scholastic year and to distant field locations during the summer. In the eyes of the founders of anthropology, this was a central part of the training of specialists in the discipline.

In the years since then, one of the most important components of the Anthropology Department's introductory course in social and cultural anthropology has been a field research project designed to help students develop skills and gain an introduction to the essential methodology of anthropology. Yet field work has continued to move away from its original goals.

With the growth in the number of students enrolled in the department (more than seven hundred students in the introductory course each semester), field work has been retained at the introductory level only in the form of individual student projects that are conducted with minimal supervision. These projects remain the single most important piece of work now required in the introductory course, and they account for one-third of a student's grade.

Despite the importance of providing students with an exposure to the methodology of the discipline at the introductory level, however, students are now faced with the challenge of developing these skills on their own, following only lecture and written instructions with minimal guidance from a graduate student instructor. While some students have been remarkably adept at developing anthropological techniques on their own, others have faced considerable difficulty. Many find themselves in troubling situations with little experience to draw from in applying skills and in dealing with the ethical and personal issues they face in the process. Some have given up or have fallen back on skills they are comfortable with while failing to develop others.

The situation that exists now in the teaching of introductory anthropology is analogous to training, say, future chemists only through lectures and sending them into the laboratory to experiment and to write laboratory reports entirely on their own.

Like students in the natural sciences hoping to do experimental work, many students enter the discipline of anthropology because they are attracted by the prospects of developing ethnographic skills through field projects. Some are discouraged by the neglect of a serious commitment to skills training that they find at the introductory level.

More disappointing to many students is that despite the growth of the discipline since Kroeber's time, even the most successful students who grasp the methodology are no longer trained to integrate more than one small experience into a picture of a community or society—the real subject matter of anthropology—the way they would have been trained if they had studied anthropology in the department fifty years ago.

This has led to consideration of whether to eliminate the field project entirely from the introductory anthropology course—a solution akin to eliminating laboratory work from the hard sciences because of the danger involved in students' learning laboratory skills without proper supervision.

As in the natural sciences, the better solution appears to be to focus more care and supervision in a separate laboratory course that is offered in conjunction with a lecture.

How the Experiment Worked

There are at least three ways of providing field experiences to beginning anthropologists (and other social science students) at the introductory level. These three options match the existing frameworks for natural science laboratories as they are currently offered in university curricula. Of the three, we chose just one as a first application.

In the course that we experimented with in the spring of 1989, we chose to aim at the serious anthropology student likely to continue in the discipline by offering a three-unit methods course along with a three-unit lecture course. The purpose of such intensive training in anthropology is to prepare students to produce complete ethnographies—written descriptions of a particular social or cultural group—which are the basic research products of the discipline and which incorporate its theoretical tools.

The two alternatives to the method of using both lecture and laboratory courses are to pitch a course on an introductory level to the general student and to offer the laboratory course standing on its own rather than in conjunction with a lecture course. For example:

- A half-time (two-unit) introductory course in anthropology (which could also be offered on its own for three units) could be geared toward demonstrating to introductory students, through their own field work, how a community works and how its various parts and activities are functionally interrelated in sometimes hidden ways as part of a larger whole.

- A short, one-unit course could focus more on specific skills and on issues raised and learned through field work, rather than on preparation of a complete ethnography or on trying to gain an overview of the whole community's workings (the syllabus is shown in Exhibit 4.2).

In 1989, the University of California at Berkeley tested the three-unit class. While most of the students were freshmen, some were older. But for all of them, it was their first anthropology course.

Proof of the course's success and a fuller description of what is possible come from the students themselves, in their reflections on the experimental course and in the papers they wrote. Their work, excerpted below, is a testimonial to their ability to master research skills, to apply theoretical concepts, to question their own stereotypes, to establish rapport with those who are unlike themselves, to grapple with the ethical issues confronting them, and to experiment with different styles of presenting what they discovered.

Some of the topics they chose to study might seem sensational outside of Berkeley, but the topics were not overreaching or scandalous or any more unusual than one might find portrayed stereotypically in the mass media. The San Francisco Bay Area is not the typical American community, but the topics that students chose were a real slice of the Berkeley environment—topics that their classmates (and teachers) were all curious about.

The titles they chose for their ethnographic field work, in random order, were

- Asian American Youth and Families
- American Education and the Individual
- AIDS and Teenagers: A Change to Be Made in Light of the New Epidemic
- Female Erotic Performers
- Racism Within the African American Community: Color Distinction and Other Intraracial Struggles
- "Deadheads"
- Japanese-Owned San Francisco Hotel: Together in Harmony—Japanese Management in America
- Social Structures in the Society for Creative Anachronism's Kingdom of the West
- Hrvatkska! An Ethnographic Study of Croatian Americans
- Relationships Through a Computer Network: AppleLink
- Women Reentering School
- Punk Rock Subculture

The students' comments on the class and segments from their papers hint at the flavor of the course and way students challenged stereotypes. The attempt by the students to reinterpret the community around them is the essence of real learning and community integration.

Some of the following excerpts are lengthy and might well be published as essays or articles on their own. They are presented here as examples of the depth of the work and thinking that goes into these projects. They show how the methods of democratic experiential education result in a kind of learning that has a larger dimension and greater quality than that acquired in traditional courses, including the basic introductory course in anthropology.

EXCERPTS FROM "THE CHANGING VALUES AND BELIEFS OF TAIWANESE IMMIGRANT STUDENTS AT THE UNIVERSITY OF CALIFORNIA, BERKELEY"

LOK C. D. SIU

In presenting my data, I have chosen to write in narrative form. I have reconstructed various experiences which my informants have conveyed to me. I feel that this style of presentation best captures the essence of the parent-and-child relationships in a Chinese home and the conflicts that the immigrant Taiwanese child experiences. [All names used are pseudonyms from life histories compiled in field work by Ms. Siu.]

JUNE WONG, "REFLECTION"

I guess I should tell you about the time I was arrested for shoplifting when I was fifteen. Yes, it's true; I had about $200's worth of clothing in my bag when an undercover policewoman caught me. . . .

I'll never forget my mother's face when she came to pick me up from the police station. Her eyes were red from crying and the color of her skin had grown pale. I could feel pain and anger in her silence. She looked at me as if I were a murderer; it wasn't until later that I realized I'd killed her pride and her trust in me. "What did I do wrong? Why was I such a bad mother? Why didn't I teach you not to steal? How did I fail?" She screamed. I kept silent because that was what I was taught—keep quiet and just listen. There was nothing I could have done anyway.

I remember [how my mother] would say to [my sister and me, when we were growing up], "You see, everything the children do reflects on the parents and the family. . . . The whole family goes wherever you go. No matter where you are, you'll always be a Wong. . . .

I often think about that day and how terrible I felt, how awful I must have been to put my mother through all this torture. She didn't speak to me for days after that, and I don't blame her. I don't think she'll ever be able to trust me in the same way again. . . .

I never intended to hurt my mother. I never expected this to happen. There is so much I have to tell her, so much I have to explain. How do I apologize?

How do I tell her I love her and that it wasn't her fault?

AMY WU, "SILENCE"
It was all very easy. . . . Just sit and listen.

Conversations? We hardly ever had conversations. Our communication only consisted of lectures (usually given by my father). The topic was always the same. He would start by asking me how I was doing in school and I would answer.

"Fine."

"You have to study hard and do well in college. It's important to get good grades."

I would nod as he continued.

"You have to set a good example for your brothers. Study hard and don't go out so much." . . .

My parents, especially my father, wanted me to be a doctor. I had majored in biology, even though I hated it; I had no choice. I don't think my father wanted me to be a doctor so I could help other people; it seemed to me that it was more because doctors are well respected by others and they earn huge salaries. He used to say things like, "It would be so wonderful to have my daughter as a doctor. People would be so impressed." It was all a status symbol to him.

My parents never really asked me how I felt about anything. I stood aside as they planned my life. I wanted to tell them that I didn't want to play the piano and that I didn't want to become a doctor, but I was afraid to speak up. I was afraid that they might yell and say terrible things about me. I was afraid that even if I did speak up, they would not hear me. I decided to remain silent.

SUSAN CHANG, "PARADISE"

America in Taiwanese, *Mei Gwo*, literally means "beautiful country." And I interpreted it in the fullest sense of its meaning; as a child I didn't know any better. Everything people said about America was positive. Naïve as I might have been, I imagined America as paradise. I imagined green grass covering every piece of land, bright flowers blooming everywhere. I saw tall trees growing on every block and people always smiling, always friendly and happy. Life couldn't be any better. I imagined clean streets on sunny days, warm breezes and ice cream cones. That was the image I got when I thought of America, the beautiful country.

My parents always talked about the "opportunities" that were available in America and how I could get a better education there. When my parents referred to opportunities, they meant the opportunity to become rich, the chance to become economically well-off.

"Your uncle left Taiwan when he was eighteen years old, with only a penny in his pocket. Now he has his own house and a bakery in Chinatown. Your cousins are attending college and earning good money. You can do the same once we get there." These were the stories my mother told us.

Flying on the plane was so exciting. Every time we passed through a cloud, I thought we came closer to America. The sadness of leaving my friends disappeared as I flew farther and farther away. I was going to a new land, a better land.

Once we arrived and got into my uncle's station wagon, I realized that what I saw wasn't exactly what I expected to see. I was only ten years old. What a way to shatter my dreams! We drove through the city, passing by a few homeless. There was trash everywhere. It was cold and windy and I no longer wanted to be here. I thought maybe we'd arrived at a different place.

When my uncle shouted, "Here we are!" I became sad and disappointed; I knew that this really was America. The name betrayed me. The stories betrayed me. I guess it was too late to leave.

As I unpacked my bags, I thought to myself: "They lied."

Excerpts from "Sex and Art?"

Kyle Stewart Miller

Erotic performers come from all different ethnicities, ages, socioeconomic groups, and so on. . . . The only characteristic that most of the workers seem to share is a relative comfortableness with their bodies. But even that doesn't always hold true. So what then *is* common among erotic performers? [Through interviews in their work environments and homes], I have found out that the most unifying characteristics are the motivating factors that lead them to this kind of work.

The most common reason for being an erotic performer is *money*. There simply are no other jobs that can compete with the huge salaries made in this field. Even many of the offers made to college graduates are not as high. . . . The bottom line is that a woman can make enough money to live a more than comfortable life working as an erotic performer. Or, like Faye [a pseudonym], work only two nights a week but earn as much as a full-time secretary paid $8 an hour.

Not only is the money good, but it can be all "under the table." This is because most erotic performers are paid entirely by tips. . . . And, if by chance the performer gets audited, the dance clubs have no records, so there is very little chance of getting caught.

This gives a sense of independence to the job, which is definitely appreciated by the workers. It's not only freedom with respect to money, but also in the way they do their jobs. The dancers are almost always left to decide for themselves how to act, how to perform. Elise [a pseudonym] does not even think of herself as working *for* the club. Instead, she feels that the owners allow her to perform there in exchange for the business she brings. . . .

Contrary to the myth that women are being controlled and dominated as erotic performers, they actually have a considerable amount of autonomy—à perquisite that I think any other kinds of laborers would like to have.

But this control doesn't walk alone. With it comes power. Just by looking at the position the performers are in, one can easily see who is in control. If at any time a man pisses Faye off, she'll just get up and leave the room *with* his money. One time, with Elise, a man started to avoid her hints for money and stalled for time. This made her so irritated that she finally blew up in his face and yelled, "Look buddy, don't think that I'm not getting anything out of this. . . . I'm exploiting you, not the other way around!" These workers not only are getting money, they're getting a boost to their self-confidence.

Of course it is also flattering, say most of the women, to have a man like to look at them. It does help their egos. But that really isn't an incentive more than [it is] a bonus of the job. However, in many of the women's cases, there is a strong sexist motive. Many of them get a sense of victory when they take advantage of a man. Regardless if some people think that it is really the men who are exploiting the women, to them, and especially to Elise, it's a way of proving that men need women. She even told me flat out, "I do it for the revenge."

The common conclusion that these people are either prostitutes or junkies . . . is probably affected by society's preconceived images of erotic performers, because the people whom I have interacted with, and the people they know well, do not conform to these stereotypes. Elise [says that] when she lived with students in Berkeley, she saw more of them doing drugs than the performers she works with now.

Do the customers really believe the person cares about what they are saying? Or do they simply not know that these women are motivated by money as opposed to real compassion? . . . The customer is paying money to be deceived into thinking that the performer is there for his benefit. This is certainly the case with Faye. . . . Faye says . . . that her work is "all one big lie." She is selling a deception.

If there is so much sexism involved in being an erotic performer, then why are there so many females who do it? The answer is quite simple, according to Elise. She believes that there is no more sexism within the sex industry than anywhere else. According to her, working as a secretary was more demeaning than what she does now. "I had to fetch the boss his coffee, and shit like that." . . . When Elise was a secretary, to challenge those who signed her paychecks would have meant losing her job, but now if a man starts saying rude things, she simply gets up and leaves.

Many stereotypes about erotic performers that are common in our society do not hold true when one examines them closely and clearly. Typical notions about who performs erotically, who watches, and why are mostly false, often because of an us/them mentality. By thinking that only certain marginal groups participate in the sex industry, the mainstream can distance itself from this taboo subject. But in fact, there are no real distinctions—all types of people work in and pay for erotic performance. It is not us and them, it is everyone in our society.

EXCERPTS FROM "PUNKS: A FIELD STUDY IN BERKELEY"

STEPHEN MIDGLEY

Everyone knows a punk when they see one: brightly colored "mohawk," black leather jacket, ripped-up jeans, boots, and a safety pin through his (or her!) cheek. Just a little sideshow oddity at the shopping mall or downtown.

In the course of my field work, I have found that punk is not entirely what it seems, and in any case, it is a much richer and more complete subculture than the public at large seems to give it credit for. . . .

Because the music is so noticeable and reactive (crying; screaming support for poverty, class, and race struggles; or sometimes nothing at all), the media has tended to concentrate on a study of punk rock music, rather than on the culture itself. . . .

While the violence of the subculture is often exposed by the general media, peaceful ideology appears frequently just out of view of the public. Many kids who devoutly support fighting on the streets see world peace and unity as the ultimate goal of punk rock.

There is a giant distinction, though, between what hardcore punks seek in the short run and what they envision for society in the long run. Very often their short-run attitudes cause them to be concerned only with having a good time, which consists mainly of getting *wasted*. Allen [a punk informant] told me that he does not mind living with this "slight" contradiction because he feels that society has much graver and more flagrant contradictions that no one complains about. . . .

Of the suburban punks, I was able to find three main groups: skaters, death rockers, and "pseudo punks." . . . Skaters, as the name implies, skateboard everywhere. . . . Skaters are almost always male, and they appear more interested in girls and drugs than in the street scene or even the bands. . . . Death rockers are mainly girls, with most of the boys in this odd cult seen as being or acting somewhat homosexual, according to several death rock girls. Death rockers dress in all black, wear veils and capes, and whiten their faces so as to appear dead. Typically they are age sixteen or seventeen. . . . Why "death rockers"? "To the rest of the world, we're as good as dead," one girl explained. . . .

Finally, pseudo punks, according to Allen have transformed punk from an antisociety statement into a fashion statement. They are characterized by wearing black cowboy boots with silver and jeans or black clothes. Bob [another informant] claims that they are typically college art students looking for "a good time."

Where is the source of anger for these kids?

Initially I believed it came from all of the pressures that the parent culture was placing on them. While I have not rejected this hypothesis entirely, I have found that much of the anger springs from the interaction between the subgroups themselves.

COMMENTS ON THE COURSE

LOK C. D. SIU

Among other changes . . . I have undergone during the past few months, my greatest achievements are gaining a new awareness of my Asian identity as well as understanding the social and cultural situations of our country.

[Through work on my research project on the changing values and beliefs of Taiwanese immigrant students], I have become so much more aware of the dilemmas that Asian American students go through as they assimilate into the American culture. . . .

It is frightening how attached I grew to my research. Though the paper started out as a project for a class, . . . I was so absorbed in my writing that nothing else mattered. In some ways, I neglected other classes in which I was less interested.

In the course of this semester and especially from writing my paper, I have learned much more about myself and, in fact, much more about my parents. I am now able to see and understand better my parents' perspective.

EXHIBIT 4.2. Social and Cultural Anthropology Laboratory Course.

An Introductory Laboratory/Field Methods Course
in Social and Cultural Anthropology
(Proposal for One- or Two-Unit Course)

University of California, Berkeley
(Awarded Educational Improvement Grant, 1989)
(Taught as Anthropology 3 Laboratory)

Purpose:
The goal of this course is to introduce students to the theory and practice of social science with a particular focus on the study of social and cultural processes and organization.

The basis of the course will be to provide supervised feedback, instruction and discussion of field skills, the ethical issues involved in working with human subjects, the relation between the individual observer and subjects, and the subjective values incorporated in particular forms of methodology and observation. A particular goal in the teaching of the course will be to deal in a coherent and direct way with the emotions that students experience in their interactions in the field.

Within a laboratory course framework, students will have the chance to:
• Receive ongoing feedback on their work.
• Experiment with a variety of approaches and then discuss the success or failure of those approaches.
• Identify areas of research, learn methods of making contacts and the various scientific and ethical implications, create a role as a participant observer, interview and develop strategies for posing questions and interpreting answers, seek access to records and other recorded or historical data, make qualitative observations, record behavior, write field notes, and analyze field data.
• Share ideas with other students and benefit from others' experiences in the field.
• Look at connections between several institutions in forming a holistic view of a community.

In addition to direct training in anthropology, the program will provide students with the opportunity to:
• Consider the realm of social science methodology and its conclusions, and to test existing theories and social science work against clear standards.
• Deepen understanding of American subcultures, ethnic groups, and institutions (building on the University's commitment to awareness of the ethnic diversity of the state's population).

- Compare models and media images with the reality of American life.
- Consider the effects of organizations on the social and cultural environment, and the role of social services in the community.

Topics:

The course will cover the following topics:
- The theory of field ethnography and the unique characteristics of anthropological methodology in the context of the set of methods of measurement available in the social sciences for measure of human behavior.
- The theory behind the course itself as a study of learning environments and socialization processes (students can participate more fully when they understand the theoretical basis of experiential learning).
- Perceptual issues of ethnography and social science research—what it means to try to "objectively" study "the other."
- Ethical issues of anthropological field work.
- Data collection methods and techniques—qualitative observation, interviewing, gaining access to records, making contacts with subjects, recording behavior, etc.
- Writing up data.
- Using and collecting historical and previous ethnographic material on field sites as well as general information in preparation for site visits.
- Theory of culture and society—how different sites relate to each other in a community, what the concept of a community is, and what the actual isolate of anthropological study is or should be. (This will be stressed in the two-unit course and will be closely integrated with the readings in lecture.)

Field Sites:

Laboratory work will be conducted at the following types of field sites:
- Factory
- Low-income housing complex/suburban community
- City jail
- Old-age home
- Alcohol or drug rehabilitation center
- Military base
- Office building
- Court house
- Psychiatric hospital
- Veterans center
- Religious service
- Inner-city high school

Options:
1) For two units: class will meet once each week for two hours of discussion and once each week, beginning the third week, for field work in the community. If possible, this course will include one overnight field trip for immersion into an unfamiliar surrounding (e.g., Round Valley Indian Reservation).

This course will differ from the one-unit version not only in the additional number of field trips and readings, but also in the special attention given to achieving an integrated view of the local community and how several organizations, structures, and types of behavior interact to make the community work as an organized whole. The goal of the course will be to prepare each student to arrive in a community as an anthropologist and to make sense out of the social and cultural environment.

2) For one unit: class will meet once each week for one hour of discussion and every other week for field work in the community.

Attention in this course will be on added skills training so that students have all the requisite skills to complete a thorough anthropological study in a specific organizational setting.

COMMENTS ON THE COURSE

KYLE STEWART MILLER

Anthro 3L is a great class, one that should be preserved from the emotionless jaws of U.C. Berkeley. It allows students the chance to go out and meet a group of people that they are not already a part of. . . . Students (and I think also the informants) are forced into a situation that, like it or not, makes them think about certain ideas and come up with some independent views. . . . I believe a good education comes not from being forced to work, but rather encouraged by the fun of it. And Anthro 3L certainly does that. . . .

Almost every other class I've been to here at Berkeley has made me feel like I'm just one of thousands and that I have no unique slant on an issue. Anthro 3L lets one break those typical restrictions and lets the student's mind run on its own. That is the reward that should be kept alive.

COMMENTS ON THE COURSE

STEPHEN MIDGLEY

When I first became interested in investigating the punk rock subculture for this course, I had little idea exactly how to go about getting the information I wanted from a group of kids that (almost by definition) hates everyone outside the group. I was not even sure if I would be able to get any information at all. . . .

The first night I went to a show, I saw a punk with a huge mohawk standing at a bus station. In the spirit of exotic adventure, I rolled down my window and offered him a ride to the show (it was about ten o'clock at night, and I knew that he must be going to the show). He accepted, and probably got more than he bargained for. . . . Of course . . . without knowing it, I had already trod on ethically thin ground, trading a car ride for information. . . .

When I went up to one group and told them I was writing for a university, [my best informant] indicated that this was one step below writing a police report. He said it is the word itself that turns punks off; school is an understandable predicament, but for punks [he said], university is an undue hardship.

COMMENTS ON THE COURSE

WILLIAM CAMBELL

At first I thought my project on Deadheads was not a very strong topic because I figured that knowing about these people had no social significance or importance. I mean, who cares about a bunch of old hippies who follow a rock band and do drugs, right?

It was not until after my interviewing that I realized that the Deadheads are not a group of burnt-out people wandering aimlessly around the country trying to forget about the "real life," but instead [are] a fairly well-organized social structure of people who do live in the real world, just in a different way.

While writing, I thought about the old saying "You can't judge a book by its cover," because of the impression the majority of society has about Deadheads without knowing much about them. I then realized that the importance of my paper is the realization of that quote, and that it pertains not only to Deadheads, but to any number of groups in our society, including punks, bikers, or just about anybody.

No project is ever over, and I hope I get a chance to do another project on the Deadheads in future years. I think that by doing so, I will learn considerably more about them, and possibly about society's perception of groups like them.

COMMENTS ON THE COURSE

KRISTIN CHIN
The Hoteru Hotel [not the real name of the Japanese-owned hotel in San Francisco that Chin studied] has a confidentiality policy against employees disclosing information about the hotel or its guests. . . . Since I knew that employees should not reveal information to external sources, I was cautious about challenging the Hoteru's authority and interviewing employees without its approval. . . . I felt as if I was risking the worker's job as well as the Hoteru's trust if it was discovered that I was conducting separate interviews. This dilemma led me to question my responsibility and obligations to the Hoteru or to any other subject [and to think that responsibility might mean compromising the strength of my research]. . . . The ideological trade-off of trust versus gains in research became an important consideration in the progression of my paper.

Ethics became an important issue when I interviewed a union representative. At this time, I was faced with the possibility of negative research effects on my informants. In the interview, we discussed information that might result in management retaliation against employees. Listening to [one] man's deliberations [on] fear of losing his job versus living with bad working conditions [law violations at a crab stand on Fisherman's Wharf] reinforced the importance of an anthropologist's responsibility.

COMMENTS ON THE COURSE

JAKE HOELTER

[As I studied users of a computer network], I did have certain preconceived notions regarding what a typical network user would be like. I thought that the users would be mostly male, teenage, and probably somewhat shy in person. I was pleasantly surprised to discover that this was not the case. The male/female ratio turned out to be about sixty/forty, and many of the regular users are in their thirties, forties, and fifties. I found that people were very friendly, and they didn't just talk about computers.

. . . [The network] encourages nonprejudiced relationships. . . . I never once heard of an instance of a person asking another what his or her skin color was.

One of the users is a quadriplegic and unable to leave his room. With [the network], he can make a lot more friends than he would otherwise have the opportunity to, and he won't be treated differently since they do not know about his disability.

———✺———

An Introductory Economics Laboratory Course

As a challenge to Harvard University's Economics Department to develop laboratory courses in economics that focused on the real activities of production and exchange, we designed a course called The Changing American Economy: A Structural and Field Approach, that fit into the existing Harvard curriculum as a sophomore seminar for economics majors. The course is divided into three kinds of topics: methodological (what economists measure and how), analytical (overall observations of economies), and structural (how economies work).

While economics is often called the "dismal science," we feel that the only thing dismal about it is the way it is taught, in abstractions cut off from the reality and excitement of how economies actually work (or do not work), with little attention to how power is exercised, and only cryptic descriptions of how gains and losses are really distributed, in terms that hide what anyone might plainly see.

The typical introductory economics course currently taught in most universities is really a course in applied mathematics and graphics. Instead of studying economic production, consumption, and labor, students study the models and pictures that have been developed by economists, learning the jargon and manipulating equations. Sometimes they use statistics, but with little idea how those statistics are computed or what they represent.

Microeconomic courses posit something abstract called "the firm" and they start with something called a "demand curve," which no one has ever actually seen with real data and that no producer has ever calculated. Macroeconomic courses discuss abstract concepts of interest rates, government spending, tax incentives, and rates of return.

Few if any of these courses deal with the actual physical mechanisms of the way the economy runs and the roles of individuals who are producing, investing, and innovating. Indeed, many of the most important questions about economics—how an economy really works, how it can be improved, and how and what are to be measured in comparing economies—are largely absent from basic economics courses.

Among those questions that we are able to reintroduce in economics through experiential work on real issues are these: How do the institutions of an economy really work? Who owns the land? Who owns the productive capital? What is produced? How are investment decisions made? How is America's workforce trained? How are its managers trained? Where does innovation come from? What does infrastructure look like? What is the real power of consumers and workers? How much competition is really in the economy? How do government and business really interact? How good are the data that economists use? What are appropriate measures of the "quality" or "quantity" of production and the "quality" of life?

The syllabus that we designed for this course is shown in Exhibit 4.3.

EXHIBIT 4.3. Economics Laboratory Course.

The Changing American Economy:
(Nuts and Bolts)
A Structural and Field Approach
Prepared for Harvard University
Sophomore Tutorial: Economics 970
Overview of Approach:

The purpose of this course is to help students examine the reality of the American economy behind aggregate data and theoretical models. By combining theory and laboratory work, students will examine the measurements that economists use and learn to collect their own data on various aspects of the American economy.

The design of the course can be flexible, responding to student interests. One way of structuring the field exercises in the course is simply to follow basic products along the path from extraction of raw materials to their ultimate sales and uses. Field work could include visits to mines, farms, or a loading dock; to a factory; to truck drivers and rail stations; to warehouses; to night markets; and to retailers. Another way to organize the course would be to follow different industrial sectors and issues and would entail meetings with bankers, views of service industries, meetings with a manager of a large firm and an entrepreneur in the same industry, and meetings with union representatives and consumer advocates.

The following readings provide the theoretical backbone of the course. A list of sample field sites is also provided.

Readings: A) *Methodological Issues:*
Edward Quade, "When Quantitative Models Are
Inadequate"
William Baumol, "On the Discount Rate for Public Projects"
Robert F. Clark, "Program Evaluation and the
Commissioning Entity"

Harold Leavitt, "Beyond the Analytic Manager"
Barbara Rogers, "The Treatment of Women in Quantitative
　　Techniques"
Robert Chambers, *Rural Development*
B) *Analytical Issues:*
John Kenneth Galbraith, *The Affluent Society; The New
Industrial State*
Warner and Low, *The Social System of the Modern
　　Factory* (vol. 4 of *Yankee City*)
Bluestone and Harrison, *The De-Industrialization of
　　America*
Marvin Harris, *America Now*
Seymour Melman, *Pentagon Capitalism*
William Whyte, *The Organization Man*
Paul Streeten, "Basic Needs"
Alex Inkeles, "As We Modernize, Do We Homogenize?"
Peter Barnes, *Who Owns the Land?*
Elton Mayo, *Social Problems of an Industrial Civilization*
C) *Structural Issues:*
Murray Melbin, *Night as Frontier*
Peter Cohen, *The Gospel According to the Harvard
　　Business School*
Robert Granfield, *Making Elite Lawyers*
Robert Reich, *The New American Frontier*
Jagna Sharff, "Free Enterprise and the Ghetto Family"

Field Sites:　Dorchester High School, Milton Academy (human capital)
Boston waste site, Boston sewer system (infrastructure)
Newmarket, Flower Market (intermediate markets)
Harvard Business School (American management)
Fish Pier (fishing industry)
Family and industrial farms (agriculture)
Lowell, Massachusetts (manufacturing and
　　deindustrialization)
Route 128, Raytheon Corporation (new industries, military
　　conversion)
Advertising agency (marketing)
Toy store, WBZ Radio (entertainment)
Hale & Dore, Harvard Law School (legal infrastructure)
Massachusetts State Prison, Pine Street Inn (human
　　resources)

5

Building Skills for the Real World

Intermediate Level Course Adventures with Xavier N. de Souza Briggs

The potential applications of experiential and democratic educational techniques in courses at intermediate and advanced university levels are infinite. This chapter provides merely a small sample of the infinite: examples of the kinds of courses that can be taught as complements to existing courses in existing disciplines, including the natural and social sciences and the humanities.

—⟨∞⟩—

Course Proposals Across Disciplines

As examples of what is possible, we have developed a list of intermediate courses that can be developed almost instantly and placed in existing educational frameworks as a prelude to potential long-term institutional changes. We provide a short description of the rationale for each course and explain how it can enrich the existing curriculum without directly competing against it.

As in Chapter Four, we devote the most time to those disciplines in which we have the greatest expertise—the social sciences—as a model for what can be done elsewhere. We also include a set of lay science courses that we believe can supplement theoretical courses for students at all levels with an interest in the sciences.

Extended descriptions of select courses show how easy it is to develop the ideas into complete syllabi and to implement them as we did on the introductory level. We present complete and detailed descriptions of two programs in particular: a social science theory course that was taught successfully at the University of California at Berkeley and continues—in its third generation—seven years later, and a public policy course at Stanford taught by three generations of students. Both courses are upper-level versions of The Unseen America, led by undergraduate students for their peers. We also describe a third interdisciplinary course, one in economic history that we developed for Harvard University.

We lead with the disciplines in the same order as in Chapter Four.

—◦◦◦—

Humanities

We apply the same techniques to upper-level courses in the humanities as at the introductory level, merely introducing more skills and a greater complexity of theories and problems.

History

Using the techniques developed in introductory-level laboratories for primary historical research, students in upper-level courses are ready to use their skills for the study of local, community, and general American history, as well as for other historical studies overseas. They can also apply their skills to empirical historical work using data sets, computers, and analytical techniques as part of the testing of theories that relate to important contemporary problems. Following are some examples of courses and the questions they address.

Changing American Communities (Cross-Listed with City Planning, Economics, and Anthropology). Are "growth" and "development" good things? How does growth relate to our demographic policies (issues of abortion, industrialization, and the changing age composition of the population)? Who controls development and land use? Why is more of our population behind bars than any other industrial country's? Who owns America's land and capital? A humanities course exploring these topics would include visits with city officials, land developers, bankers, right-to-life (antiabortion) groups, residential housing associations, and community leaders.

The U.S. Constitution: Then and Now.   The inspiration for this course came from students in Leningrad (now St. Petersburg) who asked of their own classes, "Why can't we read what Lenin read instead of what Lenin wrote?" In the United States, the purpose of such a course is to reread what the American republic's founders read or taught and to compare those principles with the historical and contemporary realities.

This is a theory and field course on American democracy as perceived in the eighteenth century and now. In part, readings would include those that Thomas Jefferson taught in his course at the University of Virginia in the 1820s (Montesquieu, Priestly, Chipman, Sidney) as well as other historical materials. The course would also include new retrospective materials on the Constitution, the Bill of Rights, and American democracy and culture.

Since students would be asked to "rethink" American democracy from the worldview of the colonists, some of the classes would be held at sites of historical importance. In Boston, for example, sessions might be held at places such as the Aquinnah (the land of the Wampanoag tribe on Martha's Vineyard), the Old South Meeting House, and Walden Pond.

Social Sciences

Upper-level courses in social sciences could easily follow the introductory laboratories, building on lower-division skills and introducing a wider variety of concepts on general theory and on specialized topics.

General

Social Science Theory and History: The Unseen America.
While The Unseen America course taught at the University of California at Berkeley ultimately found its home as an upper-division methodology course in political science, its cross-listing in four different departments—and the perspective that student instructors majoring in English literature brought to that course—gave it a unique multidisciplinary perspective. In a sense, the course combined technique with philosophy and phenomenology, testing social science itself. (See the course description later in this chapter and Exhibit 5.1.)

Economics

The following courses are not meant to replace the teaching of economic theory, and what is increasingly abstract mathematics, in economics classes. The goal instead is to infuse new life into this "dismal science" by making it as fresh a field of study as it was to the Physiocrats, to Adam Smith, and even to Karl Marx. By building on field skills developed at the introductory level, these courses enable students to see and test directly how different types of economies, different actors, and different institutions actually function, and to compare the models with the reality.

Development Economics.   Development must be at the grassroots level and start with the needs of people seeking assistance, through interaction and participation with those people. One of the best ways to validate this concept of the "positive practitioner" is to incorporate it directly into the curriculum. To do so is to develop students' skills of working in the field and constantly testing theoretical models against reality—the reality of those in need of development assistance and the reality of the organizational culture of those who provide the assistance. This is in contrast to the prevailing approach to teaching development economics out of textbooks in a classroom setting—an approach that, ironically, violates the most important concept that most such courses teach.

The following locations are among the types of field visits that could be blended into existing courses to expand teaching of concepts and skills within, say, an hour or two of the Washington, D.C., area.

- The Amish people (Lancaster, Pennsylvania) and the inhabitants of Ocracoke Island (North Carolina)—to understand the ability of agricultural and nonurban societies to maintain their cultures and protect sustainable economies

- New Castle County, Delaware—to examine the workings and needs of a class-divided company town and corporate state similar to that found in much of the third world

- Rural West Virginia and Appalachia—to explore areas of rural poverty and uneven development and to examine the needs of the population

- North Carolina—to understand the economies of tobacco farms and how political and social mechanisms interact to subsidize inefficient production of an addictive substance with no other value for consumption and export

- Colonial Williamsburg, Virginia, and Native American reservations—to consider the economies of early American economies, how they functioned, and how they changed

- Inner-city Washington, D.C.—to study an example of racial segregation and waste of human potential as a result of conflict between subcultures

- Development institutions—to explore the institutional culture of organizations in the development field, including the U.S. Agency for International Development (USAID), the U.S. State Department, the Pentagon, the World Bank, corporate law firms, and commercial banks, as a means of understanding the types of projects they choose and the way they perceive economic development and growth

Practicum in Development Planning.   The best way to learn development planning is by doing it, and the best way to understand the plans of development agencies and the institutional concerns that drive their decisions is to attempt the same tasks apart from those institutions and then to evaluate the differences.

One-semester projects could easily bring students into the field as teams to create various development plans for different sectors and populations. Students would work together to incorporate social, ethnic, gender, legal, and political issues into documents that would be presented to policy makers for conceptualizing development strategies.

Among the potential topics are those focusing on specific urban problems or on a particular neighborhood or region, on rural development, and on regional development of a particular county.

Economic History.   (For an example of how such a course might be structured, see Exhibit 5.3, which presents an outline for the course entitled Life and Death of Industries and Economies: A Field Approach.)

The Modern Corporation.   While most economics courses deal with the theoretical concept of "the firm"—comparing corporations to individual, rational economic actors—students of economics have very little exposure to the internal functioning and decision making that takes place within large domestic and multinational enterprises. A field course could close that gap.

The purpose of this course would be to answer such questions as: Who makes the decisions? Who takes the risks? Who bears ultimate responsibility? Who is the modern corporation accountable to? How does it really work? What forms of regulation and oversight are effective, which ones are not, and why? What political and social role do corporations actually play in shaping preferences, and how? Such a class would include meetings with workers, union officials, executives, public relations specialists, boards of directors, corporate counsel, regulators, stockholders, and the neighboring communities.

Agricultural Economics—Person and Land.   Much of the basis of development theory and discussion of "capitalist" versus "communist" ideology is based on questions of land ownership and productivity. American democracy is also rooted in certain notions about frontier farmers, plantation economies, land ownership of the family farmer, and so on.

A course on agricultural productivity and the issues of agriculture economies would include visits to family farms, cooperative farms, industrial farms, migrant labor camps, agricultural research stations, commodity exchanges, intermediate buyers, distributors, wholesalers, and product inspectors. It would also consider various issues of productivity and quality of life in the agricultural sector.

Political Science

Policy problems and issues can be built around several topics, and students can use field experiences as the basis for real problem solving. The Woodrow Wilson School of Public and International Affairs at Princeton University, for example, has done this on occasion in its undergraduate policy courses, as have other schools, particularly those in urban locations. These approaches can be built into regular curricula and follow introductory courses such as The Unseen America after students have developed skills and can recognize how issues are interrelated. Policy courses and workshops could be based on issues such as the following.

Public Policy: The Unseen America.   In its intermediate version in 1989, Stanford's The Unseen America focused on what it means to be unseen in America and the different institutions for dealing with marginalized and abandoned groups. The course took a problem-oriented rather than structural or institutional approach, combining political science, policy, and sociology. It exemplified the versatility of the democratic experiential model in political science through its potential application to a variety of problems or ways of thinking about an issue. (See Exhibit 5.2 and the full description of this course later in this chapter.)

The Criminal Justice System.   Beyond statistics of crime, measures of enforcement, and theories of state and civil prosecution of criminal activities are the cultural milieu in which crime develops and is defined, and the institutions that comprise the criminal justice system. A course on this topic could include meetings with and visits to a law school, a bar association, judges, trials, prisons (federal and state, publicly and privately run), alternative rehabilitation centers, mental hospitals, a public defender, the FBI, a juvenile hall, a coroner's office, and probation officers. It could also include a ride along with a police officer.

American Political Institutions: The Legal System.   Most political science classes spend little time studying the legal system as a set of political mechanisms on a par with elective government and bureaucracy. This course would focus on grand juries, civil juries, access to lawyers, private attorneys, general and other types of civil prosecutions, and the actual enforcement and workings of laws in a variety of settings.

Individuals and places to visits would include courts, law schools, judges, small and corporate law firms, legal services corporations, the American Civil Liberties Union (ACLU), community law clinics, community dispute-resolution centers, and mediators. It would also focus on the workings of the law in courts, prisons, mental hospitals, factories, and other institutions.

The American Health Care System.   A course on health care and the issues it raises—of access, quality of care, distribution, preventive medicine, insurance industry practices, incentives within bureaucracies and drug companies, and so on—can easily be enriched with field visits and research at all of the sites where these issues arise. Visits could include meetings with the service providers or users, as well as with health maintenance organizations, private and public hospitals, clinics, medical schools, private practitioners, American Medical Association lobbyists, old-age homes, drug companies, and insurers.

Universities in America.   University students rarely study the organizations in which they work. A course about universities could include visits to a historically black college, a women's college, a religious university, a public university, and a private university. It could include meetings with functional groups such as trustees, private and corporate donors, foundation heads, alumni club heads, historians, department chairs, administrators, workers and unions, police departments, financial officers, and development offices to understand how the organizations work and how they can be improved.

The Military Establishment.   Almost 8 percent of the gross national product of the United States goes to the military, a major actor in the economic and political system. But few students beyond those enrolled in Reserve Officer Training Corps (ROTC) programs know more about military institutions than what those institutions present in their own information or what scholars gather from budget analyses and journalists' reports.

A course on the military and issues of military oversight and spending could include visits to a military establishment, a National Guard headquarters, a military contractor, a university science department, a military recruiter, an ROTC unit, media organizations (to talk about their sources for military reporting), a military public relations office, veterans' groups, and homeless shelters (in which about 50 percent of the population consists of veterans who have had difficulty reintegrating into American society).

Social Welfare/The Welfare State.   The welfare state is a major topic in courses in political science, economics, and political economy, but most discussions center around abstract notions about who the poor are and how the welfare system works. A course on this issue could include visits with caseworkers, as well as site visits to food banks, homeless shelters, welfare hotels, foster care and juvenile homes, job creation programs, and aid offices. It could also include meetings with VISTA (Volunteers in Service to America) volunteers, Head Start programs, legal aid clinics, and current and past welfare recipients.

Sociology

The following are among existing sociology courses that could be enriched by greater attention to field methods.

Sociology of Law.   We were successful in implementing a sociology of law course (Sociology 167) at George Washington University in the fall of 1994. Like courses in anthropology, sociology courses are natural settings for experiential methods. We started the course with a discussion about symbols and images of law and legality in a supermarket cereal aisle (how criminals are portrayed on cereal boxes for kids), a video game arcade, and a shopping-mall toy store, and went on to field work in and around the Supreme Court and in a prison, courtrooms, and alternative dispute resolution meetings. We also visited the Acorn and Twin Oaks alternative communities in Mineral, Virginia, to study their approaches to law and to dispute resolution.

Unlike a political science class with an emphasis on legal institutions, a sociology of law class focuses more on the needs, values, and incentives underlying these different institutions; the functional roles they serve; the role of ethnicity and class; the traditional dispute resolution mechanisms in different communities; differential access to law; enforcement and applicability of law within different settings; identification of deviance; and differential punishment.

The best way to explore these issues is through site visits to institutions similar to those seen in a political science course—those that constitute the legal profession—as well as to areas in which disputes and grievances are developed and resolved and to institutions in which concepts of laws are patterned. The course at George Washington University included field work in communities, on law and its symbols and patterns in everyday life, and in different concepts of legality among subgroups and different communities. It included a focus on perceptions of law and on disputes outside of the formal legal system.

In a widely cited study of police in Washington, D.C., Professor William Chambliss teamed with his own students to ride along with police. Chambliss and the students compiled observations of how the police targeted inner-city blacks for persecution (a tactic we view as similar to the pogroms in European Jewish ghettos in the nineteenth century) and, in the process, provided a model for group laboratory projects in this area ("Policing the Ghetto Underclass . . .," 1994).

Children and the Family.   Along with readings on theory, courses on the family could include visits to AFDC (Aid to Families with Dependent Children) offices, child abuse centers, toy manufacturers, producers of movies or children's television, public and private schools, runaway youth centers, cereal manufacturers, drug clinics, custody hearings, abortion clinics, sperm banks, snack food manufacturers, and advertisers.

Sports in American Society.   To understand sports in American society requires examining the institutions that sustain them. Courses in this area could include visits to training camps, retired athletes, beer companies and other promoters, television executives, team owners, land developers, rooters clubs, cheerleaders, and physicians specializing in sports medicine.

Anthropology

Anthropology courses following introductory laboratories could focus on important and neglected American subgroups, including the following.

American Elites.   Elites are studied as personalities in history courses. But as a "class" with particular networks and attitudes, they are often shielded and unseen. Private clubs, fraternities and sororities, secret societies, prominent families, fashion centers, auction houses, galleries, preparatory and finishing schools, exclusive resorts and neighborhoods, and debutante balls are all ripe for anthropological study.

Other courses could be developed on particular topics in anthropology—gender, religion, social structure, ethnicity, and so on—with a focus on issues, groups, or methodologies.

———∾∾∾———

Natural Sciences

At upper levels, science courses could teach a number of applied skills that use experimental methods, to improve public health and increase productivity.

Biology

Fundamentals of Medicine.   While most schools have premedical courses that teach the basic principles of cellular biology and biochemistry, increasing numbers have courses on the human body that focus on sexuality. Few universities go beyond the teachings of high school health and first aid courses to actually teach basic concepts of health care and the variety of approaches to it. The purpose of a course in fundamentals of medicine would be to observe and teach the practices of various health care practitioners and technologies and to provide a better understanding of the workings of the human body.

The course would include visits to hospitals (including viewing autopsies and surgeries), acupuncturists, herbalists, spiritual and faith healers, chiropractors, and mental health practitioners. Students would be trained in basic practices of health care as "barefoot doctors" for circumstances and areas in which no health care is available.

Engineering

Primitive/Early Technology (Cross-Listed with Archaeology).

Archeology professors who have developed courses in which students go out and search for basic materials to develop stone tools should be commended. Courses in stone tool construction and metallurgy would help students develop a better sense of the prehistorical roots of human society, more fully appreciate the intellectual achievement of modern technology, and better interact with the physical world. Demonstration questions could include: How were early paints and metals extracted? How were animal fats first made into soaps?

(This course could be taught along with a similar course in material culture and human adaptation. See the section on ecology, below.)

Appropriate Technology (Cross-Listed with Development Economics).

The academic literature is filled with information about mistakes made in developing countries by transferring to them advanced technologies that simply do not work in the new environments in which they are introduced. Handbooks have recently been designed for use in developing countries that explain how to build simple engines, bicycle-driven machines, and so on, with available and easy-to-fix parts; these books are offshoots of the hobbyist manuals found at specialty stores in this country.

Development planners often find it hard to know which technologies might be appropriate to a new problem without having had experience working and building basic devices. This course would provide students with that experience.

How Things Work: Technological Principles in Practice.

Automobile mechanics and basic electrical work are usually not included as part of a liberal education because they are considered to be technical skills. Instead, the application of scientific principles is detached from the theory that is taught.

A course on how to construct and operate appliances and equipment, if taught with the principles behind the devices and demonstrations of new innovations in operation and design, is no less valid than one that teaches a language or discusses books; in fact, this kind of knowledge is often essential to advanced scientists who must design some of their own experimental equipment.

Engineering professors should be commended for recent advances in their courses that include design projects and competitions in which student teams build better mousetraps (literally), parachutes, and forms of aerial and water transport, using only basic materials.

A course in simply taking apart things that are used every day (radios, televisions, automobiles, personal computers, and so on) and then putting them back together again would be an instructive means of combining theory with practical skills.

Ecology/Environment

Material Culture and Use of the Ecosystem: A Primer in Human Adaptation Survival (Cross-Listed with Archaeology and Anthropology).   Scouting activities and "wilderness" courses teach the rudiments of basic survival techniques used by primitive peoples; home economics courses teach some of the basics of apparel making. But few courses at the university level actually attempt to teach students how to replicate the lost arts of survival in ecosystems that have been turned into cities.

This course in the use of the ecosystem would include basic plant identification and techniques of plant domestication to meet dietary needs, health remedies, and creation of basic materials. The course would also include extensive explorations of using the physical materials available in the culture for the development of shelter, clothing, and other needs.

Social Science Theory and History:
Exploring The Unseen America at Berkeley

The space below is purposefully blank. The reader should look through the syllabus at the end of this section (Exhibit 5.1), then return here and pause.

For this book, the authors of the syllabus displayed in Exhibit 5.1, Arturo Cherbowski, Jacqueline McEvoy, and Laura Harris, chose not to write about The Unseen America course at Berkeley but rather to let their work speak for itself. They offer a blank space and a challenge that becomes a lesson and a thought-provoking experience that is similar to the time spent in their class. For those who shared The Unseen America experience with them, the learning experience these three designed was one that forced students to think hard about their own biases, their individual needs, and the perspectives and perceptions that they projected in their studies of the world. In a sense, the authors turned what was originally a social science course—one geared to training students in policy techniques and to introducing them to public issues—into a study of the processes of knowledge, of formulation of theory, of political communication, and of policy making. Their choice not to describe their course themselves is, in a sense, an extension of that philosophy.

The course they taught was at the cutting edge of philosophy, literary and textual analysis, and social science theory, and it demonstrated the versatility of democratic experiential education in its potential for developing complex thinking and a broad range of skills. The Unseen America course at Berkeley was not only about American society; it was also a test of "postmodernist" theories, as well as theories of communications and processes within the classroom. It allowed Cherbowski, McEvoy, and Harris to present and test their own beliefs, including the credo that there is no one reality (as there is no one single view of their approach to The Unseen America or one on which they could all agree).

Berkeley's The Unseen America was an intellectual experience like no other. Describing a course, an experience, a learning opportunity, or a type of interaction in a few words—or even in a chapter—presents exactly the same type of challenge that Cherbowski, McEvoy, and Harris posed in their version of The Unseen America. They would not have wanted their course described in a phrase, nor would they be content with the description contained in one essay. The ability to recognize the limitations of trying to describe experience in brief and formal terms is the type of awareness and consciousness they try to raise.

Just as there are multiple views and interpretations of the lives and needs of those communities with which students came into contact in a class session of The Unseen America, there are multiple views of the semester-long sequence of experiences at Berkeley called The Unseen America.

What is the essence of The Unseen America, Cherbowski, McEvoy, and Harris would ask, that everyone shares? Can The Unseen America really be reduced to a few words on paper? Is that a fair representation of a shared experience and exchange? What description is not colored by all the subjective interpretations through ideology, background, language, and the like that all of us bring to the experience? What is "real" and what is being described and altered in a conscious or subconscious way for "promotion" and "marketing" purposes? Whose vision does any statement about the course represent, and why is it presented that way?

Looking at completed sections of early drafts of this book, Cherbowski, McEvoy, and Harris asked, "Who are the 'we' mentioned in the book? Does that apply to us? Is the 'we' of this book an inclusive 'we' or a conjunctive and all-encompassing 'we' (where every statement should apply to everyone)? Is the vision of democratic experiential education or of The Unseen America itself an additive one, or more one person's vision, format, and subjective experience?

"Doesn't this book already reflect a framework that forces and predisposes every chapter to 'fit' in a certain way," they asked, "that acts as a means of control?" What if their description did not fit?

The description of their course, then, is one provided by an outsider looking in.

The Unique Approach of The Unseen America at Berkeley

The Unseen America at Berkeley was taught in a very different way, and to a different group of students, from The Unseen America that was taught at Stanford in 1985. The Berkeley version was by and for those attending an urban public university rather than an expensive suburban university only forty miles away geographically but much farther away in all other dimensions. (The breadth of approaches that can be accommodated in the idea of experiential and democratic education demonstrates that there is something in this form of education that is self-activating and larger than the energy of any one educational entrepreneur or teacher.)

The course by Cherbowski, McEvoy, and Harris was, by design, more "democratic" than the previous version. Led by three students, it was taught to peers by peers—juniors teaching juniors and seniors, rather than a professional student teaching freshmen. And it was officially under the rubric of student-oriented courses at the University of California—something known as Democratic Education at the University of California (or DE-CAL for short).

Its goals and purposes as well were different from the Stanford course. The Unseen America at Stanford was designed to develop more sensitive and skilled policy makers and professionals as well as more adept social scientists. The hope was that students would learn to seek better measurements of American society and of social behavior in general; that they would question the variables that social scientists currently use and come up with more useful ones; and that given additional information from direct contact with their subject of study, they would look at policies and approaches that were being implemented and come up with new and workable solutions.

At the root of the Stanford course was a philosophy that human behavior (and the world in general) is essentially and eventually knowable, explainable, and predictable; that being able to predict and control events with empathy and understanding is not only possible but desirable. Furthermore, according to the philosophy, students and citizens should be involved in the world and should be active participants in this process. The view represented by the Stanford course was scientific, positivistic, activistic—and completely different from the one that Cherbowski, McEvoy, and Harris held.

This dichotomy was an outgrowth of the different worldviews of those who designed different versions of the course, and it was something that the concept of democratic experiential education not only allowed but encouraged. The Unseen America at Stanford was taught by a professional student interested in policy and in challenging political science and social science education. By contrast, Cherbowski, McEvoy, and Harris's interests were more theoretical. Cherbowski, a Mexican of Polish-Jewish descent, was interested in political theory and has since gone on to work on his doctorate (at Yale) in political science. McEvoy, a Northern Californian, was interested in literature and has pursued that field of study in a doctoral program at Duke University. And Harris, a Chicagoan, was majoring in English.

Thus, for The Unseen America at Berkeley, the key appeared to be to look at the methods of social science and to question what is knowable and whether generalizations can and should be made from limited observation. And if so, how should they be made, and how reliable are they?

The course questioned definitions of the social environment and how Americans interact with each other, how the views and biases that individuals bring can change their perceptions of what they see, and how the symbols they use to communicate further distort the reality. The course asked students to consider how descriptions are often "projections" and how interpretation is a product of contextualization—the social context in which something is observed.

Much of the teaching of postmodernism and deconstruction, or "interpretivism," has been intellectually paralyzing, making it appear that nothing at all can be measured and that intellectual discovery has little real basis. However, to believe that is to believe in a paradox. The Unseen America at Berkeley went beyond the part of the debate that stopped rational action and stymied intellectual movement. The course not only had strong intellectual grounding in its internal logic, but it also had a long written tradition in other disciplines. It was really on the cutting edge of trends in intellectual theory—forging through the "crisis of modernity" and beyond, to find what could be measured and how.

What They Did

Cherbowski, McEvoy, and Harris did more than introduce a different perspective. They made a commitment over a long period of time, they oversaw the evolution of their course, and they worked with several different student groups. Over time, they implemented a wide array of changes in the methods by which the class was taught.

They gave students more interactive assignments at the start, requiring more initiative and participation than other seminars do. In fact, the last two weeks of the course became part of a conscious strategy for empowerment of fellow students, with readings and field trips to be selected by students in the class.

Cherbowski, McEvoy, and Harris asked for weekly short essays ("response papers") as a means of eliciting a greater exchange of ideas. They ran simulations, such as the "aging game" (in which they role-played different ages), and then discussed the value and drawbacks of using such simulations.

Because they viewed educating as an intellectual exercise in itself, they also continued to experiment. For some weeks, they designed field trips and individual assignments that combined visits to places with a particular kind of philosophical discussion. To raise the issue of the ethics of voyeurism, for example, they told students to go to a place where they would feel like an outsider. In their study of "self-help," they did not focus on a policy issue but on a cultural phenomenon, to see how the self-help movement, with its books and seminars, could be explained.

Other exercises were designed for reflective looks at the students themselves as a group, to challenge their stereotypes of the group and their classmates and to explore their own social relations within the classroom as a microcosm of their relations to the outside world.

And the instructors added different communities and sites—religious institutions, women's shelters, rehabilitation centers, a self-help support group for people who had left mental institutions, and the gay community.

They sometimes reversed the notion of field visits. Instead of visiting a group of veterans, for example, they brought the veterans to the campus to hold a meeting of their support group in a university setting with the students.

Cherbowski, McEvoy, and Harris built something that possibly no undergraduates ever had built before: they built Political Science 176 and put it into the curriculum and laid the foundation for Anthropology 3 Laboratory. They crossed disciplinary boundaries to establish experiences for Berkeley undergraduates long after the three of them were gone.

Indeed, the students who were teaching The Unseen America at Berkeley in the 1994–95 academic year had no idea about the origins of the course and did not know who Cherbowski, McEvoy, and Harris were. Yet the students continued the tradition of the course, with new readings and their own emphases. This may be the greatest testament to its success.

EXHIBIT 5.1. Social Science Theory and History.

Coordinators:	Arturo Cherbowski	De-Cal Fall 1988
	Jacqueline McEvoy	U.C. Berkeley
	Laura Harris	Syllabus

Course Title:
The Unseen America: Qualitative Analysis in Social Science
Research and Policy Formation

Short Description:
This course is designed to supplement the traditional quantitative and theoretical social science approach to American public policy problems with an introduction to both qualitative research methods and data. Interdisciplinary readings will be coordinated with field trips to prisons, courts, factories, a mental hospital, etc.

Course Objectives:
1. To introduce students to the methodology, ethical considerations, and usefulness of ethnographic analysis.
2. To contrast on-site observation and analysis with written course materials in order to better appreciate the strengths and weaknesses of quantitative and qualitative approaches and means of combining the two in policy analysis.
3. To enrich students' understanding of and appreciation for the diversity and richness of American society and culture.
4. To develop and explore alternative methods of education that emphasize students' self-motivation, a free exchange of ideas, and the integration of students' personal experience.

Requirements:
Students will be required to:
- Complete assigned readings.
- Attend and participate in weekly discussions.
- Attend weekly field trips.
- Prepare weekly response papers.
- Write a small (3- to 5-page) paper describing a campus community group.
- Write a 7- to 10-page final paper.
- Give a presentation of final project at the last class discussion. (Be creative. Any medium is acceptable.)

Grading:

This course will be offered on a Pass/No Pass option to be assigned by the sponsoring professor. In order to promote the free exchange of ideas in discussion and to encourage intellectual experimentation, grading will be on a contractual rather than competitive basis. Grades will be acquired by means of "certification," reflecting attendance at discussion and field trips and completion of weekly response papers and both written assignments.

Sponsoring Faculty and Departments:

Prof. Brentano   History
Prof. Muir   Political Science
Prof. Sanders   Peace and Conflict Studies
Prof. Potter   Anthropology
Prof. Carr   Conservation and Resource Studies

Course Plan by Week

Week		Topic
1	(8/29–8/31)	Introduction
2	(9/3–9/7)	Examining Education
3	(9/12–9/17)	Perceptions of America/The Workplace
4	(9/19–9/21)	The Workplace (cont.)/Wealth and Poverty
5	(9/26–9/28)	Wealth and Poverty (cont.)/Qualitative Analysis and Methodology
6	(10/3–10/5)	The Institutionalized: The Aged/Ethical Considerations
7	(10/10–10/12)	Alcoholism and Drug Abuse
8	(10/17–10/19)	The Institutionalized: The Insane
9	(10/24–10/26)	War and Its Domestic Repercussions
10	(10/31–11/2)	War and Its Domestic Repercussions (cont.)
11	(11/7–11/9)	The Justice System: Jail
12	(11/14–11/16)	The Justice System: Courts
13	(11/21–11/23)	The Homosexual Community
14	(11/28–11/30)	Religion
15	(12/5–12/7)	Conclusion and Final Projects Presentation

Field Trips and Readings:

Week 1: Introduction

Class Meetings: Two class discussions. No field trips this week.

Readings: No readings this week.

Week 2: Examining Education

**Class
Meetings:**   One class discussion (Monday is Labor Day).
No field trips this week.

Readings: Ivan Illich, *Deschooling Society* (excerpts)
Allan Bloom, *The Closing of the American Mind* (excerpts)
Jon Wagner, "Teaching and Research"
David Lempert, "Return to Stanford"

Week 3: Perceptions of America/The Workplace

**Class
Meetings:**   Two class discussions.

Film: *All American High/A Day in the Life of America*

Field Trip: Northface Factory, Berkeley

Readings: C. Wright Mills, *White Collar* (excerpts)
Richard Reeves, *An American Journey* (excerpts)
James Baldwin, *The Fire Next Time* (excerpts)
Noam Chomsky, *The Bounds of Unthinkable Thought*
William F. Buckley, Jr., *On Right Reason* (excerpts)

Week 4: The Workplace (cont.)/Wealth and Poverty

**Class
Meetings:**   One class discussion.

Field Trip: Low income housing complex, City of Alameda

Readings: Karl Marx, *The Communist Manifesto* (excerpts)
Marvin R. Weisbord, *Productive Workplaces* (excerpts)
William B. Johnston, *Workforce 2000* (excerpts)
David Riesman, *Abundance for What* (excerpts)
John K. Galbraith, *The New Industrial State* (excerpts)
From *The Journal of Housing:*
  Terrence Cooper, "Public Housing and Architecture"
  Teresa Riordan, "Housekeeping at HUD"
From Housing Authority of the City of Alameda:
  A Guide to Housing Vouchers

Application Form
Fact Sheet

Week 5: Wealth and Poverty (cont.)/Qualitative Analysis and Methodology

Class Meetings: Two class discussions.

Field Trip: Rest home (on your own)

Readings: George Gilder, *Wealth and Poverty* (excerpts)
W. Ryan, *Blaming the Victim* (excerpts)
James Spradley, *The Ethnographic Interview* (excerpts)
Horace J. Miner, "Body Rituals Among the Nacirema"
Neil B. Thompson, "The Mysterious Fall of the Nacirema"
George Marcus and Michael Fischer, *Anthropology as Culture Critique* (excerpt)
Stephen J. Gould, *The Mismeasure of Man* (excerpts)

Week 6: The Institutionalized: The Aged/Ethical Considerations

Class Meetings: Two class discussions.

Readings: Michael Rynklewich, *Ethics and Anthropology*
American Anthropological Association, "Statements on Ethics"
Calvin Pryluck, "Ultimately We Are All Ousiders . . ."
Jules Henry, "Personality and Aging . . ."
More readings TBA

Week 7: Alcoholism and Drugs

Class Meetings: One class discussion.

Field Trip: Salvation Army Alcohol Rehabilitation Center, Oakland

Readings: Herbert Fingarette, *Heavy Drinking* (excerpts)

Mark E. Lender, *Drinking in America* (excerpts)
Marian Sandmaier, *The Invisible Alcoholics* (excerpts)

Week 8: The Institutionalized: The Insane

Class Meetings: One class discussion.
First paper assignment due.

Field Trip: Highland Hospital Psychiatric Ward

Readings: Oliver Sacks, *The Man Who Mistook His Wife for a Hat* (excerpts)
David Rosenbaum, "On Being Sane in Insane Places"
Thomas Szazc, *The Psychiatric State* (excerpts)
Insanity (excerpts)
Charles Manson, excerpts from interviews

Week 9: War and Its Domestic Repercussions

Class Meetings: One class discussion.

Field Trip: Alameda Naval Air Station

Readings: "Why Men Love War," *Esquire Magazine*
William F. Buckley, Jr., "Do You Oppose the Draft?"
Defense Monitor, "Militarism in America"
More readings TBA

Week 10: War and Its Domestic Repercussions (cont.)

Class Meetings: Two class discussions.

Field Trip: Discussions with Vietnam veterans from the Oakland Veterans Center

Readings: Harrison P. Salisburg, ed., *Vietnam Reconsidered* (excerpts)
Ron Kovic, *Born on the Fourth of July*

Week 11: The Justice System: Jail

Class Meetings: One class discussion.

Field Trip: North County Jail, Oakland

Readings: Jessica Mitford, *Kind and Unusual Punishment* (excerpts)
Irving Goffman, *Asylums* (excerpts)
John Irwin, *Jail* (excerpts)
Philip G. Zimbardo, "Pathology of Imprisonment"

Week 12: The Justice System: Courts

Class Meetings: One class discussion.

Field Trip: Berkeley Municipal Courts

Readings: TBA

Week 13: The Homosexual Community

Class Meetings: One class discussion.

Field Trip: Discussion with members of the Gay-Lesbian-Bi Alliance

Readings: Adrienne Rich, *Compulsory Heterosexuality*
Laude Humphreys, *Tea Room Trade*
Jeffrey Weeks, *Sexuality and Its Discontents*
William F. Buckley, Jr., "Who Speaks for the Gays?"
"The Kindness of Strangers," *East Bay Express*

Week 14: Religion

Class Meetings: Two class discussions.

Field Trip: On your own, go to a religious service, preferably one with which you are unfamiliar.

Readings: Émile Durkheim, *On Religion* (excerpts)
Max Weber, *The Protestant Ethic* (excerpts)
Robert N. Bellah, et al., eds., *Individualism and Commitment in American Life* (Chapter 9)

Week 15: Conclusion and Final Projects Presentation

**Class
Meetings:**   Two class meetings.
                 Final paper assignment and presentation due.

━◦◦◦━

Public Policy: The Unseen America
Returns to Stanford

If there is one great strength to democratic and experiential education, it may be that it shapes itself to the needs of its student participants and to nearby communities without any rigid preconceptions of or framework for the way it should be done, other than concern for educational quality and for the dignity of all who are involved.

When The Unseen America was taught for the second time at Stanford, by a new group of undergraduate students, these students had their own definition of unseen and their own style and approach. As these student coordinators wrote in the course syllabus, "In addition to exploring the attitudes and circumstances (that is, economic inequities) that shape a complex social reality, the course will explore the individual's experience of the subject matter."

In honoring that approach, this chapter also tells the experiences of the participants in their own personal style, in the form of a commentary by Xavier Briggs, one of three then-undergraduates who served as coordinators and teachers of the course (the syllabus for this course appears in Exhibit 5.2 at the end of this section).

While Briggs's description is more personalized than the typical explanation of the philosophy and logistics of the course, we have chosen to present it for several reasons.

First, it demonstrates how students were able to work within the institutional framework of the university and expand its possibilities in different ways. The process of curricular change and reform at the university level requires a certain amount of creativity in working within the system, as well as persistence.

Second, this story is about building on past success and using it to expand what is possible. The original course at Stanford was taught on a shoestring budget; four years later, however, the administration had already begun to recognize the value of peer learning. The original course and its follow-up had expanded what is possible.

Third, this story is also about the importance of outreach and of institutionalizing innovations so that they outlive their creators. When David Lempert left Stanford in 1985, The Unseen America course left with him because there was no one to teach it or advocate for it. Xavier Briggs describes how a brief communication about that course was enough to capture his attention and set the course in motion once again.

At the same time, transferring a course to new instructors was a difficult process. When Briggs and his colleagues passed The Unseen America on to a new generation—to their students, who taught their own version of it a year later—they were applying techniques of institutionalizing the idea, as Cherbowski, McEvoy, and Harris had at Berkeley in similar ways.

Fourth, this story also describes the kind of dedication required for innovation: how there is no prefabricated or standardized model, and how, if one did exist, it would contradict what democratic experiential education is all about. Briggs and his colleagues had their own visions, philosophies, and commitments to ideas and success that led them to shape their own approach and bring it to a successful completion.

Finally, Briggs describes how he and his colleagues were able to link The Unseen America with the concept of service learning—not only studying and interacting with the community surrounding the university, but also finding ways for students to give something back as part of the learning experience.

This is their story.

—⟨∞∞⟩—

Creating Dialogue and Growth

Xavier N. de Souza Briggs

I first heard about The Unseen America in the spring of 1988 while facilitating a workshop at a student-run conference on international development at Stanford University, where I was a junior in a self-designed program called Resources and Development. It was at the workshop that I met David Lempert, a lawyer, an educational entrepreneur, and an anthropologist. David intrigued me—as he did the entire workshop audience—not with some highbrowed exhortation on poverty in faraway lands, but with the striking account of his struggle—at Stanford and elsewhere—for a more student-focused and socially relevant education. David linked faraway problems to everyday neglect here at home in a very compelling and memorable way. I decided then that I would try to follow up on his course the following year.

It took time to develop my own goals for the class and then to work with two friends—Jim Pitofsky, a communications major with an interest in law, and Wendy Whitehill, a premed student studying human biology—to understand the experiential method and outline a possible focus. David and The Unseen America instructors at Berkeley had their doubts that I was serious about the class. Now, after having facilitated one of the courses, I can see how vital it is to be careful about replicating experiential models. David and the others were asking, "What do you want to do with The Unseen America?" Until about two months before our first class session, I simply wasn't sure.

To "do something" with The Unseen America, I worked with Wendy and Jim to create a class that would involve our interests and strengths even as it compelled and challenged a diverse group of students. We had to question ourselves and our goals as readily and constructively in the course of developing The Unseen America as we would later question our students.

The experiential format that underlay this workshop/class demanded that we be self-critical and patient at each step of the way: developing themes; ensuring that the three of us had the kind of supportive yet questioning relationship to make a team effort work; making contacts and selecting readings; gaining university acceptance for both the content and method; selecting student participants; and last (but far from least), conducting the workshop in a way that would challenge everyone involved to seek *dialogue* and *growth*.

It was these two words that motivated me and guided our experiment to give the workshop a new identity at Stanford. Dialogue and growth became challenging—even frustrating and elusive—goals when we began to confront the ethical dilemmas that seem to be inherent in learning "in the world" and outside the classroom. But these dilemmas are unavoidable in the kind of risk-taking pedagogy that makes dialogue possible.

Like Wendy and Jim, I wanted to apply all of myself to the project, not just my intellect or my limited political and social understandings. I wanted to offer a small group of motivated peers an exceptional opportunity to question themselves as they were questioning the world. And I wanted to grow along with them.

Many late-night conversations and seemingly interminable lectures in restless classrooms—these at what many consider one of the nation's top schools—had convinced me that such a learning opportunity was both needed and timely. Many of my friends at Stanford were both very hardworking and very bright, but too many felt utterly uninspired by their coursework. It's not simply that they questioned the value of the university's required courses, though that was part of their disillusionment. It had more to do with the failure of their classes—whether instructors or material or both—to show them that their academic work and their lives outside the classroom could overlap and nurture each other. Students often felt removed from the changing world around them and unable to express their own interests or develop their talents. However, to achieve—to compete with their hardworking peers—most had resigned themselves to the priorities as they were: to learn the theory and to learn to articulate the neat academic phrases whether or not they have any personal meaning, whether or not they seem a valid reflection of what really goes on in the world.

But this sense that the Stanford experience was incomplete is only half the picture. Much more motivated Jim, Wendy, and me to resurrect The Unseen America, a glaringly absent "voice," within the academic community. The other half had to do with Stanford students' attitudes and extracurricular commitments, with the pulse of college life as best we, students ourselves, saw it.

Moving Ahead and "Making a Difference"

Prevalent in the words of students, administrators, and faculty alike at Stanford in the late 1980s was the idea that "you can make a difference," that is, you can work to make things better all around you as a student and through your career.

Jim, Wendy, and I agreed. But too many of our friends were content to accept things as they are, feeling that society's ills must be too big and bad—too complex and demanding—or else somebody brighter or more capable would have figured them out already. It's not that Stanford undergraduates weren't sincere about "making a difference" (though some were indeed fairweather volunteers); it's that students weren't—and aren't— being given the message *in the classroom* as often or as convincingly as they could be.

There's something being lost here, we figured. Many of our peers were ignoring the possibility that by conscious choice they might combine their learning with "making a difference." In developing The Unseen America, we wanted to inform the Stanford University community that this often hollow phrase needed a simple addendum: "You can make a difference *if you spend some time, sweat, and comfort to find out where and how.*"

As we wrote in the class outline, "The concept of 'making a difference' is much in vogue, particularly among those of college

age . . . [but] such a well-intentioned concept needs to be constructively defined and developed." So when The Unseen America returned to Stanford, the class method had been redeveloped
out of our common conviction that good intentions are indeed
not enough, but neither is a theoretical sense of how to apply
them.

Jim, Wendy, and I wanted our students to develop a critical
approach to diverse sources of information. We looked to the nontraditional opportunities of the field as well as traditional sources of
information, including books, films, and guest speakers. We wanted
to encourage students to dream with a solid grounding in reality, to
propose tentative and flexible but workable definitions of "making
a difference." We sought to define these words for ourselves and
each other in a supportive yet challenging circle of learning and
dialogue—a circle that would grow restless over clichés and stag-
nant ideological positions, a circle that would question convenient
answers to the inconvenient questions.

We also wanted our students to believe that it was both a right
and a responsibility to share differences as equals, to challenge each
other's assumptions while building mutual respect. We came to see
that this would require considerable effort in managing discussions.
Groups that carry on genuine exchange are made, not born. How
else would there be dialogue or growth individually or collectively?

Ideas in Service Learning

To put these philosophical commitments to the test, though, we
had to organize an accredited class. We began to draft an outline
and to select tentative readings, with the goal of presenting The
Unseen America as a Stanford Workshop on Political and Social
Issues (SWOPSI). Along with other special programs that "didn't
fit" into the standard academic curriculum or could not be taught
by regular faculty, SWOPSIs were sponsored by a program called
Innovative Academic Courses (IAC). IAC provided undergraduates one of their few opportunities to be instructors rather than

teaching assistants. It was one of the few programs that were flexible enough to offer courses on important, contemporary situations (AIDS, for example) or growing areas of knowledge (such as non-Western healing), and the growth of its budget was, therefore, a sign of changing times. Whereas IAC had granted David Lempert a budget of $25 for The Unseen America four years before, we received stipends of $250 each and a budget of $150 (to which we added much-needed funding from what is now the Haas Center for Public Service).

The IAC program required all SWOPSI applicants to submit a course proposal that included the objectives of the class, the social and political content, and an "action component"—some requirement that students act on the class material. We drafted a proposal and circulated it among our personal contacts in various areas of the university: the Public Service Center, the Disability Resource Center, the Chicano Center, and so on. These groups provided feedback that was timely, uniformly enthusiastic (yet questioning), and very valuable. But we hadn't yet developed the action component that would qualify the course.

We knew that in the past, SWOPSI students had organized programs in the dormitories or discussion panels on the campus radio station. We wanted something different, something to reflect the unique approach of The Unseen America. Ultimately, it was the workshop's action component that would afford us the chance to create a version of The Unseen America unlike the earlier courses at Berkeley and Stanford.

But more important than fulfilling the requirement for a SWOPSI class, the action project we developed represented our response to one of the key dilemmas of The Unseen America and similar courses: how to give students on-site exposure to "unseen" communities, such as migrant farm workers or the institutionalized, *without being voyeuristic toward or exploiting these groups*. We were very concerned about the "ooh-ahh" effect, very worried that our students might gawk at rather than respond to the communities in which (and of which) we would learn.

We planned to address and deter this in the classroom, but we realized that in the action project we might create a different kind of connection between our students and the communities we would visit—a more substantive one. Over a ten-week period, we would be asking our students to engage various communities in the classroom and then respond to and learn from them during field visits. But we decided that through the action project, we would ask the students to go back to one community again and again, to work with a local community group such as a homeless shelter or a school classroom with the hope that the extended time in one such community would lend a fuller and more humane understanding of its specialness. How could a student who had volunteered to assist a teacher in a low-income school not have a richer experience to share than one who had only read about why children don't achieve to their potential, or one who had spent only two hours touring the school?

Narrowing the Distance: Theory Behind the Experiment

In my view, Americans who wish to be considered "educated" must make an experiential commitment that *narrows the distance* between themselves and others. Liberal education should be a process of shortening all types of distances, including those of class, race, religion, physical or mental ability, and profession. This means more than becoming politically aware. It means creating dialogue in and out of the classroom. It means removing barriers to understanding that exist because society creates them for us *and because we let them stand*.

I first heard the word *distance* used this way by the late Mitch Snyder, a man who both inspired and annoyed me (and whose methods we came to adopt as part of our educational approach). Snyder was an advocate for the millions of homeless people in our nation, as well as director of the Community for Creative Non-Violence, a Washington, D.C.–based shelter and activist organization. After listening to Snyder speak at a conference on the homeless held at Stanford in the spring of 1989, I was convinced he was hell on two legs.

Snyder gave an irreverent and strikingly unpretentious talk on American life and politics, followed by an equally candid question-and-answer session. While answering a student's question, he told us that there was no reason to be at a place like Stanford if we sincerely want to "make a difference." Snyder said that we couldn't possibly "learn" while being fed the excuses and detached theory, no matter how articulate and well read we might become. This was a hard pill for many to swallow at a conference that attracted some of the school's most concerned and community-involved students.

Snyder argued that the "ivory tower" rises to especially dangerous heights at our nation's top schools and that it inevitably creates a destructive distance (and accompanying symptoms of indifference and intolerance) between us and those we wish to help or simply need to understand. The result is that the schools' graduates—professionals in all areas of the private and public sectors—are clearly unable to offer viable solutions to increasingly complex problems. They are often unable to understand or deal with the people most affected by their decisions. And the reasons for this inability lie less in the extent of their education than in the way they have been educated.

At the age of twenty, for example, some of my college friends had already set up a disturbingly comfortable distance between themselves and those who live in what seems a different America. This distance is disempowering, because it makes them unable to relate to or communicate with a large proportion of their fellow Americans, and I don't know that they will ever want or be able to cross that gap. In this context, *distance* is more than physical separation, though that's often a central, contributing factor. Distance is the sense that our lives and destinies are essentially unrelated to those of groups whose life circumstances are greatly removed from our own, whether "better" or "worse," richer or poorer. Distance is as much a psychic and emotional gulf as it is a physical one.

Distance endures thirty-second "sound bites" on the television news; it defies the empty, unfulfilled rhetoric about social responsibility that lacks a lived sense of what it means to be "on the other side." Distance often emerges from the lecture hall (or movie theater or benefit concert) unscathed or even strengthened.

Distance is a sense of separation and self-sufficiency, rugged individualism run amok in a changing world—and a confused America—that will not comprehend or endure it. We need only look around us at the growing interdependence, the overlap, of the social, political, and economic spheres of our lives and living groups to recognize this distance as dangerous.

Many young people allow their genuine desire of discovery and growth to unravel so that their lives are centered on credentials and career. This pattern only confirms the unfair stereotype of Stanford and other schools as little more than privileged "country club" environments.

Stanford was much more than a country club to me, though I do feel that the campus setting that provided me such opportunity for companionship, reflection, and growth also worked to conceal me from communities and ideas that are essential to a working understanding of modern America. I know many Stanford students and alumni who feel this way. Even the freshmen in our workshop largely agreed that we lived and studied in what was often a "bubble" of distance and disinterest.

But we don't have to accept the bubble. I learned and grew a great deal at Stanford and through the opportunities it afforded me. I know that what I brought to the class—wonder, passion, and skepticism, for example—were as important for what I got out of them as the intellectual eminence or the good intentions of those who sat in the teacher's chair. The peers I respected most were those who were determined to *narrow the distance* in whatever way they had to in order to learn.

One of the most important things I had learned at Stanford was how to ask better questions, probing questions, revealing and unexpected questions. So I felt that with two good friends with different personalities but similar motivation, I could help other students— my peers—place themselves in the social realities that surround us.

As facilitators of The Unseen America, Jim, Wendy, and I sought to provide good questions more often than the "good" answers that we didn't have (and that many lay claim to). Our academic achievements and disappointments, as well as those of our personal lives, had convinced us that questioning dialogue would captivate and reward students more than the information exchange they were accustomed to.

We shared the view that information means little if it is not channeled into a genuine dialogue—within the self, among other students, among diverging perspectives.

My belief in dialogue-based learning "rooted in the world" owes much to the work and writing of Paulo Freire, an innovative and inspiring Brazilian educator. Freire's method of teaching illiterates in "culture circles," which he developed in some of the poorest regions in Brazil, is internationally recognized. I was first inspired by his *Pedagogy of the Oppressed* (Freire, 1970) and have more recently discovered *Freire in the Classroom* and other works edited by American educator Ira Shor (1987), with useful and inspiring case studies of the Freirean method.

Jim, Wendy, and I sought to incorporate Freirean concepts of learning and the world directly in the course. We wrote in the workshop outline, "This course is about dialogue and growth, not monologue and regurgitation." Visiting speakers were to be guests of the circle of learning, guests with a distinctive life experience and perspective to share. But they didn't necessarily have the right answers, either. We wanted students to question (in the sense of "challenge") the guests, just as they would question their facilitators (us) and each other.

We also wanted to facilitate students' critiques of the book and article excerpts they read, and we encouraged them to bring relevant materials of their own. We wanted to share our hope with each other as well as our skepticism. We challenged our students repeatedly to integrate their life experiences—their twenty-odd years of life and not just the field trips—into a multifaceted process of learning. We sought dialogue.

Getting Started

Neither Jim, Wendy, nor I liked the idea of conducting an application process. You might say that we saw it as a necessary evil. We believed—and what took place in the weeks that followed supported our belief—that the uniqueness of the class would attract many students, of which only some would be ready for the challenges. We believed that some students would be attracted by the novelty of the content and by the active hands-on approach we described. Others would appreciate the novelty but would be mature and self-critical enough to respond to the "circle of learning" concept that we wanted to create. We hoped that this latter group of students would include a few who were willing and capable of continuing the workshop in future years.

This was indeed a project whose time had come. About ninety students expressed an interest in the fifteen slots of The Unseen America class in the spring of 1989. Many more didn't bother to sign up, though they wanted to join the class, simply because their schedules did not permit it. About forty of the ninety students appeared on the first night; we were able to choose only fifteen of them to return the following week.

The feeling on that first night was electric. We sat for hours on the floor in a large circle and listened as students shared insights on college education—what it is, what it might be. They also related many day-to-day experiences of frustration and wonder, and they explained how their upbringing had shaped the learning they were doing—and not doing—at Stanford. All of this happened in a way they had never thought possible in a classroom setting.

The sense of connection was uncanny. There was a strong feeling that a support network had been found. Here was a group in which to share the excitement *and* the frustration of real learning. No one noticed as the minutes and hours ticked away. When it was time to leave the classroom—to break the circle—a group of students stunned the three of us by deciding that if they were not accepted for the class, they wanted to convene on their own, get class materials, and keep in touch with each other and the directions the class would take.

Needless to say, this made the process of selection all the more difficult. What right had we to decide someone's worthiness or sincerity? Over one long weekend, we read and reread the striking thoughts our applicants had shared on their upbringing, their schooling, their careers, their dreams. We reluctantly made the cuts, realizing that everyone in some sense deserved to be in the class.

In making these arbitrary assessments of our peers, we felt that we were asking students to pay the price of an academia that was obviously not responding adequately to their needs. "There ought to be ten of these classes," we said to each other. And the only redeeming aspect of the selection process was welcoming fifteen unique and motivated people to The Unseen America. We read the excitement in their eyes and in their voices, and we knew that in working with them we would be forced to grow at least as much as they . . . or more.

Action Projects: "Just Tell Us What You See"

The action project we developed as our special interpretation of the experiential format of The Unseen America—an approach combining voluntarism with research—allowed us to emphasize one of the most important and underutilized tools of social science: ethnography. This research method involves speaking with and observing people in their daily routines in order to understand events both from the perspective of an outsider and from the perspective of those involved.

But for untrained students, half of them freshmen, to do ethnography was not easy, and we knew it wouldn't be. Since field research methods are not learned overnight, we didn't ask for thesis-level research or formalized presentation. We guided our students in their selection of a setting for the action project and of a focus within that setting. We found it effective to let students explore for three to four weeks—letting themes emerge—and then quickly decide on foci and pursue them closely. We worked to convince students that they could "push at the envelope" of their volunteer/research projects, and that, for example, they could use written sources of information—the academic literature—to question and inform what they saw in the field. In so doing, we helped them create a brief ethnographic report—a "personalized document of learning"—on the research experience (see the syllabus in Exhibit 5.2).

This ethnography, along with the journals and weekly response papers (on various communities and themes) that we required, encouraged inquiry that responded to students' own interests and convictions. This individualized learning through critical inquiry developed even as we built a group dialogue that all could share. We spoke openly and often about experiences in the field. We did frequent check-ins with the group and conducted one-on-one meetings during office hours.

The students themselves can best convey the meaning of "action project," and why the projects were special. The following excerpts from student ethnographies illustrate the students' personal involvement in their field topics as well as their commitment to the communities they studied and in which they volunteered. There were, as we expected, many methodological shortcomings due to our students' inexperience with ethnography. But more important and to our great satisfaction, there was a great deal of *sensitivity* and *intellectual honesty*, due to our students' often inspiring desire to question and learn.

EXCERPTS FROM "ASSUMPTIONS" SECTION OF "SCHOOLS JUST LET THE CHILDREN DOWN"

MIKE SANDOVAL

I did not quite know what to think about the children at the school. I had many assumptions about the school systems of East Palmar Parkway before I went to Bering Elementary School. Would [the children] be bitter or would they be just like me when I was their age? You can read all you want about the underprivileged, but until you encounter what they are really like, it is all theoretical. Coming from a high school that was 80 percent white, 15 percent Hispanic, and 5 percent black . . . I [understandably] had many preparatory thoughts and fabrications.

Sure, I had visited poverty-stricken schools before for varsity sports and other recreational reasons, but I had never been in the classrooms during school with the students, interacting with them on an educational basis. I thought when I walked into the classroom all the children would run around and look at me as if I were an intruder. I believed they would be illiterate and almost retarded by regular elementary school standards. I thought the children would be young gang members [wearing] jackets [that signified] their ethnic backgrounds.

Excerpts from "Assumptions" Section of "Holly Middle School"

Emily Simas

Junior high is reading, writing, arithmetic, basketball, boys, bowling, best friends, cosmetics, class trips, chaos, dating, dancing, daring, gossip, girls, good times, homework, health class, and heart-to-heart talks. It is a time of transition. It is the vehicle that transports children into young adulthood, filled with confusion and curiosity. It is a frightening experience with bodies and attitudes changing at an uncontrollable rate. Junior high is a time of unanswered questions. Why can't I stay out late? Why doesn't he like me? Why do I like him? Who changed the rules of kissing tag? Why am I crying all the time?

Now add to this confusion the dangers of life on the streets, and junior high moves from chaotic to deadly. Drugs, gangs, violence, and crime are scooped out of the gutter and dropped into the middle of the playground. This is the atmosphere at Holly Middle School.

The sign at the gate reads "Holly Middle School Bears." But the only roar on campus is the nonstop shouting that rings through the halls. The only word to describe the atmosphere is volatile. Administrators know the police officers by name because of their frequent visits on campus to control gang fights.

Make Yourself Uncomfortable: Risk-Taking and Growth

On the class application, we had asked our students to sign the following learning contract:

I agree to challenge myself and those I work and learn with to question the world, to be patient, to make myself uncomfortable when it means a chance to grow, to bring the best out of others and to respect their differences, to believe in myself and in my right to know for myself.

These were difficult objectives to act on, both in our group trips and in our individual experiences in "unseen" communities. We were in constant motion to identify and deal with risks ranging from personal threats to voyeurism to misrepresentation.

For example, one female student decided to volunteer with a leadership development program in a low-income area. The program was created to instill disadvantaged youth with self-esteem, leadership ability, and an awareness of their social and economic situation, and our student was excited to pursue these organizational goals. She visited the host school once or twice per week and collected information. She presented films and helped supervise exercises developed by the project's director. She loved the children and her work, though she found the program's method frustratingly incomplete and inconsistent. She shared these frustrations with me and with the class, but she remained motivated and was anxious to write an ethnography on what was being done for the kids and what could be done differently.

Then, during the final week of her field work, she received sexually explicit telephone calls at her home from one of the children she volunteered with. She was shocked at what she considered a dangerous and very threatening attitude, especially coming from a very young boy. She had also been subject to verbal sexual harassment when completing a field visit several weeks before. Together, these incidents made her class experience emotionally draining and it made her very angry.

My own frustration was with class size and how it made it difficult to respond appropriately to her concerns. Had the class been smaller, the support we offered might have been more effective.

Other challenges were less tangible but more perplexing. Early in the class, we asked students to sign up in pairs to use a wheelchair. We felt that this experience would give students a genuine sense of the barriers faced daily by the millions of Americans who are wheelchair bound. One student would ride in the wheelchair, the other would push, and then the two would switch roles.

The discussion that followed this experience was one of the most emotional and thought-provoking we had. One student felt ashamed to be "masquerading" as disabled. He was afraid to face those with actual disabilities for fear he would be "found out." Other students used this experience to inform shopkeepers about needless barriers. One student, for example, had showed his frustration when a bookstore employee told him that he should examine the second-floor books from the first floor and call her if he found one he wanted. (The bookstore provided no wheelchair access to the second floor.) "From here?" he had asked, pointing to the art books forty feet away. In class, he shared his disbelief that the employee had expected this superhuman effort from any customer.

Our students' different life experiences and different personalities yielded, for each one, very different perceptions of the value and justification of each project. This is not a problem with classes such as ours—it is what sets them apart. The ethical dimensions of living and learning are not to be swept under the carpet or banished to some optional academic addendum. They are integral to the process of critical thinking and creative growth.

Our last field trip as a class took us to several migrant labor camps in Watsonville, California, near Monterey. Watsonville sits on the edge of the state's Central Valley, one of the richest agricultural areas in the world and also home to countless poor migrant worker families, most of whom are Mexican or Mexican American. These migrant workers are among the most invisible members of the labor force in California, if not the country.

We had contacted a migrant outreach program in town, and several program employees volunteered time to act as translators and liaisons for the class. Despite this, a number of our students felt very alien and intrusive in the Spanish-speaking farmworker homes we visited. Only three of the students were able to speak with the families directly.

At the same time, the translators afforded our students an otherwise impossible view into the world of a migrant mother, into her expectations about America and her hopes for her family. Furthermore, our students were surprised at migrant parents' generosity and warmth, which belied the seemingly subhuman conditions in which they work and live.

The visit to Watsonville, from a pedagogical perspective, was not "better" or "worse" than it would have been had the families spoken English or had our students spoken Spanish. It was simply *different*. Linguistic barriers, far from undermining the learning experience, had reinforced and deepened in the students a complex set of feelings, including guilt, anger, confusion, and respect. We felt that each of these emotions had a certain validity and significance, emotionally as well as intellectually. And so we asked students to share them in class.

The sharing of emotions, following different visits, came in words and sometimes even in song. After we visited a low-income community near Stanford and shared our profound disillusionment over elementary "miseducation," a student brought in a song about the making and destroying of that special wonder that young children bring to the classroom. For each of us, the class was a uniquely personal experience, but also an intensely shared one.

What Have We Done?

We set out to offer our peers a very different academic opportunity, and in this, I think we succeeded. Student feedback at the conclusion of the class confirmed that the workshop provided students with unique encouragement to engage the world around them in a challenging and critical way.

We had set our standards high, however, and there were disappointments. For example, facilitating discussions in a way that promotes substantive and active dialogue without establishing an "agenda" of "items to be covered" is an art that is not easily or quickly mastered. We were beginners, not masters.

The ethnographic action project, which involved volunteer work as well as research and writing, was a challenge to all of us, facilitators as well as students. We had to prod some students to commit the time and talent we knew they possessed. In the end, we were able to apply incentive "tools" that were more positive than the threat of a poor grade. We didn't offer grades, but after our students had committed an academic quarter to a project that encouraged and demanded that they pursue their own interests through field research, and after they had volunteered the better part of a university term with a local community group that needed and trusted them, we think they came away with an inner motivation and an understanding that they could only disappoint themselves by failing to give 100 percent.

The host communities, despite our initial concerns, responded very positively to group field trips and individual volunteerships. Our fears that direct student involvement in the community would invite voyeurism or provoke mistrust never materialized.

"It's a great class," said Jamie, one of our freshmen. "I can't think of anything I didn't like. I couldn't have seen any of what we learned about without taking the class. It's time consuming, but I recommend it for anyone." Nat, a junior, commented, "The key about the class is that it opens your eyes to many other worlds. . . . At Stanford, it's easy to become involved in academic pursuits and ignore [the world off campus]." I would emphasize that the class, in fact, did engage in very academic pursuits but in a way that transcended the detachment— the *distance*—that too many courses allow or even reward.

That point is worth underlining. Many students and some educational reformers labor under the illusion that book learning and experiential learning are antithetical and should therefore be divorced from one another. Our contention and the evidence of our course, partly inspired by Freirean teaching, is that formal texts are powerful tools for discovery of self and society *when integrated* with the "texts" of organized, real-world expriences. Research on school-to-work reform in America has drawn largely the same conclusion— that hands-on activity is no substitute for structured, classroom-based learning.[1] The classroom and the workplace—we might say the college classroom and the *world*—should be joined in critical, adaptive ways to meet learning goals suitable to diverse groups of students.

Students are hungry for learning that is concerned with America's complex present and future, that is intimately involved in its changing communities. Moreover, an enthusiastic (if gradual) response from many members of the academic faculty and staff reassure me that academia is waking up to the fact that young people need fundamentally new opportunities for self-motivated growth. Stanford students—like students everywhere—want to set high standards for themselves and to pursue themes *in the world* that satisfy this need.

Ours was but one experiment. But its most pronounced and longest-lasting meaning—what our former students now, years later, call "seminal" and "life changing"—may be the sense of opportunity and excitement created in a circle of learning. Our former students still write and call, emphasizing how The Unseen America opened their eyes, minds, and sensibilities to new worlds. Is this not what we want from education?

[1]See, for example, T. Bailey and D. Merritt. *The School-to-Work Transition and Youth Apprenticeship: Lessons from the U.S. Experience*. New York: Manpower Demonstration Research Corporation, 1993.

Exhibit 5.2. Public Policy: The Unseen America.

The Unseen America
SWOPSI 147—Spring 1989

Stanford University

FACILITATORS: Jim Pitofsky
Wendy Whitehill
Xavier Briggs

Overview: Why are we doing this?

The Unseen America, an original course based on an antecedent course by the same name offered in 1985 by David Lempert, is not policy focused, per se. Rather, it will integrate experiential and academic learning about communities that remain "unseen" or marginalized, whether because of physical disability, cultural and ethnic exclusion, or socioeconomic disadvantage. By "unseen," we are referring to an imposed social and political invisibility, a refusal by the dominant mainstream to acknowledge the rights and needs of America's many communities and subcultures. In addition to exploring the attitudes and circumstances (e.g., economic inequities) that shape a complex social reality, the course will explore the individual's experience of the subject matter and his/her feelings toward it. There are few "givens" to this class. Group field trips and individual action projects (with a community group) will fuel discussion. Students will be encouraged to transcend the detachment of the classroom and see for themselves what *is* and what might *be.*

Why, for example, are we unable to bridge the gap that separates us from the experience of the deaf community, and what implication does this have for social policy that affects it? What does it feel like to spend a day in a wheelchair or a migrant farm labor camp? Why do we often avert our eyes from the disabled? How can we come to better understand the viable and distinct subculture that disabled Americans represent, to respect their ability and pride, rather than pity their inability? How can most of us who have enjoyed economic and educational opportunity learn to recognize and appreciate the obstacles faced by youth in the inner city? What special challenges—racial, economic, social—are faced by migrant families? What concrete possibilities exist for serving and empowering these "unseen" communities, for shaping and implementing more-effective policies in the long and short term? These are but a few of the questions possible.

As noted below, the uniqueness of this course lies less in *which* communities or issue areas have been chosen than in the *approach* chosen to learn about them. Students will be encouraged to articulate their own questions about social phenomena—questions that may or may not be raised by the "literature" traditional to the social sciences. Inevitably, discussions and written work will involve policy issues ("solution strategies"). It will, however, be the facilitators' role to encourage a critical stance as a precursor to policy analysis or proposal.

Clearly, many facets of American life are unseen and not disadvantaged in any apparent way, but equally clear is the fact that for any ten-week course, some starting point must be chosen. The Unseen America will be guided by a "bottom-up" focus. Students will study groups whose relative invisibility has engendered social conflict and economic challenge in the larger society. While confronting large and complex problems, we will try to understand where the priorities lie and how we can "make a difference." The concept of making a difference is much in vogue, particularly among those of college age. It is the subjective assertion of the designers/facilitators of The Unseen America that such a well-intentioned concept must be constructively defined and developed. With understanding comes effective and responsible action.

Methods/Sources:
At the heart of the critical approach proposed is the deliberate effort to surround students with diverse and possibly contradictory sources of information, including films, guests, field experiences, readings (see the following list), and discussions. In a circle of learning, each source is approached with a respectful skepticism. Guests, for example, will bring valuable background and experience but will share their insights and perspectives as equal participants in a mutual process of learning and exchange, not as experts in a one-way process of dissemination. This course is about dialogue and growth, not monologue and "regurgitation."

Objectives: What can you learn?
1. To expose students, through an integrated experience of field trips, readings, and discussions, to unseen and disadvantaged populations in America. Exposure should encourage analysis as well as empathy.
2. To encourage a critical questioning of the nature of marginalization and its root causes, i.e., why is X unseen, and in what ways? Students will be given the tools for discovering the social, economic, and political dimensions of being "unseen."
3. To identify some of the day-to-day concerns and needs of these communities.
4. To propose methods of raising societal awareness and, in so doing, to stimulate more-effective public response.
5. Methodologically, to engage in an alternative approach to education, one that emphasizes self-motivation, encourages the integration of on-site observation and written analysis, and questions "expertise."

6. To enrich students' appreciation of the richness and diversity of American society and culture.

RAPTIME: Informal conversation with Jim, Wendy, and Xavier. Time to check in on action projects, share ideas on topics, propose new directions, critique, confide, laugh.

Jim _____, Wendy _____, Xavier _____.

Workshop Outline

Week 1 (April 5)—Course Introduction/Applications

Topic: Student and facilitator objectives, public service and action projects, course requirements, field trip logistics and preview, personal backgrounds and perspectives, ethnography and field research, ethics of fieldwork. Why are we/you here? Is a course like this necessary? Why is it unusual? What assumptions does it make, and which ones must be overcome? How can facilitators and students share responsibilities, e.g., be mindful of expertism, in a setting of democratic education?

Week 2 (April 12)—Examining Education

Topics: Goals of American education, alternative institutional and personal approaches, expertism. What systemic qualities of education in America serve to constrain or define its "products"? Does society transmit and reinforce values as well as facts through the schooling process? What is meant by critical pedagogy? What cognitive and emotional demands does critical education make?

Readings: David Lempert, *The Making and Unmaking of an American Diplomat* (chapter)
Jacob Holdt, *American Pictures* (excerpts)
Rick Simonson and Scott Walker, eds., *Multi-Cultural Literacy* (intro and essay by James Baldwin)
Paulo Freire, *Pedagogy of the Oppressed* (excerpts)
Ivan Illich, *Deschooling Society* (excerpts)
James Spradley, *Participant Observation* (excerpts)
Edgar Schein, *The Clinical Perspective* (excerpts)
(Recommended: Allan Bloom, *The Closing of the American Mind;* Goodman, *Growing Up Absurd*)

Field Trip: East Palo Alto high school

Week 3 (April 19)—Minority Education/Children at Risk

Topics: Minority academic achievement—sociocultural and psychological factors, segregation, affirmative action, reform, the field trip. What relationships may exist between social stratification and educational opportunity? What are the myths?

Film: *Brown-Eyed Children of the Sun*

Guests: George Shirley and Pam Bernhard (filmmakers)

Readings: Angie Cannon, "Shocking Report on California's Poverty Kids," *San Francisco Chronicle,* 2/14/89
Cynthia Patrick, "Report Predicts Tough Future for the State's Children," *Campus Report*
Charles Martin, "Bush Must Address Problems of Educating at-Risk Children," *Campus Report*
Carolyn B. Murray and Halford H. Fairchild, "Black Adolescent Academic Underachievement: Real and Apparent Antecedents"
National Committee on Secondary Schooling for Hispanics, "Make Something Happen"

Week 4 (April 26)—The Culture of the Disabled

Topics: Recognizing the culture, interpersonal relations, societal acceptance. What do the disabled want? What subgroups exist within the disabled community? What avenues of communication exist and which are needed?

Guests:

Readings: John Gliedman and William Roth, "Handicap as a Social Construction"
Robert Duke Jr., "Whose Good Deed?"
Ved Mehta, "Personal History: Among the Seven Pillars of Wisdom," *New Yorker*
Glenn Collins, "Children of the Deaf Share their Lives"
"What If You Came to Work in a Wheelchair?" (shared authorship)
David Robertson, "The View from the Sitting Position"

Field Trip: A day in a wheelchair, Juana Briones Center

Week 5 (May 3)—Civil Rights of the Disabled

Topics: Social and political movements; issues of the workplace; possible reforms; access to education, housing, transportation, and recreation; academic recognition of sign language; field experiences. What are the institutional and interpersonal effects of misunderstanding?

Guests: Debbie Allen, attorney
             Dr. Michael Dunn, paraplegic psychiatrist

Readings: Oliver Sacks, "Revolution of the Deaf"
             Test: "Myths, Misconceptions, and Reality of Disability
             Jernigan, "Is the Public Against Us?"
             Architectural and Transportation Barriers Compliance
               Board, *About Barriers*
             Letter to Ann Landers: "The Worst Handicap is Others'
               Resentment"
             Sherman Wilcox and Stephen Wilbers, "The Case for
               Academic Acceptance of American Sign Language"
             Marilyn Golden, Address to CAPED
             "FAA Would Regulate Seating of the Disabled,"
               San Francisco Chronicle

Week 6 (May 10)—The Culture of Farmworker Migrancy

Topics: Origins of migrancy in agribusiness, life in the camps, obstacles for migrant children, family life. What are the psychological and social implications of transiency?

Guests: Jose Serna (United Stanford Workers)
             Webb Ranch workers

Readings: Louisa Rossiter Shotwell, *This Is the Migrant* (excerpt)
             Ernesto Galarza, *Merchants of Labor: The Mexican
               Bracero Story* (excerpts)
             Jean Maddern Pitrone, *Chavez: Man of the Migrants*
               (excerpt)
             Jeannie Echenique, "Children's Harvest," *This World*

Field Trip: Migrant farm worker camp, Watsonville, California,
             May 11 (tentative)

Week 7 (May 17)—Migrants' Rights and Reform Efforts

Topics: Organized labor movements, education, public initiatives, field trip. What opportunities exist to make others aware and to improve life for the farmworkers? Does California agriculture need the migrants?

Readings: Ernesto Galarza, *Kodachromes in Rhyme* (poem excerpts)
Salinas Committee in Defense of Farm Workers,
Si se puede!
California Rural Legal Assistance, "Celebrating Twenty
Years of Legal Services"
Interstate Migrant Education Council, "Migrant Education:
A Consolidated View"
(Recommended: Mathiessen, *Sal si puedes: César
Chavez and the New American Revolution*)

Week 8 (May 24)—Ethnography Retrospective

Topics: Analyzing field work information, ethics and methods of writing, interviews, project wrap-up. How does an ethnography differ from a standard research paper?

Guest: Prof. William Durham, anthropologist

Readings: Michael H. Agar, *The Professional Stranger: An Informal
Introduction to Ethnography* (excerpts)
James Spradley, *Participant Observation* (excerpts)

Week 9 (May 31)—Conclusion/Project Sharing

Topics: Student action projects. What commonalities and differences existed among the communities we visited and volunteered in? What difficulties arose in trying to interact and communicate meaningfully? Is the focus on "unseen" groups a useful or problematic one? What other approaches might we have taken, and what other groups could we visit? What can we each do in the future? How might The Unseen America be taught again?

Course Requirements

Weekly "Thought" (Response) Papers:
Students will be asked to submit a 1- to 2-page reflection on one or more aspects of the material treated, drawing as necessary on field

trips, discussions, readings, guests, etc. This open-ended assignment is meant to encourage a free expression of the individual's emotional and/or intellectual response. It might be written in a "journal style" (see below) or might be more strictly analytical. These papers will not be graded (i.e., no quantitative or standardized criteria will be applied), but rather commented on for depth of thought, creativity and insight, and effort and perception.

Journal:
Students will be asked to keep a journal in which to record their initial objectives and awareness, and then to enter responses to their course experience. This private journal should serve as an indicator of personal dialogue and growth. The instructors will encourage a few students each week to share excerpts from their journals.

Action Project/Ethnography:
The main assignment of the course will be a 7- to 10-page written assignment and a brief, informal presentation ("community rap," "take it to the people") on a quarter-long service project with a local community group. It is intended that students will integrate the ethnographic tools, discussed in class and in the readings, with two or more readings on a chosen community issue. Academic and experiential sources will provide a personalized document of learning. The Public Service Center has agreed to help establish students in an ongoing program. The facilitators will provide information on other opportunities, e.g., leadership development for East Palo Alto children, literacy programs, etc. We will help you set up an alternative, but action projects should begin no later than the week of April 17. If an individual is to "know" the "unseen America," it seems to us, he or she must work side by side with the overlooked and disadvantaged fellow citizen.

Community Education:
Our last session together will probably be held in a campus dormitory. A chance to share your work and discoveries, this "community rap" outreach effort will be an open dialogue for students and nonstudents alike. Students will also be encouraged to submit their ethnographies to the host organizations. Let's give something back.

Grading:
The P/NC option alone will be offered. We seek to encourage a noncompetitive process of learning, a contractual agreement to engage the material critically and cooperatively. Given its centrality to the approach of The Unseen America, attendance at class discussions and on field trips will be

mandatory. The facilitators intend no formal check on students' completion of the reading assignments. We can recommend, motivate, and invite you to use the material gathered. It is only a starting point, though, and you may find some readings much more valuable and provocative than others. We will expect active participation in discussions and thoughtful weekly papers. Participation in an individual action project—the products of which are an oral and written ethnography—represents the final requirement for a "Pass".

—◦◦◦◦—

Economic History: A Field Approach

The adventure of economic history can be uncovered in the sites of different economies and of "living fossil" economies (premodern groups that continue to function as sustainable economic units). To understand the context in which economies function requires asking better questions and interpreting information more effectively, as well as understanding the types of historical sources to seek in order to reconstruct past economic events. Exploring living, dying, and extinct economies on-site is the way to do just that.

We designed the course shown in Exhibit 5.3 for economics students at Harvard, but it could just as easily fit into a history, development studies, American studies, or anthropology curriculum.

EXHIBIT 5.3. Economic History: A Field Approach.

Life and Death of Industries and Economies:
A Field Approach
Prepared for Harvard University
Economics Department Tutorial

Overview of Approach:
During the centuries of human habitation of New England, several different types of economies and means of production have existed in the same area—subsistence, collective, and individual agriculture; light manufacturing; and high technology. Accompanying these economic changes from one form of production to another have been major changes in social organization and life-style and in the role of government.

The purpose of this course is to take a long-term view of the American economy—to look at the decline of various industries and their replacement with others, as well as to examine the questions of how social and economic changes occur, how economies are rebuilt, and how they sometimes break down.

Readings will be supplemented with visits to historical sites and with laboratory exercises in collecting information on economic history.

Readings: A) *Theoretical Issues:*

George Foster, *Traditional Cultures and the Impact of Technological Change*

Keith Griffin, *Land Concentration and Rural Poverty*

Ronald Müller, *The Political Economy of Development and Underdevelopment*

Berle and Means, *The Modern Corporation and Private Property*

Richard Walker and Peter Gluck, *Cities in Transition: Social Change and Institutional Responses*

Barry Bluestone and Bennet Harrison, *The De-Industrialization of America*

Robert Reich, *The New American Frontier*

Joseph Tainter, *The Collapse of Complex Civilizations*

Marvin Harris, *Cannibals and Kings: The Origin of Cultures*

Jack Goldstone, *Revolution and Rebellion in the Early Modern World*

B) *Historical Materials:*

Julian Steward, *Handbook of North American Indians*

Warner and Lunt, *The Social Life of a Modern Community* (vol. 1 of *Yankee City*)

Randy-Michal Teste, *After the Fire: The Destruction of the Lancaster County Amish*

Elinor Horowitz, *Communes in America*

Stephen Thernstrom, *The Other Bostonians*

Hillel Levine, *The Death of an American Jewish Community* (Dorchester)

Felix Padilla, *The Gang as an American Enterprise*

Field Sites: Martha's Vineyard (Wampanoag Indian tribe)

Sturbridge Village (Colonial restoration)

Museum of National Heritage, Concord

Brook Farm (collective agricultural community, nineteenth century)

Lowell, Massachusetts (textile factory)

Newburyport, Massachusetts (Yankee City)

Brick industry (kilns near Fresh Pond)
Dorchester (changing immigrant community)
Family and commercial farms
Massachusetts Institute of Technology (research
   laboratories)
Computers and genes (new industries)

6

Connecting the Disciplines

National and International Adventures for Advanced Students

If democratic experiential education works on a small scale, why not try it on a big scale? The projects described in this section owe their inspiration and success to the advantages of youth: the ability to think big, to dream, and to be stubborn enough to listen to the people who say that dreams cannot come true and then pursue them anyway. With that spirit, students can extend the envelope of the possible, demonstrating the potential for projects that few universities would have dreamed of or dared to take on.

Courses carve up existing knowledge into small pieces and assign skills to units, transmitting them through the small building blocks of assignments and exercises. Projects, however, integrate skills and a variety of perspectives into interdisciplinary learning experiences, giving new meaning to the concepts of student adventures, service, and experiential learning.

Students who take on such experiences are not foolhardy. A student team testing the concepts of democratic and experiential education did head off to the jungles of the Amazon and up mountaintops and into Latin American prisons, but the group did not "run off to the jungle" or head south in search of adventure or trouble. Group members' work was the culmination of three years of preparations and several thousands of dollars of expenses to make contacts, find out what was feasible, put together a curriculum and a research plan, gain assurances from a former Latin American president (Galo Plaza Lassos) and a current adviser to one, find a means of accrediting the project, and look out for each other's safety. In designing the project, there was no need to compromise the scope of research and educational goals since they could be built in directly, as part of the comprehensive learning experience.

There are some problems and a number of theoretical and ethical concerns involved when student teams write their own development plans for a host country, as the Ecuador student development team discussed in this chapter did. (Some of those concerns are addressed more fully in Chapter Nine.) Nevertheless, the result was a success that no one expected, given that those who designed and carried out the project were "only" students. Readers interested in the quality of the student work and the results of such a project should seek a copy of the book the team produced (Lempert, Mitchell, and McCarty, 1995). The model plan that the students devised can easily be adapted elsewhere, as can the project that led to it.

This chapter describes:

- A series of new, ambitious projects that skeptics say "can't be done"
- The success of one advanced project—an international adventure in development planning for a small country, completed in Ecuador during the summer of 1988—that proved the experts wrong
- Plans to implement a national adventure in research across the continental United States—called The Unseen America Nationwide—that will offer a different perspective on important political, economic, and social issues facing the nation in the 1990s.

—◦◦◦—

Visionary Applications:
Projects for Advanced Students

The student adventures described in this book thus far only begin to touch on the realm of what is possible. Student efforts to write national development plans and to research the state of complex industrial nations through firsthand observation may themselves appear to be lofty goals for university education, but they already exist.

One can only imagine what the creativity and spirit of America's young will bring when it focuses on building and implementing the vast panorama of potential student adventures. Expect the full range of projects that students and educators familiar with experiential and democratic educational techniques can develop in the future to be astonishing.

This chapter presents a few ideas for advanced projects that leap from the imagination in the area of policy making and planning and of pure social science in the United States and overseas. They are projects that are appropriate for advanced undergraduates (or for graduate and professional school students).

While these are specifically social science approaches to issues of national scale, it is possible with just a bit of ingenuity and imagination to apply the same concepts to projects in the humanities and natural sciences. In a remarkable application of a concept that we would apply to teach social science techniques and to contribute to a national plan for revitalizing America through experiential travel throughout the United States, Douglas Brinkley brought new life to the teaching of the humanities in his cross-country travels in *The Majic Bus* with his students from Hofstra University's New College (Brinkley, 1993). Brinkley and his students have proven that a perfect opportunity exists to apply experiential approaches to history and literature.

It is up to the reader to test and to apply even more ambitious variants of the following projects.

Potential Student Adventures in the United States

Community, Regional, and National Planning. The United States is one of the few countries in the world that does not regularly undertake national public planning, even though it works to develop plans in every country to which it provides foreign assistance. The same concept of development planning that our students tested in Ecuador (described in detail later in this chapter), with similar field trips and research opportunities, is applicable in the United States.

In urban areas, important planning issues would take into account inner-city development, education, demographic planning, the effects of attracting outside business, patterns of expansion and growth, suitability of political institutions to meet citizen needs, the family, and so on. Some educators already experimented with such models in the 1960s; David Warren, one of the architects of the country's current national service program, developed such a course out of Yale University's Dwight Hall. These projects need only be expanded and geared to the realities of the 1990s and beyond.

Such studies can be expanded all the way from the scale of a small community and surrounding areas to the national level, where the issues of economic planning for competitiveness, workers' rights, and the future of America's communities can be more comprehensively addressed. An important potential application of The Unseen America Nationwide (described later in this chapter) would be to consider the production of a national plan and to include social, political, and cultural issues—to focus on particular regions, industries, problems, or communities as central themes.

While they are not really project oriented, some schools and programs have begun to develop learning experiences that expose students to several aspects of a particular region. Cornell University, for example, has developed the Urban Semester Program in Multicultural Issues in Urban Affairs. There are Urban Semesters offered by a consortium of schools in Chicago, and there are Washington Semesters, which mostly focus on the national government. What takes these programs the next step toward democratic experiential education is the application of theory and field study to benefit the community through the development of and advocacy for new policies or through the development of new institutions. (See Chapter Seven for more information on adventures for graduate and professional students.)

Community Studies. The purpose of classic works of social science conducted in the 1930s and 1940s in various American towns and cities was to map the workings of entire communities. Student teams can again contribute to political science, anthropology, and sociology by conducting their own studies of life and changing values in their own or specially chosen communities, while drawing on the techniques and data of these earlier works.

The goal of such studies is to practice social science at its best—to put together a portrait of an entire community and how it functions by just laying out the structure without necessarily making policy recommendations. Potential subjects of study in the tradition of social science include social structure, political ideology, power structure, political decision making, social networks, racial and ethnic interaction, and the economy.

Specialized Objects of Study. It is not inconceivable that students can work together as miniature governmental or private consulting teams in:

- *Analysis of an industry* that is of particular importance to an area, and its detailed workings
- *Study and analysis of a particular institution,* for example, thoroughly examining the inner structure, workings, values held, and culture of one business or institution, with attention to issues of oversight and implementation of public laws

Specialized courses in criminal justice or in business already focus in detail on such institutions and encourage student research. Not only could this idea be expanded, but its focus could be widened to incorporate a broader range of social and political issues in the study. This is what *democratic* education brings to what may already be *experiential:* it expands the intellectual content of what may exist in a narrow and preprofessional context, responding to the concerns and interests of students and the community.

—◦◦◦—

Potential Student Adventures Overseas

National Development Planning.   (See the description of the Ecuador project and Exhibit 6.1 later in this chapter.)

Regional and Development Planning.   There are several potential spinoffs from full-scale macro-development planning efforts such as the Ecuador project. Important ideas to consider are:

- *Multilateral teams*—to include U.S., European, Latin American, and host country students in a larger exchange of perspectives
- *Planning by province or region* in countries where development planning on a national scale might not be feasible
- *Regional integration plans and comparative development ideas* for countries that could potentially form an economic bloc in their regions or in which there are border tensions and common concerns

While single-issue plans (health care, welfare, political reform, and the like) are feasible and valuable, they could endanger the concept of interdisciplinary experiential education in which the whole challenge of defining the boundaries of a problem is itself a major issue for students to wrestle with.

This type of policy analysis in specific areas should be a second step—perhaps an advanced three-month project in planning after the students have already worked on the macro issues. It should be coordinated with previous student work of a broad and interdisciplinary nature in the same area.

A number of excellent programs abroad already bring students out to work on ecological issues, historical study, or archaeological digs. We want all of these projects to go one step further: to incorporate students into design and development so that they are involved in more aspects of a project than serving as laborers in routine tasks or limiting their vision to a specific, predefined goal when their interests may draw them to focus on other dimensions of a problem.

—∞∞∞—

Adventures in International Development Planning: The Ecuador Project

On August 22, 1988, five Americans acting on their own initiative— two undergraduates from Harvard, two undergraduates from Brown, and a graduate student/attorney leading the project—were welcomed into Ecuador's presidential palace to present the newly inaugurated president, Rodrigo Borja Cevallos, with a two-hundred-page document, prepared entirely in Spanish, containing the students' recommendations for the future of Ecuador.

Two days later, their recommendations were featured on the front page of one of the leading newspapers in the capital city, Quito, and lauded in a masthead editorial.

That evening, students were invited to a press conference, where they presented their views and answered questions (in Spanish) before television cameras, radio microphones, newspaper reporters, and leading academics.

That work, later translated into English, is now being placed on the shelves of university libraries all across the country, alongside works of their professors who said it couldn't be done. The book, as we have mentioned before, is titled *A Model Development Plan: New Strategies and Perspectives*, published by Greenwood in 1995.

The small group of students had entered Ecuador only three months earlier, speaking only halting Spanish, knowing little about the country and most of its people. In just three months of serious, on-site research and with relentless energy, they learned more about the politics, economics, culture, language, and history of a developing country than they would have learned in a year of classes at their home universities.

The work they produced was a development plan like no other—a challenge to plans prepared by the World Bank or the U.S. Agency for International Development (USAID) or the Ecuadorian government itself—and also an educational opportunity and experience like no other.

Most international programs place students in a classroom setting where they learn the host country's language and focus on written material. Despite being in a foreign country, students often learn more about the country's educational system than anything else and merely move from one institutional setting to another, despite their travel to a different culture.

Other programs are aimed at a different kind of learning. They place students in work brigades or on development projects in rural or impoverished urban communities, where students exchange menial labor or specific skills (such as in health or technology) for the experience of participating in community life. This approach contributes little formal intellectual content to their learning.

Despite claims of preparing students for making more-informed decisions as citizens about foreign policy, and for gaining a real understanding of a foreign culture, students on both the previous types of exchanges generally have very little contact with the U.S. foreign policy apparatus in the host country, and considering their potential skills, they contribute very little to the country.

While some students have sought internships in government agencies, development agencies, or profit-making enterprises so they can contribute as "participant observers," the nature of the work is often constrained—and student interaction with the culture limited—in these types of programs.

By contrast, the Ecuador project was an educational adventure with the features of both a policy workshop and a seminar: it combined theoretical discussion with field work and independent macro policy analysis, contributing to national debate and the search for solutions to problems in the host country.

Perhaps what the Ecuador adventure was all about is best described by the students themselves in the following materials from the project:

- The introduction to the report the student team prepared for the president of Ecuador and for public distribution in that country (Exhibit 6.1)
- Excerpts from a student log, written during the course of the summer (in the text following this list)
- The introduction and overview of the project curriculum and methods that the student team followed and the project syllabus (Exhibit 6.2, later in this chapter)

—◦◦◦—

Excerpts from a Student's Log

The following excerpts from a student's log record examples of major events that occurred at some typical and not so typical times among the eighty days of research and writing that the student team spent in Ecuador (which the students referred to as "Around Ecuador in Eighty Days"). Most students kept detailed notes of meetings and either a very brief log (such as this one) or a complete diary, or sent daily correspondence to a loved one back home.

The following log excerpts contain the student's short summaries of major events and one or two quips about a day's happenings. To make the excerpts easier to follow, capsule descriptions are added of the planned events for the week from which the log entries are taken. The full calendar as planned (there were some changes made to deal with circumstances in the field) is presented in Exhibit 6.2 at the end of this section.

SECOND WEEK—INITIAL MEETINGS AND ORIENTATION

FRIDAY, JUNE 17—QUITO. *Morning:* Visited Soviet Embassy. Met with Nikolai Andrianov in outer office—asked about Soviet development efforts and interests in Ecuador and the region; discussed Soviet views of Ecuadorian culture, types of solutions the Soviets felt would be appropriate for Ecuador's development, some questions on Soviet foreign service in general. Joked about the airbrushing on the official portrait

EXHIBIT 6.1. Ecuador and Development, a Report.

Ecuador and Development
A Plan Presented By a Student Team
to Ecuadorian President Rodrigo Borja Cevallos
(translated into English)

Introduction:

This development plan is the culmination of eleven weeks of research by five student researchers from the United States of America.

We arrived in Ecuador during the month of June, with few preconceptions and few contacts. . . .

We arrived with the goal of understanding the problems that Ecuador faces, of considering new solutions to those problems, and of presenting a few proposals that could provoke debate. We hope that at least we will be able to contribute one or two new or helpful ideas.

Our conclusions are our own and do not represent the opinions of the Centro Andino, of our universities, or of our government. We do not work for any organization and have not received funds from any institution.

We tried several times to establish contacts with Ecuadorian students at our educational level to work with us in our research. Unfortunately, we were not successful. We decided to come anyway in order to learn and to test a new type of education. As students in the United States, we are accustomed to study development in books and through lectures. We wanted to see the reality of underdevelopment directly, to test our ideas in the field, and to share our opinions in the native language of the country.

Methods:

During these eleven weeks, we visited nineteen of the twenty provinces of the country (with the exception of the Galapagos Islands).

- We traveled by bus, motorboat, plane, truck, jeep, train, and foot.
- We attended a Shuar wedding in the Amazon region and a first communion north of Quito.
- We danced and wore costumes with the Otavalenians and accompanied a funeral procession in San Lorenzo.
- We ate guinea pig *(cuy)* and larvae and drank *chicha* in rural areas, and we dined in the best restaurants in Quito, Guayaquil, and Cuenca.
- We spoke with smugglers and governors, prisoners and deputies of Congress.
- We traveled sixteen hours to meet with Texaco employees in the Amazon region, and the same to arrive at a Chachi Indian community up the Cayapas River.
- We listened to the views of the U.S. and Soviet embassies; of Peace Corps volunteers, and evangelical missionaries.
- We conversed with executives of multinational corporations, with shoeless peasants, with mayors, and with beggars.

- We visited ports and construction sites, museums and parks, sugar-cane fields and fish farms, ecological reserves and oil wells.

In all, we met with hundreds of Ecuadorians, too many to name, in all walks of life. The majority spoke to us in confidence, and we have decided to protect them by not citing them by name. We are in debt to all of them for their time and patience.

Our experiences here in Ecuador have affected each one of us. We arrived with different perspectives, but we all agree on our love and respect for Ecuador. . . .

Limitations:

Undoubtedly, a group of only five foreigners visiting a country for only three months, without an extensive background in economic development or in specialized fields (agriculture, forestry, geology, etc.), cannot cover everything or pretend to understand fully the reality of Ecuador.

Our Spanish is not perfect, and we do not speak a single word of Quechua or any other native language.

As Americans we know that we carry certain prejudices.

Our resources were limited. We shared one telephone. We were unable to visit several areas of the country due to the lack of funds for special transportation. Most of our contacts we had to make ourselves.

Nevertheless, we visited several places where the majority of ministers, ambassadors, tourists, and other development researchers never go.

Unlike them, due to our independence, we were not limited by established restrictions or by the necessity to maintain relations with specific sectors or to protect property or programs. Furthermore, we were in the position to take a wholly inclusive perspective at the macro level. We have the liberty, too, to present suggestions for structural, political, and cultural—as well as economic—reform where these affect the economy.

We present our conclusions after a process of discussion and consensus. We come from several universities, disciplines, and experiences but we share in our conclusions. . . .

We hope that this will be the beginning of future joint efforts—between students of our country and Ecuadorian students—in research both wider and deeper.

We hope, too, that someday funds will be available—from our universities, governments, corporations, foundations, or organizations in the United States or Ecuador—that will allow for the continuation of activities such as this one.

David Howard Lempert   Quito, Ecuador August 22, 1988
Thomas Abner Lewis III
Kim McCarty
Craig Ernest Mitchell
Shannon Wright

of Gorbachev to hide his birthmark, even in light of the policy of *glasnost*. [Visiting a Soviet embassy was a little uncomfortable for all of us, but different and memorable.]

Visited nearby archaeology museum (part of Universidad Católica); given special tour of collections by Dr. Petro F. Porras Garcés; asked for directions and contacts to newly uncovered archaeological sites; heard Porras's theories about pre-Colombian visits of Japanese and other Asian groups to Ecuador (wild!—need to ask other archaeologists about this) and about Asian influence on native art and culture.

Lunch: Buffet at the Hotel Colón (elegant international hotel). Briefed by other members of the group on their findings from interviews with USAID staff members. Ran into one of the French archaeology students working with Porras; asked her about her work, her views of Ecuador, and the French community here. Tried unsuccessfully to set up a meeting at the French Embassy.

Afternoon: Meeting with Leonardo Mackliff, director of the Atomic Energy Commission and head of the local Stanford club; discussed use of radioactive and other advanced technology in Ecuadorian agriculture (seems too high-tech and out of place for such a poor country).

Evening: Meeting in Old City at headquarters of Centro Andino de Estudios Económicos, Sociales y Tecnológicos (our affiliate for the project); briefing on political situation and discussion with Dr. Luis Lopez Silva, director of the institute and technical adviser in the Office of the President of Ecuador.

SUNDAY, JUNE 19—QUITO.   Quiet day—reading, planning, shopping, walking through downtown.

Invited Hilda Ruiz, longtime social worker and human rights activist, for dinner. Discussed general political issues, status of children, prisons, etc.; got list of contacts of liberation theology priests, tips on visiting prisons (wild stories about children living in prisons because parents are too poor to support them).

THIRD WEEK

TUESDAY, JUNE 21—QUITO. *Morning:* Meetings at USAID: Interviewed Patricio Maldonado, program officer; Kate Jones Patron, officer in health section; and David Alberion, officer in agriculture. Asked questions on project sites for later visit, collected data and documents, raised issues about changing emphasis of programs under Reagan administration, whether current approaches were adequate to meet objectives, and whether they were an appropriate implementation of the legislative mandate.

Afternoon: Met with Marco Antonio Rodriguez, Ecuadorian author and director of the Casa de Cultura (national cultural organization). Discussed U.S. influence on Ecuadorian values and practices, status of the arts in the country, cultural attitudes and beliefs as they might be relevant to political and economic development, relations between various subcultures, how to make contacts with other authors and artists (including women and minority/indigenous artists). Got autographed copy of one of his books as a gift; plan to leave him a copy of something I've written, as well as a copy of our final report.

Tried unsuccessfully to find a way to screen some of the Ecuadorian films held by the Casa de Cultura.

Visited Israeli Embassy to talk with Meir Mishan of the political section. (Interview was arranged with Mishan specifically after I met his teenage son on a bus in Quito. He turns out to be the top guy after the ambassador.) Discussed potential for kibbutz-type cooperatives in Ecuador; asked about Israeli role in trade, weaponry, education.

Dropped by offices of CONIAE, an organization of indigenous peoples. All principals were out of town. Need to phone again.

FOURTH WEEK

[Travel up north in the Andes to Indian village of Otavalo; to black farming community in Chota Valley; to the coast to impoverished black fishing village of San Lorenzo; then a day trip by canoe up Cayapas River to talk with Chachi indigenous peoples; then travel to Esmereldas.]

FRIDAY, JULY 1—ESMERELDAS.   [Coastal city; heavy African and Colombian influence; economically depressed region.]

Morning: Visited Combañano compound to talk with missionary priests there about their schools and role in the community. No luck. (Got into a fight with secretaries.)

Went up to Esmereldas prison and talked with warden to try to gain entrance to main area. No luck. Tried macho posturing with warden but quit when he held his ground. (Not a guy to mess with too far!) Walked around prison and observed, through a hole in wall, a guard kicking and stepping on a prisoner pushed down to the ground to do calisthenics. Left quickly. (Lesson here: Be careful!)

Got into argument with other team members about using a confrontational style to gain access and get information. Defended it as merely a tactic with certain people in certain situations, and not an attitude toward Ecuadorians in general.

Afternoon: Interviewed three superior court judges/ministers of Esmereldas in the Judicial Building about the legal system. Asked about court procedures, selection of judges, tenures, influence of political and ethnic consideration on selection and tenure, budgets, issues of corruption, and relations between governmental branches and branches of courts.

Found Dr. Wilson Cellerí, a dentist and unsuccessful candidate for Congress who represented the party of Buccaram (an extreme right-wing populist who models himself on Adolf Hitler and who finished second in the presidential election). He was also an author of a provincial development plan several years before. Interviewed him in his office on politics, development, regional issues.

Walked over to the port to look at the docking facilities. Took bus to Atacames beach (a resort); arrived at sunset. Went for a swim.

Evening: Walked around to local bars. Talked with young foreign tourists about their travels, impressions of Ecuador.

SATURDAY, JULY 2—ESMERELDAS/QUITO. *Morning:* Took local bus to airport at sunrise. Took plane back to Quito.

Detained unexpectedly at airport by Interpol (the international police organization) as part of international drug enforcement. (Very scary!) Taken to private room in airport and forced to undergo search. I think the ability to drop names of security personnel at U.S. Embassy—the people who trained and supervise Interpol personnel—and mentioning that I was headed to a U.S. Embassy party at police headquarters helped to avoid any possible trouble, like being framed. [Students had a healthy skepticism after viewing films like *Missing.* Advice for next time: get frequent haircuts or get to know the ambassador personally.]

Afternoon: U.S. Embassy Fourth of July party at the Ecuadorian Police compound in Quito. Chance to talk with police about training and about their role. Chance to mingle with the embassy community, American businesspeople, children, staff. Talks with Ecuadorians who have married Americans. (Strange celebration. Very much an apple-pie, white-suburban-America feeling.)

Evening: Rode home from party with Peace Corps volunteers visiting from their sites. Lots of contacts. Good discussion on role of Peace Corps, problems and successes; insiders' view on working with ministries on development projects and on workings of communities.

Tried to meet volunteers at their favorite nightclubs in town. Found one volunteer, also lost, looking for one club. Talked for a while. Couldn't find the club.

SUNDAY, JULY 3—QUITO. *Morning:* Group went together for the Sunday brunch at Hotel Colón (incredible, lavish spread for tourists; cost $5). Big argument with group over whether we should spend our money at a big international hotel, especially one that Philip Agee—author of *Inside the Company*—identified as having bugged rooms for the CIA. Agreed to do it once, for the experience.

Afternoon/evening: Went to see two American films for language practice (comparing subtitles with spoken English) and to combat homesickness.

Fell deathly ill at the theater. Vomiting. Diarrhea. Simultaneously. Terrible chills. Cramps. Thought it was malaria picked up from travel. Traced it instead to spoiled shellfish from the morning brunch. Couldn't sleep. [It comes with the territory.]

SIXTH WEEK

[Travel to the Amazon jungle region—the frontier.]

TUESDAY, JULY 12—COCA.   [Frontier town on Amazon tributary.]

Morning: Met with Mayor Oswaldo Flores in mayor's office. Asked several questions about relations with provincial and national government, growth policy for the region, generation and distribution of municipal revenue, history of the region.

Afternoon: Walked through town and over to military compound. Was denied entrance.

Visited family-planning clinic/health center near military compound, run by military. Talked to doctor about role of military in public health, diseases and health services in region, feelings about contraception. Was escorted out by a soldier, despite protests by the doctor.

Found the store of José Pauker Strauss, described by someone in Quito as possibly an ex-Nazi in hiding, but I could not make a judgment. We discussed his career as a zoologist and entrepreneur in the region; talked about his emigration from Germany. Dogmatic views on Ecuadorian character and development, need for strong military. Unusual views on characteristics of various racial groups.

[The team did not consider any groups or people off-limits, but always obeyed rules of decorum and didn't press where they had no business.]

SEVENTH WEEK—INDIVIDUAL TRAVEL

[Traveled alone through south.]

FRIDAY, JULY 22—SUCUA.   [Center of Shuar indigenous group, former head-hunting tribe.]

Morning: Took advice from María Ornes [Peace Corps volunteer who put the student up for the night] and set out on foot for Centro San Jose [Shuar center, reached by a hike through the jungle] and her contacts there. Walked past sugarcane fields. Found stalk in road and sucked on it.

Arrived at household of María's friend. Talked with children there, blowing spitballs at pet macaws and parrots. He was said to be off at one of his other households with one of his other wives.

Met a cattle trader along the way. Talked with him about his business and the area.

Arrived at the Shuar center. Found some old men with tattoos on their faces, from head-hunting days. Went with them on a tour of various farms and households at center. Lots of info on cultural change in the community, effects of modernization on all aspects of life. Old men described how and why health and living conditions have deteriorated due to Westernization. (Wow!)

Arrived at a household with a small guest house. Was invited to be the guest of honor at a wedding! (Ceremony was conducted both in Spanish and Shuar language for my benefit.) Was treated to a banquet of local food and *chicha* (fermented *yuca* chewed and spit back into bowls by young girls). Tasted a little better than vomit, but had to drink lots of it as not to offend my hosts. It got me a little drunk. Demonstrated wild disco dancing to the astonishment of my hosts. Got to dance with the bride.

Evening: Took all-night bus south to Zamora. Driver gave my seat away and I had to stand for first three hours; arguing didn't help. Couldn't get anyone to open windows. Sucked tobacco smoke for hours. Couldn't sleep. Had to change buses at 3 A.M. Arrived tired and nauseous in Zamora after sunrise, after registering and opening bags at military checkpoint.

How an International Policy Project Works

By following the example of the materials used in setting up the Ecuador development project in 1988, it would be possible to successfully initiate a similar project elsewhere. This section presents a selection of the major written materials used to get an international student adventure in development planning off and running.

Included is a basic tool kit—a set of how-to guidelines for describing such a project, accrediting it, choosing students, and administering it. (Note that these are just the most basic steps and should be used as building blocks rather than a complete model for a program.)

The description of a policy project in international development planning requires much more than a syllabus and a set of materials used in the past for one particular program for a specific group of students in a particular country. The tasks and coordination of an interdisciplinary team for twelve weeks of high-level work in a foreign country are equivalent to at least five course syllabi, and students must be prepared to adapt to a different style of life for three months than what they are used to in a university setting. Many if not most students require a significant period of preparation, training, and adjustment.

The process of setting up such a project—of publicizing the idea to students, selecting a team of committed individuals who can work together for three months and who have the necessary skills and maturity, making enough contacts to be able to handle any new situation that arises—and the ability to keep such a project running smoothly during the intensity of three months of research, require more ability, intuition and knowledge (intellectual and street smarts) and experience than can be presented in just a set of written materials.

Nevertheless, what follows is an excellent starting point. It includes samples, with annotation, from the project fact sheet and also administrative material. (All the items are briefly described before the samples appear.)

The Project Fact Sheet and Some Basic Administrative Information.   The Project Description in this chapter comes from the basic materials presented to potential student participants at the University of California and at Stanford, Harvard, Brown, Wellesley, Yale, and Princeton in 1988.

The Application.   The success of an advanced student adventure depends on an ability to combine the skills of field work and democratic learning, and is best when a sequence of courses (like those described in Chapters Four and Five) is followed. Since advanced student adventures are still new, students who have not taken basic democratic experiential courses need to be carefully selected for this project on the basis of their personal skills as well as their academic achievements and ability to form a cohesive and intellectually balanced team. The samples of application questions demonstrate one way of coming up with the best students for such a team.

A Week by Week Summary of Events.   Although it is almost impossible to adhere to a particular itinerary for a democratic experiential project—and the point of such learning is that students should not be bound or programmed by an agenda—advanced student adventures rely on comprehensive plans and goals. Taking into account student interests and the environment, the weekly plan (Exhibit 6.2) serves as a guide.

This plan is useful as an inspiration and model for programs elsewhere. The itinerary would need to be changed to reflect the different geographic, historical, and economic circumstances of a given country, but the basic features and goals would be the same.

The idea is to bring students into contact with all of the key ethnic groups and industries and to contrast the extremes of wealth and poverty, of governmental approaches, and of life-styles. Ideas for student projects are included in the weekly plan, as well.

Academic Content.   Included in Exhibit 6.3 (at the end of this section) is a brief list of the materials that students had to draw on as part of a theoretical base and a "curriculum" for the Ecuador project, and it can be used elsewhere. This curriculum is too ambitious for a three-month period, given the actual demands of the project—acclimating to a new country and writing a development plan. If more time were available, however, and assuming that such a program was integrated into a university curriculum and was part of a full-semester or half-year project, it would be possible to set aside time for reading and discussing specific materials in a seminar presented simultaneously with the project exercise.

Accreditation.   An international development policy project (or other projects like it) can be accredited within an existing undergraduate curriculum in several different departments for a given number of academic units.

The policy of most universities is to offer one unit of academic credit for one week of academic work overseas. Because of the various components of the program and the corresponding academic fields, students can have an opportunity to choose their emphasis and put together a credit package totaling twelve semester units using the accreditation suggestions given here.

❧

The Fact Sheet

The following are excerpts from materials presented to student applicants.

WHAT IS THIS ABOUT?   This is an educational opportunity like no other, offered for the first time during the summer of

1988. Participants will have the chance to write a five-year development plan for Ecuador—a small South American country with most of the characteristics of the third world in microcosm: banana companies, oil exports, indigenous peoples (formerly headhunters), highlands, jungle (the Amazon), and coastal plains. The plan will be read by USAID, by at least one private development organization (Catholic Relief Services), and possibly by government ministries. Participants will have the chance to meet in the field with embassy officials, Peace Corps volunteers, multinational executives, religious leaders, and politicians.

This is a chance to see exactly how a country works (or doesn't work) from top to bottom, and with the help of Ecuadorian university students, to use a full array of academic skills and wits to offer suggestions on how to make things work better.

This is an educational opportunity for students who are tired of reading what somebody else has written about reality without seeing it firsthand, for students who are skeptical of armchair policy making, and for those who believe that education can and should be used to make a difference in the world (and that it's worth trying).

WHOM IS THIS FOR?   This is a pilot program for up to six U.S. students from the top universities and—if it is possible to coordinate—six Ecuadorian students. Juniors and graduating seniors (who have clear graduate school or employment objectives after graduation) are eligible.

The ideal candidate for the program is idealistic, independent (but able to work on a team toward a common goal), committed to intellectual life, and able to speak passable Spanish (two years of college Spanish is usually adequate). Knowledge of Ecuador or a background in development studies or Latin America is not required (and in fact could even be a handicap to clear thinking).

Although social science skills will be most helpful, no particular major or background is essential. The team will be interdisciplinary. Intellect, skills, and energy are key.

WHAT IS THE RELATIONSHIP OF THIS PROJECT TO USAID AND TO OTHER ORGANIZATIONS IN ECUADOR?   An important goal of this project is to maintain sufficient independence to guarantee the academic integrity of the work. All potential donors to the project are aware that this is a student team; an educational project maintains formal independence from any nonacademic institutions.

There is some future possibility of organizing the program to create stronger links with USAID. This is not intended to lessen the project's independence but to create an additional credential of some résumé value for student participants (with the possibility of funding on a contractual basis, as if the team were a professional consulting group). The current arrangement is to meet informally with USAID officials at the beginning of the project period, at which time the officials will explain special research interests they are not able to pursue internally on their own. Students will have the option of incorporating any or all of these issues in the five-year development plan. The complete work will be presented to interested officials at USAID.

Before the team's work is delivered to any organizations (governmental or nongovernmental), the team will meet to discuss the desired use of the finished product and the types of information exchanges and agreements it will make. No agreements will be made that could compromise the intellectual integrity and independence of the team's work.

WHAT ARE THE RISKS INVOLVED IN THE PROJECT?   The major risks are intellectual ones. Students will likely have to deal with paradox, uncertainty, conflicting values, and possibly ethical issues on how research is conducted and what will be done with it. Students will get all the support they need from instructors and fellow team members.

Team members must accept the possibility of getting sick, and of still having to work hard while sick, but health should not be a major worry. Top medical care is available in Quito.

This is not a program for students expecting to work in antiseptic offices, but it isn't survival training in the wilderness, either. Students should be ready to put on a business suit for a meeting with government officials one day, and be ready to walk through banana fields the next.

Notes for Future Project Leaders

Most of the goals stated in the Ecuador project were achieved as planned, though it was and is difficult to achieve every aspiration of such an ambitious undertaking. This is just an outline of what is possible.

It proved impossible, for example, to coordinate with a group of Ecuadorian students during the summer, even though contacts had been made with a university in Quito for this purpose, and even though such an arrangement is certainly not out of the realm of what a project like this could include. Ecuadorian academic schedules were out of phase, and our Ecuadorian contacts had not publicized the project effectively. In the future, running such a project during the fall or spring term would make it easier to achieve the goal of working as a bilateral teams.

While some of the students sought research funding from their universities, academic credit was not the major draw for the initial group of students; research opportunities, learning, and adventure were.

The total cost to students (not including tuition charge or instructor fee) was $600 for airfare and $600 for the three months of living and traveling abroad. Tuition to run a project like this again would need to include a portion of instructor living and travel costs ($1,200) plus some overhead for setup and salary.

While the students' report was not used as part of any USAID projects, it did include commentary on U.S. programs. Extra copies of the student plan were left for the U.S. Embassy, the Peace Corps, a previous president of Ecuador (delivered personally), human rights groups, indigenous peoples' organizations, the Ecuadorian government arts council, several think tanks, and the mass media. As a published document in English, its influence will likely be felt in other areas and potentially in other countries outside Ecuador.

Application Questions

The following are excerpts from the application questions.

INTANGIBLES

- What do you dream about doing after college (or do you not dream)? You do not need to write a patterned application answer about the type of job you wish to hold in five or ten years, nor should you feel limited to giving practical or socially acceptable answers. Explain what you reach for.

- How do you spend a typical day? How would you spend it differently if you didn't have to worry about meeting institutional requirements or other external constraints?

- What types of things do you pick up to read in your spare time?

Don't go hog wild on these questions. The purpose is to get a feel for the types of things you are curious about and how you structure your interests. The implications of these questions and of your answers, however, do go far beyond the purposes of this application.

TEAMWORK

- List five of your all-time favorite books and articles— those that both excite you and are your intellectual reference points and that you wish more people would read. Briefly explain why. (If you are a member of the final team, you will be asked to bring these pieces with you, both as a way of helping you to retain your sense of perspective and identity in another culture and as a forum for debate.)

- Assume that you are a member of a twelve-person international scholarly team, and you are reporting to the U.S. president and Congress on the advisability of a national economic plan for the United States—whether one should be created and the issues that such a plan should address. As part of your fact-finding mission, list five communities, five industrial sites, and five individuals that you would want to visit to help raise the broadest and most informed range of issues (for example, a Navajo-Hopi reservation, Watts, Angela Davis, Orange County, Robert McNamara, Noam Chomsky, George Wallace, Oral Roberts, Tennessee Valley Authority, Silicon Valley).

We require this section of the application because the Ecuador project demands both independence and the ability to share the benefits of your knowledge and perspectives with other students and to engage in intellectual exchange.

EMOTIONAL/THEORETICAL/CONCEPTUAL

This section requires you to write a one-page essay. (You can answer in an outline form, though, if you wish.) This will give you a chance to think about real problems you might encounter in the field, rather than writing a phony-sounding essay about "why I want to go to Ecuador" or "how this fits into my career plans" or "how my personal goals and aspirations will contribute to saving humanity." You are also being spared the unpleasant task of finding some overworked and already cynical professor or graduate student to say nice things about you in a reference letter. This is not that kind of program.

In answering these questions, you should understand that your thought process is more important than your particular answers. There will be no effort to stack the group with any particular set of values, but we will try to ensure that interesting debate takes place on issues such as these.

BRIBERY.   As a researcher you are, of course, interested in collecting as much accurate information as possible in the search for truth. The information you collect (or the ability to gain access to a particular environment—for example, a prison—or to a service that will help you in your work) can be used to help Ecuador. What types of trades for information do you consider appropriate? Which do you consider bribes? Where do you draw the line between a trade and a bribe? Can you define the difference between a "fair exchange" and a bribe? Consider the following on a continuum: bringing small presents, treating someone to drinks or dinner, and giving American cigarettes and direct cash payments. Consider also performing small favors (like buying things in a duty-free shop for someone) after you have already gotten the information. Also, consider other implications of these acts for both individuals and society.

INTERACTING WITH THE NATIVES.   You are at various types of ceremonies in Ecuador, marking the opening of, for instance, a new bridge or a new school, and as an honored guest you find yourself in the following situations. What factors weigh in your decision of what you will do in these situations?

Foods

- You are offered roast guinea pig on a stick to eat (Cuenca, Ecuador).

- You are offered a drink of Jivaro beer made from prechewed yams and saliva (Oriente, Ecuador).

- You are offered coca leaves to chew on (Andes region).
- You are surrounded by malnourished (calcium-deficient) children looking up to you, and you are offered a bottle of Coca-Cola to drink because you are an American (anywhere in Ecuador).

Endorsements

- You are asked to stand on the podium at a school and pose for a picture with a local official who is the friend of the president's (the school is named after the living president) and who, a local Peace Corps volunteer tells you, has used a private police force to take land from the native peoples (a hypothetical).

Notes to Future Project Leaders

It is difficult to design an application process to choose students who are at once committed, capable, able to deal well with adversity and intense pressure, and who have strong interpersonal skills and the ability to deal comfortably with paradox. When experiential projects are introduced in several steps of a curriculum, greater numbers of students will be ready to join in advanced projects without such screening. Until then, successful selection is crucial to the success and enjoyment of a project. These projects are not for everybody.

This application was difficult and time-consuming by design; it was meant to serve as a barrier to all but the most serious students. At the same time, it was also designed to be a learning experience from which students could benefit, even if they were not selected. Rather than being invasive of privacy, the application was intended to help students see themselves and problems in the developing world more clearly.

As an incentive for honesty and as a means of promoting discussion, all students selected for a project were told in advance that they would be given the complete applications of fellow team members, something that also helped them break the ice with each other and prevented the group leader from holding a monopoly on information.

EXHIBIT 6.2. Week by Week Events for the Ecuador Project.

Week by Week Events
(Ecuador Project Goals)

Preliminary Week—Prior to Departure

Location: Campus in the United States

Topics: Issues in National Planning (By and For Whom?)
Introduction to World Economy, Development Issues
Social Sciences—Paradigms and Ways of Thinking
Introduction to Field Research Techniques and Ethical
   Issues
Group Process Issues
Philosophies of Education
Preparation

Field Trips and Meetings:
Group orientation (health hazards, culturally sensitive
   issues, etc.)
Discussion with psychologist about stresses of culture
   shock, group process issues, methods of mutual
   support and conflict resolution
Practice field work in Spanish among local Hispanic
   community
Meeting with Ecuadorian immigrants, returned
   volunteers, local experts, consulate, recent
   returnees, etc.
Preliminary library research for sources unavailable in
   Ecuador (Ph.D. dissertations, other English materials)
   and for views in American press about Ecuador

Weeks 1 Through 3
Location: Quito, Ecuador

Week 1—Orientation to Ecuador, Introduction to Development Issues

Topics: Development Theory and Issues
Techniques of Field Research
Ecuadorian Economy and Development Plans—
1981–1985 and 1986–1990 5-Year Plans; USAID
CDSS; World Bank Plan; UNDP Assessment

Field Work: U.S. Embassy (USIS, Pol. 1, Econ., Commercial Attache)
USAID
UNDP, World Bank, IADB representatives, if available
Ministries of Health, Agriculture, Education, etc.
Research sites (university, think tank, and public libraries)
Points of interest in city

Week 2—Government and Business Leaders

Topics: Democratic Theory and Process
Social Science Theory
Ecuadorian History and Politics

Field Work: Congress and meetings with party leaders
Judiciary
Courts
City government
Executives (including representatives of a foreign hotel
and National Bank; lawyers)
Human rights groups

Week 3—International Community and Cultural Leaders

Topics: Foreign Policy—Theories and Institutions
Ecuadorian/Andean Literature
(Continue topics of previous weeks)

Field Work: Embassies of Brazil, Peru, U.S.S.R., P.R.C., Cuba,
France, Israel (if possible)
Foreign journalists
Religious leaders
Authors and artists
Educators
Local media

Project 1: Toward the end of Week 3 and through the beginning of Week 4, students will work on their first project, done individually, which they will present both written and orally to the group. Each project must include library research and field work and should have some potential for fitting into the group's 5-Year Plan for Ecuador.

Possible topics include: The demands and base of a particular political party; an aspect of the legal system; youth politics or problems; the political, economic, and social role of the church; urban marginals/underemployment; the functioning of the civil service; the role of a particular ministry; Central Bank credit or loan policies; the status of women in the economy; the role of prisons and prison life in the economy; the black market (the Asian/Colombian connection); or a focus on a particular organization or policy.

Week 4 (End) Through Week 7 (Beginning)—Group Travel

(Travel will be in either one group of ten or two groups of six, depending on available funding and on the logistics of travel in particular areas of the country. If travel is done in two groups, the groups will meet frequently to share information and to mix participants.)

Topics: Indigenous Peoples, History, Economic Institutions
Theories of History/Culture Change
Social Psychology—Intergroup Conflict, Attitude
    Change, Diffusion
(Continuation of previous topics)

Field Work: (In each site)
Missionaries (Salesians, etc.)
Field volunteers (Peace Corps, UNDP, German and
    French volunteers)
Local government officials
Ministry representatives
Landowners
Unions and local political groups
Fishermen, farmers, laborers
Indigenous peoples (through anthropological contacts or
    other representatives)
Visits to company towns, development projects

Geographic Areas and Locations (for Ecuador):
Coast—Guayaquil and northern coastal villages (including
    Esmereldas, visits to Guayaquil prison, Standard Fruit

Company banana plantation, possible archaeological
sites)
Oriente—possible short jungle trip from Mera or Coca
(visits to oil companies, palm oil plantations, mining
towns)
Andes—north (Otavalo) and south—probably through
Cuenca and Ingapirca

Week 7 (End) Through Week 8

Project 2: Students will begin their major projects during the end of Week
7 and during Week 8. These projects will contribute toward the creation of
an overall 5-Year Economic Development Plan for Ecuador, to be written
in Spanish and English.

The projects should be done in groups of two. Students will be free to
travel anywhere within the country in completion of the projects and will be
required to make their itineraries clear to the Instructor and to check back
with the Instructor on a regular basis. Facilities in Quito will remain available at all times for student use.

Students will return to Quito after their first week of field work to discuss their work with the group. They must present written notes, with an
introduction and conclusion (or tentative hypotheses and conclusions) to
the group, and must discuss their projects orally.

Additional curricular materials will be available to students in Quito for
help in both theoretical issues and methodology.

Topics for the major project may be determined in any way consonant
with a development plan. Students may choose to look at economic sectors,
regions, cultural groups, economic and political institutions, international
issues, or other macro-level demographic or environmental issues. Students
must choose a topic for Project 2 that is from a different disciplinary area and
requires different disciplinary skills than Project 1. Students will not be
expected to choose a topic in their areas of expertise, and should feel free
to develop their strengths in areas where they may have little background.

Students may also choose to work on a number of shorter topics in
lieu of one long study.

Methodology for the project can include interviews, survey research,
statistical analysis, or any other social or natural-science modeling or evaluation technique.

Ideally, but not necessarily, the topics will be integrated into a cohesive group proposal.

Weeks 9 and 10

Students are to continue their projects, with modification, during Weeks 9
and 10.

The Instructor will travel to meet with each of the groups for at least one day in the course of research in order to provide supervision and technical assistance.

Week 11

Students will meet during the final week to finish writing and editing the group's 5-Year Development Plan. The group will also prepare edited copies for USAID, Ecuadorian ministries, and local media, as well as any other organizations making agreements with the group to provide research assistance in exchange for sharing in certain results.

Week 12/Postproject

Students will be asked to communicate with the Instructor following return to the United States (once in early fall and once in spring) to comment both on observations made during return to the United States and on a short assigned reading (in the form of a short paper or letter), and to discuss readjustment issues.

Students should set aside a short period of time around the New Year in the event that the group's work is of such caliber that there may be potential for editing and publishing the team's findings.

Note to Future Project Leaders:

While it was and is impossible to adhere to such a demanding academic schedule in twelve weeks given the uncertainties of a foreign culture, this outline served as a way to begin weekly group meetings and to plan events and strategy. (For comparison with how such a project actually works in practice, excerpts from the student log presented on the preceding pages show the actual schedule of events on selected days in Ecuador.)

The purpose of frequent written projects is to prevent students from being overwhelmed by the writing of an entire book in a foreign language during their last two weeks in the country (which they were on the Ecuador project, even though they managed to complete it). Since none of the students on the Ecuador project chose to receive academic credit through their universities (they were there for the learning experience, the adventure, and the chance to contribute to Ecuador), the requirements for the three written projects were waived, and efforts were focused on the writing of the development plan during the students' last two weeks in Ecuador.

EXHIBIT 6.3. Academic Content and Accreditation for the Ecuador Project.

Academic Content

Topics:

Development—Theory and Issues
        The Classics (Russett, Harod-Dumar) and
           Dependency Theorists
        Planning Issues (By and For Whom?)
        World Economy Issues/International Economics
        Measurement Issues—Relevant Variables and Hidden
           Ideologies ("GNP," "Productivity")
        Pragmatic Issues
           Cost Benefit Analyses
           Population/Demographics
           Marginals
           Health
           Agriculture/Land Reform
           Energy/Resource Use/Environment
           Women
           Education Policy
        Administrative Industrial State (Appropriate Model for
           Development?)

Foreign Policy—Theories and Institutions
        Theories of Foreign Policy (Allison, Lenin, etc.)
        Game Theory
        The Public and Foreign Policy Making
        U.S. Foreign Policy Statutes
        Institutions (U.S.)
           USAID
           Department of Defense
           Embassy/State Department
           Peace Corps
           CIA/NSA
           USIA
        International Laws
        Institutions (International)
           UNDP
           Foreign Embassies and AID Programs

Human Rights Groups (including IRC)
Journalists
Labor Unions
OAS
Multinational Corporations
Lenders—World Bank, IADB
Foundations
Church
Soviet Policy and Interests in the Region

Democratic Theory and Process

Centralization and Decentralization
Participatory Democracy Issues
Social Contract/Coasean Bargaining (Role of Individual)
Bureaucracies/Problems of the Administrative State
Philosophies of Education (Education and Culture)
Public Administration/Control Systems
Law of Corporations, Other Institutions

Social Science Theory

Consciousness Raising (Paradigms—Kuhn, Capra,
Pribram)
Macro Abstractions (Structural Functionalism, Systems
Analysis)
Relevant Variables
Historical Processes and Theories of History (Spengler,
Toynbee, Tolstoy, Marx, Malthus)
Revolution Theories (Demographics, Mobilization,
Psychological Theories)

Social Psychology

Attitude Change and Influence Processes
Group Process (Development Sequences)
In Group/Out Group—Regulation of Conflicts
Intercultural Perceptions/Nature of Prejudice

Ecuadorian History, Institutions, and Cultures

Incan Civilization and History of Other Indigenous Peoples
Colonial Ecuador
United States and Latin America
Present Status of Indigenous Cultures
Andean Literature and Arts

> Economic Institutions (Tourism, Mining, Agriculture, Drugs, Oil, etc.)
>
> Governmental Institutions (Government Structures, Political Parties)

Techniques of Field Research

> Intercultural Perception
>
> Negotiation
>
> Interviewing

Spanish—Technical Language Skills

Note to Future Project Leaders:

This buffet menu of ideas and skills is in part a reflection of the interdisciplinary nature of an experiential project but also recognizes the rich learning opportunities that it presents. Once projects like these are adopted in existing university settings and fully accredited, such an enriched learning experience as presented here will be feasible.

Presenting the full range of materials for use in a complete experiential development planning curriculum for an international student adventure, beyond this short outline, would take several pages. The list above is just a summary of the key topics and some of the better-known authors in the field.

Alongside the theoretical materials, there is a second set of curricular materials running in parallel, with specific information on the country in which the project is taking place—from World Bank reports to ethnographies to travel books to short biographies of key individuals in the country that the students might meet.

The theory, the particular skills, and the information about the country and region are only part of the "curriculum," however. One of the keys to successful learning is to have a library on hand for students to refer to for theory, discussion, and citation, which they do. Students on the Ecuador project provided their own readings—in literature, philosophy, and social science—which they brought along with them, and they contributed to the group's intellectual experience as part of democratic education.

During the course of the project, students also continued to contribute to the team's library, acquiring reference materials for use by the team and by future project teams. Indeed, development of the curriculum is an ongoing process that invites and incorporates student involvement.

The following brief suggests how such a curriculum might be accredited by existing departments within the framework of a traditional university.

Accreditation

Development—Theory and Issues
Disciplines: Development Studies, Economics, Political Science, Anthropology
Credit: 3–4 units

Foreign Policy—Theories and Institutions
Disciplines: Political Science
Credit: 2–3 units

Democratic Theory and Process
Disciplines: Political Science, Industrial Engineering
Credit: 2–3 units

Social Science Theory
Disciplines: Social Sciences, History, Anthropology, Sociology, Philosophy
Credit: 1–2 units

Social Psychology/Culture Conflict
Disciplines: Psychology, Anthropology, Sociology
Credit: 1–2 units

Ecuadorian History, Institutions, and Cultures
Disciplines: Anthropology, History, Latin American Studies
Credit: 2–3 units

Field Research Methods
Disciplines: Anthropology, Sociology, Industrial Engineering, Social Sciences
Credit: 1–2 units

Technical Spanish
Disciplines: Spanish
Credit: 2 units

The Unseen America Nationwide

If it can be done on a small scale in communities in the United States, and if it can be done in a small country like Ecuador, then why not all across America?

The concepts of democratic experiential education are such that they can be applied on almost any scale in almost any context, with adaptations for student interests and goals of learning.

What do America's urban dwellers know about farmers in Middle America, coal miners, and Southern border towns? What do farmers' sons and daughters know about the problems of the inner cities? What do suburban Californians know about the aging cities of the Northeast? What do the sons and daughters of Boston Brahmins (prominent old Boston families) know about the nouveaux riches of the West? What do Yankees in the 1990s know about the new South?

Students know the media stereotypes of Southern sheriffs and Bible Belt politicians, of dope pushers and welfare mothers in the ghettos, of factory workers in Detroit and along the Texas border, and a host of other images. But who are Americans as a people? Where is America going? What is America all about?

Field techniques can easily be applied in a social science project in the United States on a national scale—on an educational fact-finding mission that touches on all forty-eight contiguous states in an attempt to sample the reality of American life from top to bottom and from coast to coast. Compared with previous projects, the logistics are harder, the costs are higher, the distances are larger, and the personal risks may be greater. But so is the need.

What could participants do on such a project? What could they produce to give back to the country?

They could write a national plan for the United States—or discuss whether or not the country should have some sort of national planning that incorporates social and cultural issues and perhaps political reform as well.

They could write a book of ideas for political, economic, and social reforms, along with predictions for the nation's future.

They could write about little-known projects that are working all across the country, and about new ways of thinking. They could spread the word.

They could produce a series of short articles, essays, pictures, and poems to be sent every week to newspapers and magazines all over the country and then compiled into a book.

They could identify and then write about the myths and realities of American life—the myths that Americans live by and the reality that can be seen by those who care and dare to look.

As part of democratic education, depending on the skills and interests of the student group—whether it is composed of undergraduates, graduate students, members of the community, elected officials, celebrities, authors, or any mix of these—the team can determine its goal as a group.

Such a project could include some special opportunities, too, that are difficult to include in a regular course on a campus setting, when students' schedules are shaped around classes and employment.

Students could spend a few days in different types of service projects to gain exposure to various groups, but in ways that encourage everyone involved to make a contribution directly to the community while still learning (a pro bono aspect of the course). This applies an idea that has already been tried successfully as part of The Unseen America course at Stanford in 1989 as well as in the growing number of service-learning projects.

Students could also have the chance to sample the work life of Americans in different jobs across the country by working as participant observers or following alongside those at work. Many universities have already developed "spend a day with alumni" programs for students wishing to test certain professional careers. Former Wisconsin senator William Proxmire, among others, has spent days with his constituents at factories, working on the line, to gain an appreciation for their tasks. Taking part in such a project three or four times during the summer would be eye-opening for all involved.

Deciding What to Look At

There are several different approaches to studying the "whole" of the United States in a short time. Deciding what to look at and why is itself part of the learning experience and a major component of the learning and participant adventure of The Unseen America.

Some students suggest, "Pick ten communities and spend a week in each" (but which ones, and why?), and others suggest just focusing on a couple of states or one or two regions or a couple of sample industries. Still others want to focus on certain issues that already suggest a political bias—to concentrate on social service programs or the poor and dejected, to the exclusion of the middle class and the wealthy.

But the goal of learning is to understand everything—to look at what is "unseen" as well as to try to gain perspective on what seems familiar. It is to take a "vertical slice" of life (rich and poor) and to try to solve problems. It is hard to put aside the tendency to fall back on the familiar or just seek out the exotic, to work just through contacts, to avoid what we think we already "know" or understand, or to turn the project into a mere road trip or vacation. But part of the educational process is to expand these concepts on a national scale.

It is also hard to cram such a grandiose research project into the three-month summer period between semesters. This is a project that really needs to be undertaken over the course of a semester or more. For students to understand the concepts of democratic education and the responsibility it entails—and to prepare emotionally for the intensity of the field experience and the skills it requires—takes either time or previous preparation as well. Indeed, we faced some of these difficulties in the Ecuador project—with students missing rendezvous points and being out of contact for two or three days, with internal rivalries and jealousies, and with relationships and family issues outside the project sometimes interrupting the team's plans. But we found ways to resolve these problems.

Given the size of this country and the difficulty of access to many places, the research itself requires a year of preparation—of thinking about issues and about places to stay, reading up on the United States, and making contacts.

That is not to say that the project cannot ever be more than just a tour. *The Majic Bus* (Brinkley, 1993) and the Ecuador development project are two different examples that prove that it can be done successfully.

What follow are the basic building blocks to do it.

How The Unseen America Nationwide Would Work

The Unseen America Nationwide would work much the same as a student adventure in international development planning, with a few differences.

The following are the basics on how such a project could be structured; they are supplied in the same format used in the previous section on adventures in international development planning.

The Fact Sheet—The Goals of a Nationwide Project. The Unseen America Nationwide is presented in the fact sheet as a model project to take place over a summer, which is shorter than the project should be but possibly as much time as will be available when the project is tested for the first time.

Week by Week Events. The week by week calendar (Exhibit 6.4, at the end of the chapter) lists the types of places that could be incorporated into a project outline and explains how the project would be conceptualized for a twelve-week summer session or a semester.

Student Projects (Proposed). Student requirements for the project (Exhibit 6.5, at the end of the chapter) could include writing a series of essays every week and sending them to national newspapers that were following the team's progress. These essays could all be put together at the end of three months and could be interspersed with some longer essays with more theoretical content, putting the team's observations into perspective and adding recommendations.

To do this project right means setting up a kind of mobile office—with easy facilities for typing (such as laptop computers), telephone messages, and fax transmission. Team members might also choose to work in photography, videotape, audiotape, or another creative medium. How to do this—and how flexible an itinerary would have to be to coordinate all of the student interests and the various meetings—is part of the challenge of the project design.

Academic Content.   There are a number of topics that could be discussed and many types of materials a student team might refer to while traveling across the country.

The sample theoretical materials presented in Exhibit 6.5 are in addition to a file of materials the team would carry about the individuals and sites it visited.

Accreditation.   One approach to accrediting a field research project across the United States is presented here. Given the components of the program and the corresponding academic fields, students should have the opportunity to choose an emphasis and put together a package of semester credits totaling twelve units for twelve weeks of work (see Exhibit 6.5 at the end of this chapter).

The Fact Sheet

The following are excerpts from the fact sheet.

WHAT IS THIS ABOUT?   Participants in The Unseen America Nationwide will have the chance to travel across the continental United States and to write a series of essays addressing key issues facing the nation in the 1990s and beyond.

> *Should the United States have a national economic plan? If so, what social and political issues should such a plan address?*

Further,

> *What are the major issues facing the United States in the 1990s? What steps are necessary to revitalize American society?*

This is a chance to see exactly how a major industrial country works (or doesn't work) from top to bottom, and to use a full array of academic skills and wits, in a team effort, to offer suggestions on how to make things work better.

This is an experiment in democratic education. It is an educational opportunity for students who are tired of reading what somebody else has written about their country without having a chance to see it firsthand; for students who are skeptical of armchair policy making; and for those who believe that education can and should be used to make a difference in the world—and that it's worth trying.

WHOM IS THIS FOR?   This is a program for students who have thought about starting a nonprofit organization, writing the Great American Novel (or making a definitive statement about America through any other artistic medium), running for elective office (not for ego's sake but to do good), doing investigative journalism, working within the system to achieve political change, redesigning the American educational system, rebuilding communities, defending the rights of others, leading a political movement, writing a book of proposals for reforming America, or developing a new social theory.

The ideal candidate for the program is idealistic, independent (but able to work on a team toward a common goal), responsible, sensitive, and committed to intellectual life.

Juniors and graduating seniors are eligible.

Although social science skills will be most helpful, no particular major or background is essential. The team will be interdisciplinary. Intellect, skills, sensitivity, and energy are key.

WHAT CAN THIS PROJECT REALLY ACCOMPLISH? *IT CAN CHANGE THE WORLD* . . . a little.

Participants who are willing to put in the work, aim high, never give up, and believe in the project can have an impact.

Can this group present its findings to the president of the United States? Appear on national television? Help generate new legislation? Change the nature of American education?

That's up to the participants.

WHAT WILL A TYPICAL DAY BE LIKE? Students might wake up in a mansion, a homeless shelter, or a youth hostel. Participants might have breakfast in the dining room of a state capitol building with an assembly member, at a truck stop with big-rig drivers, or in a soup kitchen. They might spend the day on an Indian reservation or with an Amish farmer, in a coal mine or a movie studio, in a county jail (just visiting) or at a county fair. They might be vomiting their lunches in a morgue or a coroner's office, at a mental hospital, or a Ku Klux Klan rally. They might be stuck in a laundromat, or on an eight-hour car ride in the desert with a flat tire or in a traffic jam, or just on a pay phone making calls to confirm future meetings. Or participants might stay up all night to visit a wholesale market and get a feel for a city at unseen hours, and then sleep during the day.

There won't be a "typical" day. What each day will be like depends on students' interests and energy in designing the project.

There are certain things that the team probably won't do. The project lasts only ninety days—with the goal of covering forty-eight states and writing and presenting findings. That is very little time.

This is not a trip to visit a student participant's Great Aunt Hilda in Wichita Falls or all of the participants' high school friends. This is not a trip to do all of the shopping or sightseeing that participants have been postponing. Parades, museums, national parks, amusement parks, and so on, are great fun, and they will be incorporated into the program when it can be run for six months to a year. In ninety days, there just isn't time.

When it is a choice between visiting Watts or going to a Dodgers game, talking to César Chavez or going to the beach, visiting a dance school in Harlem or going to a play in Times Square, going to a Soldier of Fortune convention or a circus, the choice should be very clear. The program is designed to see the "unseen" America.

There will be days when student participants will be absolutely miserable and believe that what they are attempting is completely futile. There probably won't be enough time to really think through issues in the way participants would like. Students will be bombarded with something new every day and may feel completely disoriented and unsettled. Several things participants see may be upsetting or uncomfortable, but there may be little time to recover. Participants probably won't have a chance to absorb many of the ideas they are exposed to. Students will probably have a delayed reaction to a lot of these things, which will hit them when the project is over. However, the project makes the best use of the time that's available.

During the last two weeks of the project, participants will probably write fifty pages of ideas and suggestions that they may slave over in 95-degree heat and high humidity. There may be no publicity. Perhaps not a single policy maker or journalist will ever read what the students write. Participants on the project team will do it just because they believe that the future of America might be worth the effort.

The Unseen America Nationwide is an advanced version of experiential education for juniors and seniors, an extension of The Unseen America courses, and one of a series of programs at different levels that may eventually be part of an integrated social science curriculum using laboratory and experiential methods and complementing traditional textbook and theory courses. The Unseen America Nationwide is the "showcase" program of the series—tackling the toughest issues in the most ambitious way on the largest scale with the highest potential for visibility with the most select group of students.

WHAT RESPONSIBILITIES WILL STUDENTS HAVE ON THIS TRIP AS PART OF DEMOCRATIC EDUCATION?   Students will be responsible for participating in all stages of the program. Each team member will arrange lodgings for the group for approximately ten days of the trip; arrange sites for ten days (approximately fifteen locations/people/interviews); lead their share of group meetings; add to curricular readings; contribute to the preparation and dissemination of the written group project; help prepare meals and transportation; write thank-you letters; and care for the health, safety, and personal well-being of other participants. It is not expected that students already be expert in these tasks— just that they contribute the time and energy toward completing them.

Students must agree to be sensitive to the needs of others in the group and to organizations and individuals they meet in the field, and to refrain from doing anything that will jeopardize the future of the project.

Student members of the team will participate in the signing of a group contract that will commit them to all of the above and other terms to be mutually agreed on. [See the sample contract in Resource A.]

The only real agenda that participants should have for this project should be the search for truth and the testing of ideals. No hidden agendas (for example, money-making schemes or searches for job contacts) will be permitted. Nothing that jeopardizes the safety of other participants or the potential future of the program will be allowed.

Student participants should be able to refrain from taking unnecessary risks with their personal health—those who don't care about their own health may not be conscious of the need to care for the health of fellow participants—and from participating in any illegal activity that carries the slightest chance of implicating any other member of the team.

Participants should think that intellectual activity is fun. Anyone looking for an escape will get on the nerves of fellow teammates.

Project participants should have the ability to handle adversity well, laugh at mistakes and at life itself, and help others laugh at themselves. Participants should know how to put others at ease and to let others know how to put them at ease.

Students must also agree to share in the blame if something goes wrong and to actively seek solutions when problems arise, rather than trying to blame others or giving up.

Students must agree to voice their disagreement with group decisions and discuss their disagreement openly and in a timely and constructive manner, without avoiding issues or choosing to be silent.

Participants who are looking for an authority figure, either to tell them what to do or to take the blame when things go wrong, will not find one in this program.

WHAT WILL THE COMPOSITION OF THE STUDENT TEAM
BE LIKE?   Ideally, the team will be balanced by gender and
by major (no more than two students from any one major),
and will be diverse in ethnic and socioeconomic backgrounds.
A major concern will be to find people who are energetic,
enthusiastic, and able to work well together, and who have
strengths that will complement those of the others.

Student participants need not be U.S. citizens. Those who
are successful in making this project work will likely pave the
way for future efforts between bilateral teams (for example, a
joint U.S.–European or U.S.–Latin American student team
exploring The Unseen America).

EXHIBIT 6.4. Week by Week Events for The Unseen America
Nationwide.

Week by Week Events
(Projected—Presented in Topic Form Only)

Overview:
Where does a trip across America start and where does it end? Should
it be done in one circle? Should it be done in a huge zigzag across the
country from north to south to north to south, finally ending up on the
other side of the country from which one started? Or should it be done
in a circle and a loop—across the country along the southern route,
returning along the far north, and then going back across through the
middle?

How does this mesh with the geographical realities of the U.S. climate, roads, and places to visit?

Is it really possible to do this in three months, or should it really be
done in
*   A six-month program for additional units of credit, with additional time
    devoted to research and writing, as well as further time for field trips
    to Alaska, and possibly into Mexico to consider U.S.-Mexican rela-
    tions and regional economic and political issues in greater detail
*   A four-month program consisting of three months during the summer
    and an additional month during December/January, when students
    will pursue independent field projects, conduct additional library
    research, and/or reconvene as a team to put together a cohesive and
    more detailed piece of written work

- A three-month program with reduced writing requirements during the summer, with the receipt of full credit to follow the completion of a longer written work during the fall, upon return to the campus.

These are all questions to be considered in designing such a program. One approach—a twelve-week version—might include the following general list of topics and sites:

Preliminary Week—Prior to Departure

Topics: Issues in National Planning (By and For Whom?)
Social Sciences—Paradigms and Ways of Thinking
Introduction to Qualitative Analysis—Field Research Techniques and Ethics
Group Process Issues
Philosophies of Education
Perceptions of America (Course's Antecedents)

Field Trips and Meetings:

Group Orientation
Discussion with Psychologist About Group Processes, Methods of Mutual Support, and Conflict Resolution
Practice Field Work
Preliminary Library Research and Collection of Materials
Some Negotiation of Itinerary

Weeks 2 Through 12—Location and Itinerary to Be Determined

Topics: (See Proposed List of Courses and Topics)

Field Work: (Types of Sites, Meetings, and Some Suggested Areas of Interest)
Economic Organizations/Issues:
Key industries (auto, steel, coal, high-tech, military)
Industries of interest (tobacco, alcohol, advertising/market research, tourism)
Government corporations (TVA, lotteries)
Farms (industrial, family, communal)
Factories
Unions/workers (including migrant issues, leadership)
Professional associations
Underground economy
Company towns
Legalized gambling (Nevada, Atlantic City)

Political Institutions:
Local and state government
Congress
Regulatory agencies
Planning commissions
Legal and penal system (state and federal)
Military installations (Paris Island, Citadel)
Think tanks
Media
Foundations
Cultural Issues/Groups:
Native Americans/autonomous areas
Religious groups
Mexican border/migration
Rural subcultures (e.g., Amish)
Urban subcultures
Counterculture
"Groupies" and cults
"Periphery"/"Underdeveloped Regions":
Rural (e.g., Appalachia)
Urban (e.g., Harlem, Watts)
Cultural Institutions:
Entertainment industries (Memphis, Los Angeles)
Art and publishing (New York)
Social clubs
Educational system (private and public)
Social Problems/Community Service Organizations:
Drug and alcohol rehabilitation
Women's and children's help centers/shelters
Runaway and juvenile care
Self-help and support groups
Homeless shelters
Environmental and resource use
Individual Perspectives:
Artists/writers
Retired politicians and statespersons
Dissidents
Entrepreneurs
Popular symbols

Recreational Breaks:
National parks

Library Breaks:
An attempt will be made to schedule two or three library breaks of five- to seven-day duration at major public libraries (e.g., Library of Congress) or university libraries, so that students can catch up on course reading, collect statistical and written material, pursue additional field work in the region, and work uninterrupted on their projects.

EXHIBIT 6.5. Student Projects, Academic Content, and Accreditation for The Unseen America Nationwide.

Student Projects
(Proposed)

Project 1:
Approximately at the end of the third week and through the beginning of the fourth week, students will work on their first project, which they will present in both written and oral form to the group. Each project must include library research, can include field work, and should have some potential for fitting into the group's answer to the question, "Should the United States have a national economic plan? And if so, what social and political issues should it incorporate?"

Possible topic areas include a particular social problem, land use issues, the status of a particular cultural group, projections for a particular industry or region, and government structure or intergovernmental relations.

Project 2:
During the summer, students will work continually on a series of short projects that will be due in part at the end of the sixth week. Each short project must be a piece or series of creative work—stories, poems, journalistic essays, photographs, and the like—based on the group field visits.

The purpose of this project is to encourage students to interact with and consider themselves as in relation to other Americans, to ponder their place in and different aspects of American life, and to try to present those feelings in a medium other than a standard analytical written approach.

Project 3:
Students will begin their major projects during the end of Week 7 and during Week 8. These projects will contribute to the creation of the final group report.

Topics for the major project may be determined in any way consonant with the issue of national planning. Students may choose to look at economic sectors, regions, cultural groups, economic and political institutions, international issues as they are relevant, and other macro-level demographic and environmental issues. Students must choose a topic for Project 3 that is from a different disciplinary area and requires different disciplinary skills than Project 1. Students will not be expected to choose a topic in their areas of expertise and should feel free to develop their strengths in areas where they may have little background.

Students may also choose to work on a number of shorter topics in lieu of one long study.

Subject to geographical and logistical limitations, methodology for the project can include interviews, survey research, statistical analysis, or any other social- or natural-science modeling or evaluation technique.

Ideally, the topics will be integrated into a cohesive group proposal.

Edited copies of the group's findings may be prepared and presented to various media organizations, scholars, and policy makers, as well as to any other organizations making agreements with the group to provide research assistance in exchange for sharing in certain results.

Participants should plan to set aside a short period of time during the year in the event that the group's work is of such caliber that there may be potential for editing and publishing the team's findings.

Academic Content

Overview:
It isn't easy to read in a car driving across the Rocky Mountains or Death Valley. (Who would want to, anyway?) It may not be personally or even intellectually desirable to spend an evening in a motel room or in a host's apartment reading theory when one could be asking questions and exploring a new environment to gain a greater insight into how people in another part of the country live. Nevertheless, there should be a strong academic component to an educational research project across the United States.

Even if in the compressed time of three months there is not enough time for research, planning, and contemplation, it is important to have a readily accessible library of reference materials available—in the collective minds of the project leader and the students as well as in written form.

The advantage of running the project over a longer period of time, or limiting it to students who have had the benefit of prior democratic experiential courses in which they were already exposed to theory and have developed skills, is that it reduces the pressures on students to choose between book learning and experience when they are in the field.

Topics: *Social Science Theory:*
Consciousness Raising (Paradigms—Kuhn, Capra, Pribram)
Macro Abstractions (Structural Functionalism, Systems
 Analysis)
Relevant Variables and Hidden Ideologies ("GNP,"
 "Productivity")
Measurement Issues/Cost-Benefit Analysis
Politico-Economic Systems:
Market Economies Versus Planning
Planning Issues (By and For Whom?)
Administrative State/New Industrial State
Economic Development Theory (As Applicable)
American Economic Institutions:
Agriculture
Small Businesses/Entrepreneurs
Corporations
Factories
Professional Associations
Labor Unions
Foundations
Media/Advertising/Market Research
Government Corporations (e.g., TVA)
Etc.
*Democratic Theory and Process (American Political
 Institutions):*
Centralization and Decentralization
Participatory Democracy Issues
Social Contract/Coasean Bargaining (Role of Individual)
Bureaucracies/Problems of the Administrative State
Philosophies of Education—Education and Culture
Public Administration/Control Systems
Law of Corporations, Other Institutions
Game Theory
Institutions—Military Installations
Regulators
Think Tanks
Media
State and Local Government
Etc.
Social and Cultural Change:
Attitude Change and Influence Processes
Group Process (Development Sequences)
In Group/Out Group—Regulation of Conflicts
Intercultural Perceptions/Nature of Prejudice

Historical Processes and Theories of History (Spengler,
  Toynbee, Tolstoy, Marx, Malthus)
Social Change Theories (Demographics, Mobilization,
  Psychological Theories)
Techniques of Field Research:
Intercultural Perception
Negotiation
Interviewing

Accreditation
(Components of the Unseen America Program, Corresponding Fields, and Possible Credit)

(Lists of possible topics for each component and a program summary are presented earlier in this exhibit.)

Social Science Theory
Disciplines: Social Sciences, History, Anthropology, Sociology,
              Philosophy
Credit: 1–2 units

Politico-Economic Systems
Disciplines: Economics, Political Science
Credit: 2–3 units

American Economic Institutions
Disciplines: Anthropology, Economics
Credit: 3–4 units

Democratic Theory and Process (American Political Institutions)
Disciplines: Political Science, Industrial Engineering
Credit: 3–4 units

Social and Cultural Change
Disciplines: Psychology, Anthropology, Sociology, History, Ethnic
              Studies
Credit: 2–3 units

Field Research Methods
Disciplines: Anthropology, Sociology, Industrial Engineering, Social
              Sciences
Credit: 1–2 units

7

Applying Professional Expertise

Adventures at Graduate and Professional Levels

Most of the advanced national and international projects described in Chapter Six can be developed for graduate and professional students as well, on a much higher technical level.

The same approaches can be combined and developed in different ways, to meet different community needs, to focus on different problems and skills, and to appeal to students with different interests or goals. Joint teams of professional and graduate students would not only bring the concepts of democratic and experiential education into professional and graduate education, but would also reinforce the importance of interdisciplinary approaches to problems and of the notion of service.

In a sense, this is the beauty and the strength of democratic experiential education. It shapes itself to new circumstances rather than relying on arbitrary disciplinary or bureaucratic definitions of what is useful and required in a curriculum.

What follows are four types of democratic experiential projects that can be developed in professional schools—public policy schools, law schools, business schools, and graduate programs—to run alongside existing curricula to strengthen them, give them added dimension, and spark student interest. In fact, students in these specialties could only benefit from participation in interdisciplinary projects across professional disciplines. In projects generally viewed as business development, graduate students and law students could raise issues of ethics, long-term development, and impact on the community. In projects viewed as legal development, business students could address issues of economics and institutional structure, while graduate students could concentrate on issues of social networks and relationships.

The four types of projects we propose are the following:

- Microenterprise development initiatives, incorporating small business development and the management of small credit institutions, as a new kind of clinical project in minority and depressed communities
- Small business development overseas through export/import training
- International teamwork on law and development and law and policy
- Development planning, legislative drafting, and government and institutional restructuring at the international, national, and local community level

In some respects, schools are moving in this direction already but have yet to take the larger leap. An idea that has worked especially well with law students, and recently in business schools as well, is to establish university-affiliated clinics; however, little effort has been made to combine these activities with other disciplines to look at larger issues of impact on the community and of relations between the university and the community. In law schools, for example, faculty, practicing attorneys, and students work to provide low-cost legal services in low-income communities while students gain experience as student attorneys. In business schools, professors and students act as consultants to small businesses and nonprofits. Not only do these projects benefit the community, but they sometimes fund themselves if recipients are charged nominal fees for services. We foresee a time when all professional schools follow the clinical model of the teaching hospital, which has long been a part of professional training in medicine and can easily be adapted to law, business, and policy schools, and the projects we propose are complementary to that vision as well as to existing curricula.

The democratic experiential programs can be shaped to meet specific curricular needs of professional students, but the projects themselves are not confined to or defined by single disciplines. Each project could and should involve students from different disciplines and professions, all working together. In many ways, the skills needed in the professions—law, business, social science, and international development—all merge when applied to real problems. Each school could use these programs by applying different emphases and linking them in different ways with basic courses. (For a complete description of a model business curriculum that incorporates and integrates these ideas in a coherent program of study, see Lempert, 1994.)

The following pages explain how each of the four types of projects listed above could be designed.

<hr/>

Microenterprise Development Initiative

For Whom: Business, law, public policy, and graduate students

Where: Inner cities, rural areas, and developing countries

The idea of clinical projects for legal assistance and small business advising can apply to teaching finance and other management skills as well, to add the skills of credit allocation and banking to a project that could actually fund itself.

Much of the attention focused on improving the business law curriculum at prominent law schools is currently directed toward the needs of large domestic and international institutions. However, an equally pressing need for investment planning, labor-management advice, commercial transaction assistance, and capital exists in the inner city, in rural areas, in developing countries, and among minority businesses. All of the same skills found in the business law curriculum, and more, could be taught in such a project, while helping the community.

In urban areas, such a project would involve students and the community in rebuilding the inner city. This project is designed to address the outward migration of capital from the inner cities and the disappearance of small, community-owned businesses in a climate in which small banks are failing.

What Students Would Learn

This project would train students in the skills of business planning, structuring financial and employment agreements, making loan decisions, providing financial advice to small businesses, monitoring impact on the community, and researching the workings of existing credit institutions and laws.

The project also would work synergistically with the practica in development planning described in Chapter Six as well as in the more specialized projects professional and graduate students described in the following pages. It would begin with community needs assessment, identification of counterpart agencies, outreach, and other development skills.

Why It Should Work

During the past few years, the idea of small-scale credit institutions providing small sums of money has become a reality, filling an economic niche that major financial institutions have chosen not to enter.

In a speech given on the Cambridge, Massachusetts, PBS radio station, William Burrus, director of Acción Internacional, a lending organization aiding small businesses in developing countries, estimates that "the largest untapped credit market in the world" is in small minority-owned businesses in both the United States and developing countries (which are usually denied capital due to the discriminatory credit practices of major lending institutions).

The expertise required to run such a project is already available. Nonprofits like Acción Internacional, Trickle-Up, and Spring-Board, modeling themselves on the Grameen Bank, a small lending institution started in Bangladesh several years ago, have demonstrated that such projects can not only be successful but that they can generate income at market interest rates that can continually be put back into the organization or redirected to new types of programs. This project has the potential to generate enough capital to be not only self-sustaining, but profit making as well—to generate an independent source of capital that would fund a whole array of democratic experiential courses and projects.

How It Would Work

The project would work in several phases. The first phase would be assessing the particular needs of a microregion in the inner city and the potential for small business and community development. The second phase would involve designing and opening a small credit institution, run by students, faculty, and the community and modeled on the South Shore Bank (a community bank in Chicago) and other community-based financial institutions, and acting as a lender and a community assistance program. The continuing phases of the project would involve monitoring the operations of the institution and assessing change in the microregion.

Setting up such a project both as a course on small business development and credit policy and as a functioning nonprofit credit organization (not a bank because of banking regulations) is not as difficult as it may sound. Community groups are ready to offer technical assistance, and there are several potential sources of outside initial capital from government and foundations. It requires beginning with community outreach, setting up an organizational structure, and raising initial capital with the joint effort of faculty, students, and community.

The typical loan amount needed to sustain a successful small business is

- $5,000 to $20,000 for a small business in the United States
- $100 to $500 for a youth-run business in the United States
- $100 to $500 for a small business in the third world

With an initial capital endowment of just $100,000, the project would ultimately involve fifteen to fifty students per year and at least ten businesses.

=✶✶✶=

Export/Import or
Local Business Development Overseas

For Whom: Business, law, public policy, and graduate students

Where: Developing countries

The next logical step, after establishing a small credit institution, writing international development plans, and advising small businesses, is actually to try to run a small international business.

Already, students have opportunities in many universities to manage small operations, and a number of educational programs are based on teaching the skills of running small businesses. Few of these opportunities have actually made it into university curricula because of the conflicts of interest that occur and because of the time commitment.

Developing small export/import businesses, however, could serve as an educational tool as effectively as a legal clinic or small credit institution could. It could generate income without demanding educational or ethical sacrifices.

Such a project should not take the place of a macro–planning strategy but rather can be used in coordination with the strategy as a means of financing. As part of the learning experience, students would take into account the various ethical and social issues involved with their participation in a money-making enterprise.

Export/import opportunities enable students to do more than develop business skills and—if taught as part of a democratic experiential curriculum—cultural sensitivity. They also carry the expectation that the products developed would be indigenous goods made with appropriate technology. The goal would not be to repatriate profits but rather to use the money within the region, for students and as an aid to the local economy.

Cooperative farming efforts have already been established overseas as experimental university projects, but they are not suggested here. A project that is geographically limited faces potential problems with long-term survivability and is much more difficult to stop and start (that is, to staff with students year-round, particularly between academic terms, and to use as a teaching tool) than a series of small trade opportunities that do not require owning or working the land but merely buying and selling to meet market needs.

International Teamwork:
Law and Development, Law and Policy

For Whom: Law, public policy, and graduate students

Where: Industrialized and developing countries

Law school graduates, policy school graduates, and social scientists often find themselves in policy and advisory positions, making decisions with implications for the cultures and political economies of peoples thousands of miles away, whom they have never met.

A different way to educate would be to put together a development team of students to produce

- A set of draft laws, codes, or constitutional provisions to achieve particular goals in legal reform, infrastructure, and enforcement.

And/or

- A general macro plan or a specific regional or sectorial plan for presentation to a host government and development agencies. The plan would incorporate a comprehensive approach to political, social, legal, and economic development.

In these adventures, students would have a chance to examine legal issues in their social context and to evaluate enforcement, incentive structures, the relation between law and society, and the workings of institutions in which law plays a role (prisons, mental hospitals, reserves for tribal minorities, export processing zones, and so on).

Student research projects could be directed toward drafting constitutional provisions and legislation or proposals for development agencies that would address local problems and meet the needs of specific constituencies.

Among the types of projects that a team could effectively address and integrate into a set of proposals are researching constitutional reform, protecting minority cultures and land rights, managing decentralization and/or privatization, monitoring multinational operations, enforcing existing laws, restructuring the courts, improving legal education and public awareness of law, and working for land reform.

A school could ultimately set up projects in several countries, on a rotating (and potentially ongoing) basis, involving five to ten students on each project team.

=⧼o⧽=

International, National, and Community Development Planning

For Whom: Business, law, public policy, and graduate students

Where: Inner cities, rural areas, and developing countries

Not only can national and international student adventures in development planning be offered to advanced undergraduates but they can also take on even greater depth and significance for graduate and professional student teams.

The goal of the development plans is to incorporate social, legal, ethnic, gender, and political issues into documents using state-of-the-art research techniques. These documents would be presented to policy makers for conceptualizing long-term strategies for community development.

Planning projects can be run on a variety of scales: putting together a student team for a long-term development plan for a city, providing a regional plan for a county or state, or addressing national planning issues in a project across several states.

For example, a planning project for graduate and professional students in particular might take the form of an urban problems workshop in local government law. Including law and policy students on an urban research team would present them with the opportunity to develop comprehensive alternatives in the form of specific legislation for revitalizing inner cities as well as for the restructuring of city administrations and institutions. This is something beyond the capabilities of an advanced undergraduate team but appropriate for professional and graduate students.

All in all, the projects outlined in this chapter are only the beginning of what is possible in graduate and professional schools. We hope will have a chance to follow this book with one describing our complete vision of model curricula for law, business, and policy schools, curricula that apply the concepts of democratic experiential education.

8

Back to the Campus

Making Adventures Part of Residential Life

The student adventures described in the preceding chapters are classes and projects designed for university students. But the philosophy of student adventures and of democratic experiential education is not limited to one type of process or even to learning at one particular stage of life.

Many of the ideas of experiential and democratic approaches to education can be adopted at other points in the educational process: in elementary schools and high schools (where they are currently more likely to be found, ironically, than in higher education) and in adult and continuing education.

At the same time, the ideas of democratic and experiential education can also be applied outside of the formal educational process that takes place in institutional settings in blocks of time called classes.

For undergraduate students, for example, waking up in a dormitory room in the morning, attending campus parties, and eating in dining halls are part of a larger educational context. On many campuses, living environments have been defined for students, but they can be redefined and reshaped as educational student adventures.

This chapter describes ways of bringing democratic experiential education directly into student residences, in the context of the traditional campus setting.

The University as a Living Laboratory

More than a century ago, Leo Tolstoy expressed a vision of universities as theaters and museums, attracting those with curiosity for samplings of intellectual pleasures. He was on to something.

In a university setting, experiential learning does not have to be only off campus. It can begin in student residences as part of learning what it means to create a model community; the residences can be used to invite visits and ideas from neighbors, who are not always likely to view a university as being linked to their lives and concerns.

There are a variety of models of residential life at some of the top universities in the country: residential college systems with individual print shops, theaters, libraries, darkrooms, pottery kilns, kitchens that can be used for cooking classes, squash courts, weight rooms, even small teahouses or canteens. These facilities are wonderful for building a sense of community, for making the scale of the university accessible and livable, and for making educational opportunity available in the home.

However, the idea behind these models of residential life can be taken one, two, or several steps further. The potential for residential education has hardly been tapped. Residential speaker series, discussion seminars, and residential-based courses are one way to do this. There are other ways as well, in which students could use skills in different disciplines. Among them are the following.

Museums

Why shouldn't the university be a living museum? When, for example, as a tribute to student art and free speech, Professor Kennell Jackson inspired a week-long T-shirt museum in Stanford's Branner Hall, it led to a larger question: "Shouldn't students have a place where they can exhibit their art and expression on a regular basis? Shouldn't space be set aside, not only within existing university museums, but in the major residences themselves, for museum exhibits?"

The learning that goes on in researching a paper and presenting material in a written form is the same type of learning that goes on in preparing a museum exhibit. The difference is that the museum operates in three dimensions and is a source of discussion and the result of a team effort, while the other is two-dimensional and in black and white.

Among the multidimensional educational approaches possible in the university are the following.

Anthropological Exhibits.   These exhibits could highlight intriguing aspects of American culture or the life of subcultures and minorities— even portraying the "ordinary" features of university life in a way that makes them a topic of discussion. Students at the University of Vancouver, for example, have designed their own displays in the university's anthropological museum. Display cases in libraries at places such as Harvard have been available for exhibits of artifacts, including materials from Russian law and legal life ("Pepsi-stroika," set up by the main author of this book in an exhibit in the Langdell Law Library in 1991). Existing university museums, libraries, and residences are perfect places for an explosion of exhibits.

Historical Exhibits.   Universities have archives and stored materials, but most students do not get to see them. A better idea is to set aside one room in each different dormitory or residential college and use the rooms as the sites for rotating exhibits about different periods in the history of the university. With period furniture and decor, for example, the exhibits could chronicle how the rooms were used over time. The exhibits would be a source of interest to alumni, who would be attracted back to the university to present oral histories (and perhaps personal artifacts) of student life there during particular periods.

Universities can and should take the step of establishing special museums dedicated to student history—a student-run museum that would not only portray life at given periods but also set aside displays for technological discoveries by students at the university. This would be something empowering and integral to the goals of participation and good citizenship.

Artistic Displays.   Most student residences have special meeting areas—lounges or dining halls—in which artwork is displayed. The exhibits are usually of the sternly threatening, gloomy face of some university benefactor or forgotten professor. Those walls could be put to better educational use, with changing displays of both student artwork and photographs and university collections. Explanatory materials posted with the collections could provide short seminars in art for those who entered the rooms.

Artistic displays do not need to be limited to lounges, either. Some of the exciting work includes murals that students have produced on their bedroom walls—work that is invariably painted over by the university. While not everything put on a student wall is art, some of it is and ought to be saved and recognized. A certain number of works should be protected by the university for future generations of students to experience in their own rooms.

Turning University Resources into Educational Tools

Beyond the residences, the university environment is still a fertile ground for experimentation and intellectual education. Among the potential uses are the following.

Botanical and Experimental Gardens

Most botanical experimentation at universities is locked away in special greenhouses presided over by faculty. Some land immediately adjacent to university living spaces could be put to a more educational purpose than the current typical prospect of grass, shrubs, or cement offers. Gregor Mendel discovered the laws of heredity by planting peas in a monastery garden. There are quite a few things that students might learn by trying different techniques of their own in their own gardens adjacent to their residences. While such approaches are already common in agricultural and forestry schools and in biology department greenhouses, the idea has yet to expand to the liberal arts school, where it could serve well as an educational tool.

Should student houses also have their own fish farms, aquaria, zoos, and ecological advisers (to help students explore finding and preparing edible plants, animals, and fruits on the campus)? Eventually, yes.

Radio and Video Documentaries and Dramas

Most of the equipment for producing academic work in any medium other than the written word tends to be kept locked up in a couple of university departments and available only through special requests or only to majors in those departments.

This is very odd. Even in public high schools, students have access to movie projectors to make their own films and can use video equipment for class productions (or for weekly television newscasts in the school lunch hall). The price of basic equipment is not prohibitive. It should be available in the university residences, not only for use in developing skills in drama and communications but also as a way for students to supplement the written presentation, which currently seems to be the only medium acceptable in university disciplines other than the film and communications departments.

Craft Shops (and Skills Workshops)

Anyone visiting a restored colonial village in one of the original American colonies is transported to streets of blacksmiths, weavers, and cabinetmakers. Those villages contain a sense of community that is missing today. In universities, there are often communal living situations, but few students have the opportunity to make themselves feel useful and to use their hands when their minds need a break. Why not take inspiration from our country's founding mothers and fathers?

If a dormitory can have its own library, printing press, and computer room, it can also have its own automotive and mechanical repair shop, sewing and weaving rooms, and other modern craft areas. While local merchants might want to drive them out of business, or while some entrepreneurial students might want to use the facilities to make profits, it is both therapeutic and educational for individuals to have the chance to learn some basic skills, in a noncertified, nonthreatening, unregimented way, when they just feel like exploring something new.

There is more to a university than just preparing students to be factory workers or symbol manipulators and to buy mass-marketed consumer goods. The skills of self-reliance should be reintroduced and restored, not just in technical programs for students who are being trained as machinists, auto mechanics, or other skilled workers, but for all students.

Entrepreneurial Adventures

While we have proposed in the previous chapters that university projects provide opportunities to develop professional skills off campus, many of these skills can—and already are, in limited ways—being applied and developed on campus. We encourage universities to provide more of these entrepreneurial adventures.

Student Businesses

Although space may be limited, and although there may be several ethical issues involved in choosing one enterprise over another, one of the best ways to develop student initiative would be to create room for small student-run and student-developed businesses. Sup-

port for such businesses would break the company-town environment of some private college campuses and even challenge the
monopolies that the one or two existing student-run stores may
have on student business. (Perhaps profits could be put back into
some general student fund to hire or invite educators with business
experience). This idea has worked on a micro scale in the form of
coffeehouses, canteens, and services. It deserves to be expanded
into a larger educational tool through which the university demonstrates concern for competitive markets and development of student skills rather than just for monopolistic "efficiency" and
short-term profit.

"For the fun of it," what follow are some other tips on the more
mundane ideas that work.

Specialty Speakers Series

With a shoestring budget and some imagination, it is possible to
bring the outside world onto campus in a way that is up close and
personal.

If they are asked in the right way, all sorts of people—celebrities, sages, and just interesting characters—often take it as an
honor to come for dinner in a dining hall or for a chat or speech in
a residential lounge. Often, they will even pay their own way.

By using Stanford's and Yale's name recognition and some
initiative, the authors of this book were able to invite former
presidential candidates to drop in, along with authors, musicians,
and entrepreneurs, often for the price of a phone call or of a
stamp and an interesting piece of stationery (the Yale "Minds
that Matter and Matters to Mind" series, or the "Branner Hall
Speaker Series").

These are do-it-yourself operations—picking up members of
Congress in someone's 1958 Ford, for instance, or getting into a
slight car accident with a former presidential candidate, or inviting
a folk singer to look at student rooms—in which students get to see
the more human sides of people they only read about.

Given existing university resources and structure, one of the best ways to take on these projects is to take Teddy Roosevelt's attitude of gambling on success: send the Navy halfway around the world while exhausting its budget, just to convince Congress to pay to bring it back. When a good idea has already been initiated, even without funding, there are usually extra funds available from "somewhere" if deans stand to benefit—from added recognition when prominent figures come to campus and pose with the deans during photo opportunities, for example. When told that a former chancellor of West Germany would soon be visiting as a result of a student phone call, a law school dean at Stanford had an excellent incentive to find funds for the event. "Whom are you bringing next: Mother Teresa? The Queen?" the same dean asked.

The trick to making such projects a success is to stay alert to whomever might be passing though town or living nearby. Something in the same vein, which has been tried unsuccessfully but which still has possibilities, is "Celebrity Dating." Well-known contemporaries might come for a "date" in the dorms if invited in the right way. If not, it's their loss.

Special Invitations

It is simple, inexpensive, educational, good for relations between the university world and the real world—and it is fun—to invite alumni for closer relations with students.

It is easy to invite alumni, as well as faculty in lesser-explored disciplines, to give talks or to meet students over lunch. However, the atypical "role models" who are usually invited by the university administrators as a quid pro quo for their donations, or by lecturers as a means of establishing their own networking, are not that intellectually interesting. Rather than fall into the trap of just bringing in famous or rich alumni who talk about how to follow in their career paths, students can take the opportunity to invite much more interesting guests. Alumni selected for their expertise and special insights can be excellent educators and fun to meet or put in the hot seat.

9

Coordinating Adventures

Questions, Answers, and Practical Tips

This chapter is meant to be a practical guide and reference; a how-to for setting up democratic experiential student adventures. It is written in question-and-answer form, to be skimmed rather than read, and to be used as a handy detailed reference when confronting particular issues.

To overcome pitfalls and to achieve success on the first try requires special insight in how to go from theory to implementation. The questions and answers in this chapter are presented in the order of concerns that one might face in setting up new courses and programs: who should be an instructor, how to choose sites for group field work, the roles and concerns of students, the special requirements of advanced projects, and finally, how to accredit such projects and to fit them into the university. Interspersed are tips about what makes the projects self-activating, how to keep courses fresh and inspired, how to maintain educational quality, how to troubleshoot potential problems, how to make projects self-replicating, and how to deal with ethical issues and dilemmas that are likely to arise.

These are some of the toughest questions and critiques that we faced and that advocates of democratic experiential education are likely to encounter. Being ready to answer these questions with persistence and good humor will make the task of implementation that much smoother.

General Questions

If democratic and experiential courses are "self-activating," are there any guidelines or limitations on who should teach them? Only those who are willing to follow all the guidelines of democratic experiential courses should attempt them. A standardized curriculum that is exactly the same for every instructor will not work, nor will simply grafting on one or two features of democratic experiential education.

Instructors must be comfortable with the theoretical material as well as with the skills that the course or project aims to develop in students. They must also be comfortable as leaders in the field settings, so that they can convey confidence to students. Because of the nature of some of the interactions in the field (visits to a psychiatric ward or a jail, for instance), instructors must be particularly sensitive to the individuals they visit, and they must be able to treat students as individuals, so that students are free to talk about their concerns. In the same way that the quality of one's experience in student adventures depends on all of the other group members, much of the success depends on the dynamism and ability of the group leaders in this same way.

The teaching of experiential democratic courses must be personalized. It requires that instructors put themselves at intellectual and emotional risk as much as their students. Instructors need to be friends and counselors to their students. They also need to be assertive, critical, and secure enough to constructively challenge students to confront the material and the difficult issues before them, even when it is confusing or even unpleasant.

Finally, since one of the keys to interpreting field data and perfecting one's skills in field methods is that researchers be sensitive to their own biases, instructors must be particularly conscious of their roles as instructors. They must limit the authoritativeness of their own judgments in field settings. There may be no "right" answers to what students learn and observe. Instructors should view themselves as resource people, facilitating a dialogue of learning, rather than as lecturers imparting information.

How should project sites and curricula be selected? Topics and visits should be fun for participants, and should be in areas in which they have few or no preconceptions other than what they are ready to challenge.

At best, locales should be those on which there is an existing journalistic and academic literature but with which most of the students have had little or no contact. Factories, prisons, indigenous communities, and political institutions, for example, are all aspects of academic study and are the subjects of academic questions raised every day in the classroom, but few faculty or students take the time to study them in everyday life. This makes such locations excellent sites for student adventures.

The process of selecting sites is itself part of the learning and is a source of "experimental data" because it raises issues of research objectivity and representativeness. Project sites should be chosen neither completely at random nor through personal contacts. Introducing preexisting biases into the learning experience distorts it, but dropping into a place with no backup research makes it less meaningful for learning.

Finally, it is important to keep in mind the difference between educational adventures and mere adventures. While a travel bureau might lead individuals to factories or Native American reservations, academic field sites should be places that can yield insight into particular social problems or research issues.

What can be done to protect student safety? The "unseen" is not necessarily the safest place to visit. Still, the risks inherent in exploring the unseen can be greatly minimized. In a sense, the nature of experiential courses themselves, by building bridges into the community with groups of students, works toward increasing the safety of students and the community.

One of the advantages of class visits over independent research (besides the critical importance of a common experience that students can discuss and learn from together) is that there is strength in numbers. Students do not need to walk alone into America's boardrooms or violent ghettos in order to see them. They can go as a group to places about which they have some advance knowledge.

While advance arrangements can create biases by giving hosts time to prepare and to hide what they prefer that outsiders not see, making some prearrangements is an important way to minimize risks and improve the use of limited time. Rather than talking to drug addicts on the streets, it is safer to go to a clinic or hospital. Rather than knocking on the doors of mansions or exclusive private clubs, it is safer to call them in advance.

It is important to know how to avoid going where one is not wanted, to be sensitive to the people being visited, and to ask hard questions while trying not to threaten or push too far beyond one's welcome.

These preparations do introduce biases into studies, and they can make students more likely to research "institutions" or controlled settings than people in their daily environments. That is inevitable. These courses cannot exist without some risk—and some potential for tragedy—but they can be designed to reduce the greatest dangers and therefore ensure that such programs will continue and that participants are as safe as possible.

How can student adventures ensure a sensitivity to moral and ethical issues and protect against invasion of the privacy of the people visited? It is important to address concerns for sensitivity and ethics at the outset and also to remember that inevitable conflicts and the way they are used as learning experiences are part of what makes the courses self-activating.

Sensitivity goes beyond reading required articles on the ethics of field work in a syllabus and taking part in abstract discussions in a classroom. In some ways, ethics can be taught only through interaction, observation, and discussion about the feelings of everyone involved, participants as well as the people they visit. Situations inevitably occur in which values are at odds and questions arise as to what sorts of behavior are correct. There is no "right" answer. The only real answer is to make sure that discussion of these issues, when they arise, is used as a learning experience for the class.

Consider two examples.

When Stanford students simulated being handicapped by spending a day in a wheelchair in a shopping center, a man in a wheelchair who had been talking with them watched them walk away at the end of the day. The man yelled at the students, feeling deceived. That was an opening for a real discussion on ethics and sensitivity.

Similarly, a Stanford student pretended to be homeless by spending the night in a homeless shelter. He was then reminded by an instructor that he forced a real homeless person to spend the night on the streets so that he could satisfy his intellectual curiosity.

There is no way of insulating the projects from the reality that students will make mistakes and hurt some people unintentionally. This is part of the balance of learning in the community, in which students can also bring joy and encouragement to others.

In the end, it is important to aim for a fair exchange and, where possible, for more human contact rather than less, so as to increase exchange. If possible, it is important for student groups to give something back, whether it is sharing their own experiences and answering questions about their own lives, volunteering time for service work at places they visit, or amplifying the voices and concerns of those they meet in other forums.

How large should classes be? Class visits and projects should be limited to between four and twelve participants. This limitation is out of concern for the communities and sites visited and the quality of exchanges between participants and hosts. Hosts must feel comfortable, and meaningful exchanges and learning are best promoted through contacts with smaller numbers of people. Similarly, discussion and expression of dissenting student views are easier in small groups. Trust and mutual respect are also easier to create and maintain in smaller groups.

How can the courses and projects be implemented cost effectively on a mass scale if class size must be limited?   Democratic experiential courses cannot be implemented on a mass scale in the same way that lecture courses can. These courses are not like standard "factory" methods of education. However, this does not mean that student adventures are more expensive than the factory methods. There are ways to run them cheaply, as the model projects described in previous chapters prove.

Democratic experiential courses provide the perfect opportunity for peer learning. With appropriate direction from faculty sponsors, graduate students (on their own) and undergraduates (in groups of two or three) can teach these courses, often as part of their own academic experience (that is, on an unsalaried basis). Even at generous student instructor wages, a university would still come out ahead, as our own financial projections demonstrate.

How can the intellectual content of the courses be assured to be adequate and equivalent to that of other courses?   The syllabi in this book, the quality of student work produced in classes, the depth and breadth of student discussions, and the audiences that some student work has received—as well as the seriousness with which that work has been taken—speak for themselves—so do the number of faculty in different departments sponsoring these courses and projects and so do the student testimonials about what they have learned. Academic reputations can be bet on it.

Though the success of past experiments is presented here, the real evidence can be gained through empirical experience; readers are encouraged to test such approaches themselves in the educational contexts in which they are most familiar. Plans that are designed in good faith, with careful reflection, and that include readings, exercises, discussions, and projects oriented toward a particular goal will likely exceed the standards of most other courses.

The real question is, "Is the intellectual content of nonexperiential and nondemocratic courses adequate to the challenges of modern societies?"

Following up on the previous question, what hard and useful skills do students gain in experiential education that can be measured and that can attest to the quality of these programs? Experiential education projects stress reenforcement of previously learned skills along with the acquisition of new skills. Indeed, we would urge that more courses be evaluated in terms of the skills and conceptual abilities that they impart, rather than merely in terms of the length of the reading list or the use of traditional materials on the syllabus or the status of the professor teaching the course. In general, which skills are strengthened depends on the curriculum and the instructor. Specialized skills involve data analysis, use of language, particular areas of study (such as government finance, ecology, technology, commercial policy, or banking), engineering and scientific principles, social modeling, experimental methods in sociology, and so on. At the same time, the methods of democratic experiential education themselves introduce training in an additional set of important skills. Among the skills stressed are the following.

- *Writing.* The writing that students do in experiential courses is very targeted. It has to appeal directly to specific audiences— policy makers, the media, foundations (in appealing for funds for a student project), and so on. Students write promotional materials, press releases, legislation, policy briefs, descriptions of research methodology and findings, and other types of documents in these projects. They develop very specific applied writing skills.

- *Public speaking.* On projects, students not only may have to defend their policy recommendations before large audiences but their interaction with people they visit also demands that they develop their speaking abilities. This is something that a good instructor helps them to improve.

- *Interviewing.* This sometimes neglected skill, necessary for lawyers, businesspeople, doctors, and so on, is at the heart of experiential learning.

- *Negotiating, participating in successful interpersonal relations, consensus building, being flexible and adaptable, and understanding diplomacy.* These essential democratic skills are built into the very design of democratic experiential learning.

- *Critical thinking.* Students in experiential courses have to develop their cognitive abilities because there is no other way to reconcile the conflicting perspectives they are exposed to.

- *Accepting responsibility.* Through sharing in the design and implementation of site visits, syllabi and class projects, the consideration of the ethics of different interactions, and the work of a team, student participants are given more than responsibility. They learn that accepting responsibility is essential for the projects to succeed.

Do students do the readings in field courses? If not, how can they be encouraged to? Students in experiential classes are currently caught in a difficult learning environment.

Democratic experiential courses demand a lot from students—not only in time and in thinking but also emotionally. Some field visits—to a prison, a homeless shelter, or a mental hospital, for instance—can be devastating experiences. What experiential courses mainly do is shatter illusions. Emotional experiences often take a long time to process (we address this issue in answer to a separate question below).

When students are taking four other courses and are also asked to take several hours for a field trip and then a discussion, there are no "bad" consequences for students in democratic experiential courses other than the fact that their learning experience will be that much shallower than it could be. Grading students on whether or not they do readings is difficult to do. Even if it could be done objectively, it would be difficult to ascertain what was being measured and why.

The role of the teacher or facilitator in democratic experiential learning is to discuss as many of the ideas from the readings as possible in a way that is relevant to what students observe, so that students are motivated to see the value in doing the readings and to give students positive rather than negative incentives.

Often, students who have not done the readings during the experiential courses do specific readings after the course has ended, when they have more time. The battle is not with lack of intellectual interest but rather with lack of time.

If need be, there are always traditional methods to fall back on. Some instructors of experiential courses have tried weekly "response papers," asking students to think through some of the issues they had to confront in the class during the week and to put them in writing. Students can also be asked to address different authors' perspectives when synthesizing their own written or oral responses to the week's topic.

How can community colleges, or schools in which students are working part- or full-time, schedule experiential courses?   The reality of experiential courses is that students are often dependent on the goodwill of individuals and institutions, and this can create a conflict of interest between what students want to know and the kinds of questions they feel they can ask without jeopardizing their ability to return to the same site. In addition, individuals meet with students at times and in ways that are most convenient to those individuals, and this can make scheduling difficult.

In many cases, there are so many opportunities for field work that it is possible to tailor courses to students' schedules. However, these courses do demand that students have greater flexibility to reorient their schedules on short notice so that they can participate in field outings.

The best solution may be to schedule two or three different field exercises on the weeks when it is impossible to conduct field work during the scheduled time for class sessions, and to split up the class for discussions afterward.

We recommend that students refrain from devising their own exercises and pursuing them individually or in pairs until they are able to begin final projects incorporating what they have learned. Individual field work encourages "dry labbing" (false reporting), disrupts the continuity of the class as students conduct different exercises during different weeks, and almost completely undercuts the learning experience. The internship model and the independent laboratory model exclude the most important component of democratic experiential education: the ability to discuss a common experience and the different research strategies that members of the group applied in the course of that shared experience.

How can students be given greater responsibility in a field course?
Since an important goal of democratic education is to help students develop a sense of initiative and confidence in field work, the role of the student must be built directly into the curriculum. Student responsibilities can be placed directly in a course syllabus or written into a group contract for an advanced project. (For a sample contract, see Resource A.)

The syllabus for The Unseen America course at Berkeley successfully included the following requirements:

- After the first two weeks, students are given the responsibility of leading discussions on a rotating basis.

- On or about the fifth week, students are asked to visit a particular type of setting on their own, in which they should have little or moderate difficulty. An example might be: "Visit an old-age home of your choosing. Spend two hours there. In discussion, we will talk about how you went about making contacts, which institutions you chose, whom you spoke with, what you asked, what you observed, and how you made those decisions."

- During the second half of the course, students are required to set up a group field trip of moderate or greater difficulty and to select a reading for the class. This also serves as part of class discussion.

In peer-taught courses, what prevents student instructors from using their power over other students to defeat the ideals of democratic education? This danger already exists with faculty instructors; in such situations, students have little opportunity to appeal. In courses with student instructors, students can appeal directly to the professor sponsoring the course. In general, the power differential among students in peer-taught courses is lower than in traditional classes, and peer pressure is a disincentive to the abuse of power.

However, there is a better solution, one that reduces the potential for abuse of power, no matter who the instructor is. The solution is to offer these courses (and all courses) on either a pass/fail or a contract-grading basis. In contract learning, students can often aim for a given grade based on their participation in a set number of required class exercises, rather than on some subjective and arbitrary measurement of the "quality" of their work.

Are students really ready for such challenging experiential projects? It is true that not every student is ready for a specific experiential or democratic education project or course. For this reason, the courses and projects described in this book are presented at different levels of difficulty and for students with varying experience with this approach. Democratic experiential courses and projects carry different responsibilities and expectations that need to be carefully geared to student abilities. As with other skills, no one can be expected to understand experiential or democratic approaches immediately; but students can be taught such approaches.

In some respects, American culture and the expectations in our educational system might appear to doom programs that rely on students' initiative, curiosity, and intellectual interest. Some young people do take advantage of poorly designed experiential projects and use them as an excuse to do minimal work with minimal thinking.

Rules and responses exist for dealing with the problem of a few students trying to manipulate the course agreement. At the same time, there is no way that a specific course or project could survive if such an attitude were endemic among a majority of the students—that is, if the expectations of and responsibilities given to a student group were geared too high.

Until programs are well established, democratic experiential courses can and should be treated as special and select, with students applying for a limited number of spaces. Since interaction with the community requires a particular sensitivity, the courses should be open to students who will likely commit the greatest energy and bring a serious sense of purpose. Once the ethos of the programs spreads, then a greater number of students will likely use the opportunity wisely and create an environment in which active and responsible participation becomes the norm.

Finding capable and responsible students has not been a problem so far. Student demand has outstripped the ability to fill it. At Stanford, for instance, ninety students expressed interest in The Unseen America course taught in the spring of 1989; only fifteen spaces were available.

To expand on the previous question, do students really understand the concepts of democratic education—setting their own standards and being responsible for their own curricula and learning? Might this just promote indulgence of their worst instincts, encouraging long drawn-out processes in which nothing is accomplished and inviting tyranny of the majority? Chaos or abdication of the role of faculty, leading to mob rule by students, is not the goal of these programs. When projects are structured correctly, such problems are not likely to occur.

Misinterpreting the concept of democracy can certainly lead to inaction or chaos. This is why it is important to follow a set of principles and underlying concepts similar to those outlined in this book, and to stress them as often as possible and as necessary in the duration of the course. (See the chapters in Part One and the sample contract in Resource A.)

The participatory and consensus aspects of democracy are particularly difficult for students to understand because Americans are not used to exercising them other than through very limited forms, like voting once a year. Even universities have not taken the lead in making these opportunities available. Thus, for many students, taking responsibility or giving responsibility to others can be scary and difficult at first.

Part of the problem lies in the context in which democratic education programs may be carried out. Just trying to do something open in a system that some students distrust carries the potential for students to take out their frustration on the freer, more democratic setting of democratic experiential education, where they can push the limits much further. That does open up the possibility that some students will attempt to manipulate the class or subvert educational goals.

Democracy and openness must be limited where they threaten an individual or where they threaten the group's ability to carry out programs. This is the role of group leader or facilitator, and student instructors do not abandon the role of holding students to high standards and demanding that they do their best.

Giving up ultimate authority is not the solution and is not what democratic education is about. It is important to fail students who do not keep up their part of the bargain. What is different in democratic experiential courses is that the bargains are negotiated up front, and achievement is more objectively measurable than in most other classes. Democratic experiential classes are also more flexible and provide greater opportunity.

How can students who have had no teaching experience develop the difficult skills required to manage classroom discussions effectively and facilitate community meetings?   Xavier Briggs, who as a college senior was one of three instructors in The Unseen America course, provides a few simple principles that he followed and that can help student instructors manage discussions more effectively, even on their first attempt.

I think of facilitation as consisting of these multiple roles and functions (which can be split if there is more than one student leading the course or project):

- Being a gadfly
- Gatekeeping
- Validating;
- Clock watching
- Synthesizing

Gadflies *challenge* group members by provoking them with questions and statements; they add life to the dialogue. Gatekeepers *balance* the input of various members with time for "housekeeping" announcements and, where appropriate, lectures or presentations by guests; they can step up and out of the flow of discussion to ask, "What is missing or appropriate here and now?" Validations *encourage* and *reassure* group members with statements like, "That's a helpful idea—can anyone build on Maria's suggestion?" or, "Don't hold back, John. Develop that thought! We need to hear from you." Clock watchers *track* the discussion to ensure that objectives are pursued effectively in the time available; they remind group members when things are off track or when time is running out and the most critical issue has yet to be addressed. Finally, synthesizers *bridge* and *relate* ideas to make the discussion more productive. To do this, they use summary statements and questions that ask the group to link ideas.

The key point is that these roles can, to some degree, be allocated among two to three group members as well. Doing so empowers participants to take ownership of the discussion and to recognize and support their peers' learning.

Also important is to debrief afterward. Discussion management is learned by doing and reflecting. Have a partner watch you and the group. Ask your partner to offer specific insights on how well you performed on key discussion-management functions. And remember not to expect too much too soon. Good facilitators are made, not born.

Finally, remember that conflict can be used to sustain high-energy, thought-provoking exchange. Any group can overdose on it, but conflict itself is not a sign of breakdown.

How do students deal with their emotional reactions to what they see, and is there a need for any special preparation? Learning can be an intensely emotional experience, particularly when students face unpleasant realities and directly confront their own strongly held beliefs. That is particularly true of experiential courses, since much of what students see and experience can shatter years of misconceptions and shielding.

It is important to set aside time for the class as a whole and for individual students to deal with their emotional reactions to what they learn as well as to some unpleasant experiences they may encounter outside of the classroom. Male prisoners in a state prison yelling obscenities at female students, the stark poverty experienced by migrant farm workers or homeless families on American soil, the tears of Vietnam veterans, and even harassment of female students by young people they meet in group homes are not usually damaging experiences, but they may be traumatizing. It is important to talk these issues through, in a helpful and healthful way.

One of the biggest mistakes that can be made in trying to introduce the advanced projects (on both a national and an international scale) is to assume that students can deal effectively with all the demands and rigors of a project in a period of three months without attention to emotional needs. Even for the project in Ecuador described in this book, three months was not enough for students who did not have prior overseas experience or were unfamiliar with the demands of a loosely structured learning environment.

The goals and demands of the advanced projects can overwhelm students. In the model Ecuador project, for example, participants were confronted with the following demands:

- Cultural adjustment in a country that was composed of several subcultures in a variety of climates (jungle, coast, mountains, city, countryside) as well as unseen subcultures within the familiar environments (for example, urban prisons)

- Daily communication in a foreign language
- Participation in a democratic educational experience that was unlike the strict, traditional classroom setting to which the students were accustomed
- Work as a member of a noncompetitive team
- The need to learn and develop field research techniques
- Ethical issues of political and social interaction with Ecuadorians in a very diverse society
- Production of a policy document for government officials

This is a great deal to ask in a short time. It is unfair to push students to absorb the full amount of information with which they are confronted and to push them to consider their values and to think about a new type of education in the course of three months. This is not enough time for students to air concerns, deal with their emotional needs, and relieve stress.

Risk taking—intellectual and emotional—and active participation in the planning and execution of a project are essential parts of the educational experience of a major policy project. But students need to feel comfortable enough to work and think. They need time alone just to reflect or read; they need opportunities to rediscover themselves in what can be an intimidating and confusing array of experiences.

For this reason, it is essential to lengthen the amount of time devoted to such projects, to train students in advance in field skills and in the approach of democratic experiential learning, and/or to screen students extremely carefully.

Issues Specific to Advanced Projects

How can advanced projects be adjusted so that enough time is allocated to meet all the objectives?   One solution—once projects are known to more students and are more fully accredited and integrated into university curricula—is to run the projects during a four- or five-month academic term, rather than only during the three months of summer.

Another solution is to require students to do project-related work during the term preceding the field work.

Other problems could likely be solved by focusing on group issues, democratic education, and techniques of field work for several weeks before departure. Many students do not understand that democracy implies responsibility, sharing of views, and respect; nor are they familiar with contractual obligations or commitment. Yet it is possible to give students a taste of these concepts by starting work as a team several weeks prior to departure in joint fund-raising and planning (travel arrangements, sites, and equipment) and in sample field trips (visits to emigré communities, returned Peace Corps volunteers, consulates, and so on).

Asking students to sit in a classroom setting for further lectures and book learning on the areas they will visit is not the answer. The kind of students who would sit through such preparations as a prerequisite may not be the kind that can be part of an interesting student team. Further, too much classroom preparation can lead to biases, stereotypes, and false analyses.

Once forms of experiential (social science "laboratory") classes and forms of democratic interdisciplinary education begin to take root at universities at the introductory and intermediate levels, they will eventually help prepare more and more students for advanced projects.

What is the project leader's role in the advanced projects? The role of project leader or facilitator is one of guidance and not authority. The leader provides a library of materials for students to consult as an "informal curriculum" on all topics that might arise, pushes students to ask probing questions but also to consider ethical issues, demonstrates various methodologies for which curricular materials are available, helps facilitate discussions and site visits so that students derive the most benefit from their time, provides help on formulating strategies and applying various disciplinary approaches in the field, and questions theoretical assumptions and "givens" while seeing that the group still adheres to stated objectives.

Isn't there an arrogance in the belief that students have a right to try to influence policy at a high level in the United States and abroad? It is a democratic right (duty, actually) of citizens in the United States to participate actively in policy making and to work to benefit the country.

Those who travel overseas on democratic experiential projects and try to share the benefits of their views in the form of recommendations do not enter into politics in any way that violates U.S. or host country laws, and do not comment on areas of political concern in which the U.S. government or an international organization is not already interfering. If it is wrong for students to comment on host country politics, then it is probably wrong for organizations like the World Bank International Monetary Fund, representatives and diplomats of the U.S. government, multinational organizations, and religious groups to interfere in them also.

U.S. citizens' votes already have an impact on other people's politics since U.S. governmental bodies make important decisions overseas every day, often with less-accurate information than students can collect and with less ability for independent judgment and reflection. What better than to add to the plurality of voices and to give meaning to the concept of democracy? Those who are preparing themselves as future U.S. ambassadors, foreign service officers, multinational executives, and international development bankers may perhaps be better informed and more sensitive after completing a democratic experiential project than are some individuals who now fill these posts.

There is a key element missing from industrialized countries' international projects that should be corrected to make these projects more sensitive to host countries and to combat the paternalistic arrogance inherent in "top-down" development models imposed by foreigners. Indeed, the goal of our student projects is to combat the substitution of the armchair ivory tower theories and models of world bankers, government officials, and corporate and academic leaders for firsthand knowledge of the aspirations and needs of real people whom these officials and leaders never meet and refuse to hear. The students and leaders in our projects may be outsiders, but we seek to incorporate as many voices and views as we can.

There are advantages and disadvantages to involving host country students as part of student project teams, but this involvement is our goal. We recognize the political risks that host country students may face for taking certain positions; the potential biases resulting from the socioeconomic status or ethnic background of host country university students who are included in a project team; and the difficulty of working with an educational system abroad. It is important, nevertheless, to try to arrange for participation with host country students on projects in the future.

Finding funds for host country student participation, arranging relevant contacts, and overcoming structural barriers to participation make this difficult, however. Indeed, the students most likely to participate in host countries are privileged urban youth of the dominant ethnic group, who may have little interest in the concerns raised by outsiders seeking to be objective. We continue to seek ways of overcoming these obstacles.

Are advanced project teams in any area long enough to develop true rapport and understanding, or are they really engaging in academic tourism? Aren't experiential student groups really objectifying the people that they visit and making them into objects of study? These are important questions that go right to the heart of the ethics of university curricula in general as well as to the heart of what democracy is about, how it works or does not work today, how educated Americans can best "do good" in the world, and how different cultures relate to each other. Leaders of student adventures have differing views on these subjects. In fact, this is why they take different approaches in designing and teaching democratic experiential courses.

The answer lies in the amount of time spent discussing these same questions. They are questions that must always remain in the curriculum of an experiential education course. If the questions do not come up on their own, instructors are not meeting their responsibility.

Do student teams treat all groups that they visit equally, or do they give special consideration to (or stay away from) those groups that are richer and more powerful? No one "owns" democratic experiential courses and projects. By its very nature, democratic education breaks the link between university funding and judgments on student advancement. Students are not beholden to particular donors or to the biases of the institutions in which they work.

The role of instructors is to help students see the unseen in their own backyards, so to speak, and to encourage them to see things they would not normally see or that they see but are unlikely to consider very deeply. At the same time, students have the ability to contribute to course design by expressing their own curiosity and by planning explorations of areas they wish to know better.

For those students who have not been exposed to U.S. and international elites and who would be more comfortable meeting with the excluded and dejected, the goal of student adventures is to break down stereotypes that may not be based on experience. For those students who are comfortable moving among the elites and who have had little exposure to poverty in the United States and elsewhere, the goal is to help them confront their stereotypes and lack of firsthand information.

Experiential courses aim to expose students to a vertical slice of life—a slice that includes the poor and the rich, the glamorous and the downtrodden, the established and the dissenting. All are legitimate groups for study. It may be impossible to improve one's communities without understanding the interests that are common to all groups and the responsibilities that each group bears for existing problems.

Implementation

What will make universities more likely to accredit these programs, given faculty resistance to relinquishing control over students, to crossing disciplinary barriers, to indoctrination, and to change? Some universities, such as Harvard, retain long-established barriers that make it impossible for students to develop their own courses and unlikely that interdisciplinary, democratic experiential courses would ever be adopted by an existing department. This is a very difficult problem. Perhaps only the generosity of a major donor, specifically earmarking funds, could change the policies that favor the established method.

In many cases, university departments are not structured in a way that allows for the initiation of interdisciplinary, experiential, project-oriented learning. Other institutions, due to the way faculty have been selected for generations or to the way in which they are compensated and judged, often lack the contacts with the local community required to arrange field research. Further, they often do not have the expertise or the time to develop teaching skills in experiential and democratic learning.

In some universities in which these courses and projects have been tested, faculty find them threatening. The projects receive more publicity than many other courses since they are visible in the community and since students are excited and like to talk about their experiences. Such courses also encourage students to take a more active role and to challenge what they are being taught in other classes. That can be threatening to professors.

For student adventures to succeed, it is important to find a way to expand the pie of resources going to universities and to bring interest to courses that already teach skills. Certainly it is important for students to learn particular skills in basic courses so that they can comfortably apply those skills in the field. In most cases, experiential education is complementary to other kinds of learning.

Some skills are learned most effectively in a classroom setting and with a textbook, while others are best learned in the field. Once skills are learned, they must be used and applied in the field. Democratic experiential courses encourage students to learn more practical skills and to do more theoretical work. It is exactly this interaction between theory and experience that creates greater demand for and skill in both.

While barriers to instituting such courses and projects have been higher than they should be (the more time spent working through the bureaucracy, the less time spent enhancing learning and sharing the educational benefits of experiential education with other students), such courses are meeting the needs that several university committees and national studies of higher education have identified. It is important to toss the rhetoric back at administrators and faculty who espouse it and to show that democratic experiential courses actually produce results that they can share in.

As one example, one of the leading public universities in the country—the University of California at Berkeley—experimented with and ultimately adopted two courses described in this book. The university did this because the courses fit in quite nicely with the stated goals of the faculty themselves. Even if faculty do not take the first step, they can often be held to their words. What may sound like faculty rhetoric often can be used by those who seek change to hold administrators and faculty to their stated missions and to cooperate with them to expand what they would not have developed on their own, as happened at Berkeley. We found the following encouragement, for example, in administrators and faculty members' own words.

- The Committee on Academic Planning identified the university's mission as one of research and of providing opportunity for undergraduates to participate in the gathering and analysis of information. These were described as the basic activities of a research-oriented university.

- The university's Task Force on Lower-Division Education, headed by Dr. Neil Smelser (Department of Sociology), called for *interdisciplinary programs* requiring students to synthesize material from different fields, to supplement current specialized disciplinary offerings; *recognition of ethnic, racial, and cultural diversity* through providing more "educational experiences that are simultaneously meaningful, broadening, and integrating"; *humanistic education*, in the sense of considering knowledge in the context of the "natural, moral and spiritual aspects of the human condition," through "infusing new resources into teaching and research in the humanities and social sciences"; and *problem-oriented courses* that would supplement traditional information or methodology courses with applied work and that would "focus on such topics as bureaucracy and freedom, the fate of democracy in large industrial societies, and the political implications of ethnic and cultural heterogeneity."

The central purpose of democratic experiential projects is to meet these goals, and we held the university to its own declarations.

Is there a national network or clearinghouse for projects like The Unseen America, a way to join an ongoing project or seek help or advice from someone who is running one?   While there are currently a number of organizations dedicated to service learning and to experiential education (generally internships), this book represents one of the first comprehensive approaches to democratic experiential education. While the information presented in this book may be incorporated into existing organizations in the future, the authors have incorporated their own nonprofit (Unseen America Projects, Inc.) and are always reachable individually through the alumni offices of the schools in which they developed their programs.

10

Remaking the University Through Democratic Experiential Education

Allan Bloom is right that young people in today's universities and in American society "must navigate among a collection of carnival barkers, each trying to lure [them] into a particular sideshow" (Bloom, 1987, p. 339).

The battle for change is often a competition over stories, with different groups trying to fit actions into the text of an acceptable story or changing the story to fit a particular action. Bloom (and those who oppose him in the ritual debates over higher education) has used a particular story for his own purposes in attempting to move education in a particular direction, seeking to provide continuity to old texts and provide a sense of security and familiarity by stressing powerful symbols.

While the manipulation of symbols may be less important than the actual quality of education and the educational system's ability to meet certain objectives, the debate over symbols often determines whether or not any opportunity exists for a real test of new ideas. Thus, students, academics, and members of the public who wish to see democratic experiential education gain ground at American universities need to understand how to turn arguments in the current debate back against themselves and to demonstrate the strong link between traditional democratic and civic values in America and democratic experiential education, just so that the reforms can be judged on their merits.

Overall, improving the educational system is as much a question of politics as effectiveness of programs. It requires understanding the incentives behind the operations of higher education and then building the constituency outside and inside education that will enable reforms to compete with, outdo, and eventually replace the current system. It requires recognizing the institutional and cultural depth of the problem and that it is important to work within the institutional culture to restore the mission of the country's educational institutions.

To be effective in educational reform is to recognize that there is a battle to be waged on two fronts—one requires fitting proposals into familiar stories about the country's values and about education, so that the proposals fit easily into existing mindsets, and the second requires proving the benefits in ways that meet the most important financial and structural concerns of those within the system. Both battles need to be fought simultaneously because they reinforce each other. We think we can succeed where others have failed because we have a way to engage in both battles.

Since much that happens at universities now is about the manipulation of abstract symbols rather than about real experiences, for reformers to move the system toward democratic experiential education means, ironically, that they need to be adept at the very task—abstract symbol manipulation—that they find distracting. They are put in the position of having not only to manipulate symbols but to manipulate them even more effectively than those who are masters of the technique and who oppose change.

This chapter provides some suggestions on how to win at that game by turning the debate back on itself and by appropriating symbols of democracy and educational quality in a way that demonstrates how much more effective than traditional education democratic experiential education really is in meeting the objectives that traditional educators claim they support.

Once ideas for reform are placed within the existing structure, using existing rules, these ideas, if designed correctly, can grow and slowly compete against existing forms without compromising their essence or creating major disruptions. Such change is much more likely in places where existing structures are vulnerable—where there is already recognition of the need for some sort of change and where the costs of inaction are mounting so quickly that doing nothing would be more harmful than taking a risk on a proven idea. We demonstrate in this chapter how democratic experiential education meets these challenges.

We start by drawing attention to one of the many great ironies in the debate: how history has been distorted within the university to achieve ends opposite of those intended. Take, for example, one of the great mainstays of the system of higher education, the tenure system, which many older faculty and administrators use today to protect their positions, invoking the American democratic tradition of free speech and history.

In the United States, the tenure debate had its origins in 1900 at Stanford University, where students would develop The Unseen America almost a century later. In 1900, Jane Lathrop Stanford, the wife of the university's founder and benefactor, fired Professor Edward A. Ross for researching her family's railroad interests during an era of monopolistic practices and political corruption. The American Association of University Professors backed Ross as part of its vision that faculty roles—during the Progressive era—ought to include the use of knowledge to investigate issues of public concern and to benefit the public (Sammons, 1995). Today, by contrast, the tenure system has been mythologized to support faculty members who teach in traditional ways and dissuade their students from such independent lines of inquiry as that conducted by Ross. Indeed, one might ask, what is it that Bloom—or those who challenge him—do today to honor the memory of Professor Ross and to encourage such independence among their own students?

In applying the history of Western enlightenment and the birth of democracy to democratic experiential education, one finds that the Western intellectual tradition has long been marked by writings and models seeking a liberating and humanistic education. It is from these traditions that educational reformers have often sought inspiration, as we have, and we seek to bring these traditions to public attention once again.

Similarly, the Latin American philosophy of participation—drawing from the work of scholars like Paulo Freire and based on communications, relationship, and community—merges with North American democratic traditions in its concept of education and a participatory democratic society.

To see this is to go directly to the source of Western educational traditions and to reflect on the two models of education—the prevailing view and the democratic experiential view (described throughout this book) and then to add a touch of business and administrative savvy, seeing how modern institutions currently work and how our proposals are more efficient and effective.

Drawing New Meaning from Tradition

In Athens, in the early days of higher education, Socrates sat outdoors on one end of a log, and a student sat on the other end. This model is considered by many to be the educational gold standard. While this is the model invoked in classrooms like Bloom's, that model has been lost. While Socrates's methods of questioning are still used, much of the quality of the interaction and the idea of dialogue has been stripped away in the modern classroom of lectures, papers, and tests.

Similarly, Rousseau's concept of democracy based on the social contract—an idea of governance beginning with the needs of the individual through a contract, rather than with the needs of institutions—was tied to a caring and liberating philosophy of education (which Rousseau described in *The Social Contract* and *Émile, or On Education*, both first published in 1762). Yet while Rousseau is still cited as one of the intellectual founders of modern democracy, the principles of the social contract have been completely inverted in the modern university.

Thomas Jefferson, perhaps America's greatest statesman-intellectual, put many of the concepts of his own liberal and practical training into the design of the university he founded in Virginia, not only in the curriculum but in its entire design. Yet the University of Virginia today, with its emphasis on lectures and book learning, would hardly turn out a modern-day Thomas Jefferson (Jefferson, 1971).

In nineteenth-century Russia, Leo Tolstoy, revered in American university classrooms for his writing, was among the first to scold modern universities for turning education into what he viewed as a series of military exercises and little more than amusing but meaningless ceremonies performed with utmost solemnity. Tolstoy designed his own model school in which children were put in contact with nature and allowed to follow their own interests. Yet despite his teachings in other fields, little of Tolstoy's approach to education is incorporated in the institutions that teach his work, either in the United States or in other industrial societies (Tolstoy, [1863] 1967). Renowned American universities that once practiced quality experiential methods have abandoned many of those practices for reasons that made sense in the past but that make little sense today.

Dewey's view of the fundamental connection between education and society, which has been a rhetorical lodestar for American university education, has faded in practice (Dewey 1944). Herbert Hoover, one of Stanford University's first alumni, recalled in his autobiography his experiential field trips and the close student-faculty relations at Stanford in its early years—features of the university that have since disappeared (Hoover, 1951). Willard Hotchkiss, dean of the Stanford Graduate School of Business in the 1930s, praised the sort of interactive learning that placed students in actual business environments where they could test theory directly, and he tried to bring that approach into the newly established school. Today the Stanford Graduate School of Business, ranked among the top programs in the country, adheres to a different model, in which firsthand learning is replaced with simulation in the form of case studies on paper.

Although America's commitment to higher education in the 1960s resulted in greater experimentation, most of the models that were developed then to incorporate existing knowledge on improving educational quality have also all but disappeared some thirty years later.

The story of democracy and effective learning that is told in the universities is hardly reflected in the methods used to transmit it.

Remaking the Structure of Higher Education

To understand American universities and how they can be changed is to go right to their hearts—to see how they are structured, where that structure is cracking, the principles that are at their core, and the approaches that could be employed so that new ideas succeed and institutionalize themselves.

The Structure of American Universities

Behind the rhetoric about educational "quality" and "values" is an economic reality that administrators and trustees know much better than they know the lofty words. For new ideas to succeed, those who hold the ideas must address the bottom line, explaining how the new ideas would save the universities money or how they would generate it in a way that would make the new ideas much more effective than current approaches. Here is an outline of that explanation.

The traditional university system of lecture halls and factory methods well served the economic system of large institutions characteristic of the late nineteenth and early twentieth centuries. But as mass industrial forms of production begin to reveal their inadequacies for the twenty-first century, organizational structure is changing. Sustainable growth is increasingly dependent on forms of economic organization that inspire creativity, greater productivity, greater accountability, and better use of resources. For economies to remain productive, flexible organizations must have the opportunity to compete against the large economic institutions that are beginning to monopolize their industries. Such monopolies are losing their incentives for innovation and productivity and will ultimately fail to meet society's demands (Toffler, 1980; Harris, 1982).

However, to understand why the factory model continues to dominate in the university—and why it will for some time, even beyond its usefulness—is to understand the political economic reality of modern society that keeps systems afloat long after they begin to fail.

For years, the university has done well at training organizational people and in pleasing its donors—the organizations and their representatives who have benefited from the university's services. Indeed, the entire process of education, production, and consumption remains part of an interlocking chain. The university has been effective in placing students in large institutions and training them for entry into the labor force with large institutional employers. At the same time, professors serve the economic system in which the large business and educational institutions are embedded, consulting for business, engineering products, and providing basic sciences. Donations for special professorships and to specific programs have brought the views of those who own productive wealth directly onto the campus, shaping its structure in a way that has brought the university closer to the needs of the large institutions and individuals with accumulated wealth. The locus of influence and control over the university has been reflected in the selection of university trustees, regents, and administrators and in campus policies.

The stability of this system has been its strength. To change it requires challenging and competing against many of these links, and against the institutional wealth and networks they represent, as well as working with those constituencies that recognize that this system is breaking down. In the industrial state, all of the potential critics are weak—small businesses, workers, and consumers—compared with the power of large industries and organized wealth (Mills, 1956; Galbraith, 1967).

University funding—the key to its structure—comes from a number of sources, many of which have maintained certain methods and outlooks that are less conducive to learning than to serving other interests. Much of the funding, for example, has come from the U.S. military budget as part of the development of weapons technology and the planning of military policy (Feldman, 1989). Much has come directly from multinational corporations, with resulting influence on the curriculum, through earmarked gifts and research grants to professors and, as documented by Senate committees as early as the 1930s, through direct propaganda efforts and bribes, with no federal efforts to change this pattern (U.S. Senate, 1935). At many campuses, royalties on university research—with the mixed potential for important contributions to society as well as for conflicts of interest—have brought in millions of dollars—in 1993, more than $25 million each at the University of California and at Stanford (*Yale Alumni Magazine*, "Tech-Transfer and Income on the Rise," May 1994).

Some funding comes from direct sales of items that the university produces or offers to students, with the related distortions on the educational process and the nutritional content of student diets. University shopping centers and cafeterias have given licenses and exclusive contracts to soft-drink companies, fast-food chains, and other conglomerates to sell their products, a process that the *Chronicle of Higher Education* referred to recently as the "Campus Cola Wars" (Blumenstyk, 1994). Marketing of students as athletes and sales of services have also long been part of university operations.

Tuition payments hardly cover basic costs of universities—less than half, in fact, even at private schools charging $20,000 in tuition. Hence the need for these alternative sources to meet expenses and build endowment capital and the need to rely on those who manage and grow the endowments and to incorporate their philosophies into general administrative decisions. Historically, many small experimental universities that have not sold their operations to outsiders or saved and protected their capital have gone out of business, no matter how well they fulfilled their educational mission.

Total endowment capital in U.S. universities amounted to $73.9 billion in 1992, with most major universities investing their endowments in real estate, large often multinational corporations, and corporations in which their trustees are managers or directors. Though conflict of interest has been raised when those same directors reap the benefits of stock sales, there are few laws or pressures to stop the practice, because this is the essential logic and design of the system (National Association of College and University Business Officers, 1992; Blumenstyk, 1993).

Much of the investment in the past was at least in domestic corporations, or even tied into the industries close to the universities in which companies operated. Today, however, the multimillion-dollar endowments of American universities, rather than being invested in the communities where the universities are located, are invested in multinational corporations and in wholly foreign corporations that do not employ Americans, and in real estate. Roughly 4 percent—or $3.1 billion—of American university endowments goes directly to purchase stocks and bonds in foreign corporations (3.2 percent in foreign stock and 1 percent in foreign fixed income) (National Association of College and University Business Officers, 1992).

Given this system of funding, it is easy to see why the university remains ill suited to the twenty-first century. With university endowments placed into the stock of large corporations that increasingly have no tie to their communities, university administrators and trustees have a greater stake in the success of these corporations—and exert greater influence on the faculty and curriculum—than do either the community or the students.

The role of a university president is not to innovate or educate but to serve as a broker between these groups in an interlocking network of universities and large organizations (Whyte, 1956). As these organizations increasingly disregard community interests and augment their political and economic power, there are fewer educational institutions left to prepare citizens for a more productive, sustainable economy and a more effective political system. To promote a competitive economy and political system requires a greater distribution of political and economic power, which is completely in the opposite direction from where the current system has been heading. It requires training students to run their own businesses, oversee existing large governmental and nongovernmental organizations, and hold them accountable to the public interest.

Yet even as the dangers on the horizon become apparent, the structure of the system is locked against reform, continuing to fulfill the institutional objectives that were created decades ago for an entirely different economy. The whole structure of the university, embedded in its funding and administration, is designed to serve these growing, interlocking, and increasingly distant organizations and to maintain them as they are, even as they grow all the more inefficient and out of touch with society's needs. Instead of training citizens for democracy, the university's role becomes one of funneling obedient workers into large organizations over which they have little control and even less understanding (Roszak, 1979; Illich, 1971).

While the ethical issue of the intellectual independence of the university from large organizations is occasionally a topic of discussion, the debate is usually over how far the relationship between the university and industry has gone, over the decline of basic research to fuel the applied work that companies have been effectively subcontracting out to universities. The process of concentration continues unabated, with moves to make the links even stronger and to gear universities toward training students in even more basic technical skills and toward research needs. While these links are all productive in the short run, the relationship between the university and large organizations continues to stifle other kinds of training that are essential to sustain the system over the long run (Barrow, 1990; Cordes, 1992).

Where the System Is Breaking Down

Only now has the educational system begun to face increasing criticism and cutbacks. At a time when businesses now recognize the inability of the educational system to train competent workers for the changing work environment, graduate programs become filled with foreign students because of the inability of American university graduates to compete, and declining general productivity creates public alarm and dissatisfaction with institutions in general.

At the same time, the lack of feedback from students and community in university operations has already resulted in increasing waste and improper investments of scarce resources, within the university as well as in governmental and economic institutions outside of it. Tight resources have forced a reexamination of university operations, but the debate continues to be dominated by the same managers who created the problem.

Consider just a few examples of mismanaged resources at the country's top universities— examples familiar to students but rarely publicized and rarely acknowledged by the universities themselves:

- In the mid 1980s, Stanford University received a donation of several million dollars for journalism and built a new Department of Communications on its quadrangle. Yet at the same time that the new department was being built, most of the student publications—a magazine and an alternative newspaper—were going out of business due to lack of funding; only a single newspaper remained. A tiny part of the donation—$100,000—would have endowed a student publication *in perpetuity*, giving dozens of students the opportunity to learn journalism by doing it. Instead, the money was invested in bricks.

- In the early 1990s, Yale University received an offer of millions of dollars from the Bass family for "humanities" (money since returned). Most of that money was to be for the hiring of professors to teach literature and classics courses. Little if any was to go to "humanity"—helping privileged students learn to understand and appreciate (or to create real institutional change for) others unlike themselves or to incorporate study of poetry and the arts with immediate interaction with people living in the culturally rich communities one or two blocks away from the Yale campus. In debate over the terms of the offer, such alternate use of the money never entered the general debate. New "ethics" programs at Harvard and elsewhere have followed the same scenario, while those who shape these programs express genuine surprise at the public's not seeming to support their concepts of "humanities" and "ethics."

- Recently, Harvard Law School raised millions of dollars in the name of "diversity"—including $3 million from Reginald Lewis, a black alumnus. The money went for construction and resulted in larger offices for professors, more money for faculty pet projects, and more funds for conferences; little was left for diversity or for benefit to the community. Most of the capital was to be spent rather than invested in long-term changes. The result was little overall change to the curriculum or the school, and little improvement in "diversity."

- In the late 1980s, Stanford University used several million dollars to build a student learning center near the School of Education. At the same time, the university cut all funding for student-taught courses in the SWOPSI (Stanford Workshops) and Undergraduate Specials programs. The money spent on the building could have been used to endow dozens of student-taught courses *in perpetuity*. Instead of opportunities for curricular diversity and teaching, all that students have now is a building.

The mismanagement of university capital and the growing recognition that universities are failing to meet public needs (and even the long-term needs of industry as identified by business leaders themselves) would seem to be the perfect opening for a new approach.

If creative educators could link their ideas for teaching and learning with better ways to invest and save money, they would likely be able to jump into an intellectual vacuum in the debate and shift the agenda. Good ideas have failed to make the connection in the past, but new strategies could make the difference.

The Keys to Institutionalizing Success

Many field-based programs, nontraditional forms of learning, and democratic classrooms have disappeared in the past thirty years, despite much hoopla when they were introduced in the 1960s and 1970s. By contrast, clinical programs, internships, and some field laboratory courses continue to grow.

Studying these successes and failures suggests that several different attributes determine the survivability of educational innovations in universities and can be shrewdly applied to promoting critical reforms. In a sense, reforming educational institutions is not that different as a political and managerial challenge from promoting any other type of institutional change. Proposed reforms must compete successfully with what exists—meeting underlying goals more effectively, with less cost, and without threatening existing individual and institutional interests while also finding a "political" constituency that benefits from and backs the change. In the field of educational reform, programs need to demonstrate that they possess the following:

- *Standards*. They must meet existing standards and teach skills at least as effectively as existing programs.
- *Structure*. They must be clearly structured and well defined.
- *An institutional stake*. There must be administrators or teachers already in the university structure who stand to benefit from the projects (or who will not oppose them).
- *An outside constituency*. There needs to be a constituency outside the university that benefits and supports the programs politically and financially.
- *Cost effectiveness*. They must either save money or generate financial support.
- *Self-replicability*. They must have the ability to replicate themselves and outlive their founders.

The lessons contained in these characteristics can be applied in the following ways.

Standards. One of the vulnerabilities of many educational reforms in the 1960s was that they were perceived—in many cases correctly—to exist for a political purpose rather than an educational one. They did poorly in meeting evaluative standards.

The challenge to courses like Underwater Basket Weaving—the stereotypical failure—as perhaps being relevant to students or demanded by them but not meeting existing standards may have been political, a means by which university faculty kept outsiders out and students powerless. But the challenge also reflects the reality that some skills are more useful than others.

In order to survive, new courses and programs must not only meet the standards of whatever educational criteria may be thrown at them (something that requires that they cover a number of bases, given the subjectivity of many existing criteria), but they must also be oriented to teach particular skills. Even better, if some of those skills are already being used in the marketplace, the courses that teach those skills will have a greater chance of survival (even if the ultimate purpose of the skills is either to help the people who learn them contribute to the establishment and success of new institutions that will compete against or to help the public to hold accountable existing institutions).

Criticism of courses that are weak in teaching practical skills is as valid when applied to new courses as to existing ones. Some of the experimental colleges that attempted merely to teach the "great books" were short-lived because they failed to improve upon or increase the repertoire and quality of skills that students were receiving. They focused instead on content and on a particular mission. Reading is a critical skill, but it is only one of a full range of skills that citizens need for modern life. Similarly, programs that focus on living and learning environments and choice but do not establish a set of new standards for measuring the skills they teach have also been quick to fold.

Courses in social science open themselves up to similar testing for their transmittal of real skills of applying scientific methods and concepts, while courses in "humanities" need to be held to the achievement of humanistic goals. Rather than teaching new sets of books, they also stand to be measured on their ability to introduce students to new methodologies; methods of hypothesis testing; skills in data presentation; and/or civic skills of influence, negotiation, and persuasion. Meeting these standards is a form of ensuring survivability.

Structure. The critique that many of the experimental programs of the 1960s lacked structure and focus is also often a valid one. In attempting to break free of the rigid confines of hierarchy, sterile classrooms, and rigid grading, many schools rushed to permissiveness and hurt their own causes.

Unstructured environments are a boon for individuals who are already self-disciplined, who have positive goals, who are skilled in negotiation and consensus, and who can take advantage of such freedoms and use them constructively. But the reality is that the majority of Americans were not raised or trained to do this. They need to be prepared for exercising new responsibilities and freedoms, since this is also a learned skill. Removing all of structure immediately can lead only to collapse.

Professor and former U.S. Senator Harrison Wofford conducted one of the most detailed studies of experiments with the open-classroom and consensus approach at the State University of New York at Old Westbury, in trying to explain why it failed (Wofford, 1973). In these experiments, letting students question everything as a basis for beginning their learning, without even having a set of rules for how debate and decision were to take place, forced everything into conflict, debate, and ultimate deadlock.

This is not to say that the idea behind the approach is a failure—only that the methods themselves must be introduced more gradually and with realistic expectations based on knowledge of behavior. To make the approach work is to set minimum rules for structure and to continue to increase freedoms as students progress in achieving objectives. At the same time, it is essential to recognize the importance of some experimentation and "private enterprise" in learning and that students should have a plurality of educational methods and learning opportunities. Enough resources need to be available for experimentation, so that the design and testing of new democratic and experiential projects do *not* depend on majority rule and consensus. Entrepreneurs, for example, rarely survive the consensus decisions of committees.

One of the biggest fears of modern institutional life and institutional authority is disorder. This explains the rush to the tyrannical order of large classes and to an administrative structure of rules and requirements. The most viable alternative is not an elimination of all rules but a recognition that a different kind of order can emerge using a different set of goals and starting with different premises about students.

An Institutional Stake. Perhaps the greatest barrier to sustainability of university reforms in the 1960s was their lack of integration into existing institutions. Many experimental programs were tacked on as alternative universities within the university; they were field programs or alternative curricula taught by adjunct professors or led by students. While much in the alternative curricula may have been better than that taught by professors who had been raised in the institutional enclave of the university, existing institutional constituencies did not have a stake in the new programs and had little reason to promote or protect them. Professors and administrators correctly viewed these programs as threats to their authority and, potentially, to their jobs, and they turned against them.

Trying to give existing groups a stake in such programs is difficult. For one thing, they have been so burdened with existing responsibilities that they do not want to take on any others. For another, they have no reason to experiment with something they do not themselves create. Since the unfortunate reality is that many academics are themselves fearful and shut off from the outside world—through choice and experience—they are unlikely to take any risks to support changes that open up the ivory tower.

This is a very difficult problem, but reforms that have become institutionalized have found ways around it. One way is to create new courses that complement existing ones and that rebound to the benefit of existing authorities. Laboratory courses, for example, can run parallel to theory courses, even though they may ultimately be capable of replacing or engulfing them. Student-taught peer-learning courses can be placed under a professor's hierarchical direction, creating the illusion that they are controlled and providing the real benefit of success and good publicity, while under little real control and requiring little faculty time.

Tying new projects into existing research seminars, promoting the discovery of data, and creating potential for impact on real problems are also potential methods of subsidizing the research and visibility of a professor or department. Such activities can lead to recognition and financial support.

An Outside Constituency.   It is for good reason that many Americans have turned against the university. They see that they receive little benefit from the enclaves of scholars and students in the middle of many of their communities. In many ways, the greater experimentation in the 1960s created an even larger gulf between students and their communities because it often allowed students to retreat into the arcane or unleashed their energy without direction rather than inspiring them to study broad intellectual questions in ways that could benefit others.

Among the programs that have managed to survive, however, are those that are linked to the community and from which direct benefits flow in one or both directions. Clinical programs are an idea that is in the right place at the right time. The idea of students providing low-cost professional services to the community has been the best advertisement for such programs and has increased visibility of the university in the community. At the same time, contributions from the community for these services provide continued support for the programs. Internships and service programs also provide a flow of resources back to the community. Other interactive and field programs create a dialogue and demonstrate community benefit.

The potential in this area has barely been tapped, in part because it may threaten authorities in the community. Providing services and aid to the disenfranchised while questioning existing policies is a potential threat to the powers that be. But it is also essential to increasing funding to the universities and general community support while restoring the effectiveness of democracy and a sense of community in those areas.

Cost Effectiveness.   One of the problems of many valuable reforms in the 1960s was that they created a strain on university resources. While closer interaction between students and teachers is recognized as important to educational quality, administrators have continually sacrificed quality for the "efficiency" of factory methods of education in which students are merely viewed as another "input."

While many reforms have been stifled by the belief that they will end up increasing costs, traditional methods of lecture and readings are actually more costly than many potential reforms that demonstrate a higher quality of education. The reason is that universities have paid a premium for control and hierarchy.

Clinical programs and internships are a success because they are partially financed by the community and because they transfer part of the educational process to the community. Law students working in the courts are being trained by professionals and judges, and the programs are financed by clients' legal fees and student labor. Students on internships are educated in the workplaces and may receive salaries for their efforts, again reducing university costs.

Similarly, student-initiated peer-learning courses under faculty sponsorship effectively transfer the responsibility for education to students themselves and away from paid university employees. Increasing the use of field projects has an effect in the same direction, reducing the use of classrooms and costly facilities.

Self-Replicability.   The final key to the survivability of new programs is designing them so they can outlive their creators. This is one of the most difficult tasks in reform, and one that is difficult to achieve in a society that focuses on individual achievement and success. Too many courses and programs disappear when their initiators retire or leave the university, because the courses were identified with and built around particular people rather than around ideas. Many good programs initiated in the 1960s disappeared when the founding professors no longer taught them and when none of the skills and incentives for running the programs were disseminated to students and administrators.

Projects that survive are those that not only have strong constituencies and sources of funding but are self-activating or self-replicating. The best chance of success for university courses occurs when they can be taught by students in the absence of faculty to lead them, in which a syllabus or guide to a program contains all of the information necessary to run it successfully, and when one group of students can quickly find and train a next generation to carry out a certain program.

Applying the Lessons

Many of the innovations in experiential education in the past and present have tried to link curricular change with economic and social productivity, but their success has only been partial. Experiential learning—and, more recently, service learning—have been linked to productivity but not to overall democratic change or to the real source of university funding and structure, which dilutes their impact and makes them vulnerable to criticism.

Current efforts—including the recent service-learning initiatives—tend to bolster the most inefficient features of the university rather than create an alternative to challenge them over the long term. While that has made these efforts politically viable in the short term, it has also prevented them from going any further in meeting real needs and in fulfilling the scope of the possible.

Consider the following programs, which are well intentioned and serving wonderful goals but ultimately limited in their potential by their inability to change the existing university structure.

- President Clinton's initiative for service through the Corporation for National and Community Service, modeled on Rutgers University's Walt Whitman Center for the Culture of Politics and Democracy, has added the concept of internships and courses on service to the curriculum.

- Northeastern University, in Boston, has built service learning and internships into the curricula of its undergraduate and professional schools.

- Stanford University's Haas Center for Public Service and Cornell University's field and service programs are among the efforts at top universities to stress the idea of service as a part of undergraduate education.

- A number of universities are networking through Campus Compact at Brown University to spread the idea of experiential programs. Internships have been a mainstay at many campuses and have been promoted by organizations such as the Partnership for Service Learning, the National Society for Internships and Experiential Education, and the Institute for Experiential Learning and on the primary and secondary school level.

All these programs have a common weakness that limits their long-term influence. They do little to change the source of university funding, the ties of administrators and overseers to the interests of large organizations, and the goal of the university in training its graduates to fit into those institutions.

The internship or service approach to experiential education is seen as an add-on to the curriculum rather than an integration within it to democratize learning or allow for training in other critical areas, such as making institutions accountable, increasing individual initiative, and fully promoting creativity and entrepreneurial ability that would lead to different career paths.

To their credit—which is substantial—the internship and service approaches serve as gap fillers and a means of patching up the existing system rather than as an adjunct or an experiment for those outside the hierarchy. They provide outlets for student frustration, though they do not affect the source of the frustration. They provide opportunities for service, though they do it in a way that often places students directly within large structures as volunteer employees in merely a different kind of institution. They fill the gaps in society left in many respects by the institutions that students are trained to fit into but not improve.

The recent success of these service-learning programs is bittersweet: sweet because of the opportunities it creates for students, bitter because of what it reveals about U.S. society from a larger perspective. In some ways, the idea of service learning has become an inexpensive substitute for funding the basic services that the society used to provide—legal services for the poor, outreach, and other basic and equal-opportunity rights—but that now are either underfunded or no longer funded at all. With paid professionals no longer filling those roles and providing the needed services, it has become the role of students to provide the labor. The burden has been shifted to students to address the symptoms of social decay, with the rhetorical hope that it will be young people who will work directly on changing the system that has created the problems.

Students have become the new laborers in the social service field. In this work, they learn their place as employees in organizations (as interns) rather than policy makers, while also learning to treat symptoms without addressing the larger issues. Three-quarters or more of their time is still spent in lecture halls and traditional classes, preparing for life in large organizations; they spend the rest of their time helping those whom that system leaves behind.

This approach is still more effective than other "radical" alternatives that would completely transform the university or prepare students for an imaginary society—and this is not a criticism of the approach but a call to go further. The larger vision begs for an approach that is somewhere in between the internship and the open university and that builds on the success of service learning.

To introduce a form of experiential learning that is also democratic and prepares students for full roles as citizens and as economically productive members of society requires large amounts of ingenuity, vision, and persistence. It requires an understanding of how the university and the society in which it is embedded really work and where they are headed. It requires paying attention to university costs as well as to funding.

Changing the Economics Behind the Structure

The key to remaking the structure of the university is to begin with changes in how its money is earned and invested. Changing the links between the university and community and introducing democratic experiential education on a significant scale require changing the linkages in the process of university funding—in both directions, from university to funders and vice versa. Simply following good economics could make democratic experiential education work on a large scale.

Several years ago, there were active debates in the university community, with mass student demonstrations, over whether universities should invest in companies doing business in South Africa. Despite the raising of important questions, that debate rarely reached the issue of exactly *where* universities have public responsibility to invest their endowments and how those investments affect university policy and curricula.

Consider, for instance, what would happen if a university decided to shift its endowments away from foreign investments, and even away from large corporations, and into smaller businesses in the very communities surrounding it. Consider what would happen if the endowments were spent on trying to create jobs and build local communities rather than in supporting the large organizations that often exert monopoly power over or drain those communities.

As soon as the university's source of funding becomes tied to the success of small businesses in the community, so too would the university's priorities be shifted. A different set of linkages could create a more democratic culture and promote a different type of education to help build the community and secure those investments. Soon, the goal of university managers would be not only to make the cities safer for students and to serve the community but also to provide opportunities for students to learn real skills.

How could that happen?

One of the most neglected but profitable sectors of the American economy is small business development. Even though loans to small businesses could generate market rates of interest to the lenders, prejudicial loan policies such as red-lining (that is, refusing to make loans in certain inner-city districts because of blanket assumptions about risk levels in those districts) and the tendency of business leaders from the ranks of large organizations to have political and economic decision-making power have left many small businesses without capital.

Since professors' and administrators' salaries are often drawn from the earnings of a university's endowment capital, one of the first things educators could do—in a coalition with students and neighborhood groups—is to request that the endowments from which the faculty draw their earnings be reinvested in small businesses in their own communities.

Now, universities own shopping centers and real estate in their communities from which they draw a profit (and in which they sometimes restrict or drive out competition). They could just as easily invest in small businesses in their communities. That is the first step.

The amount of university endowment funds invested in foreign corporations alone, $3.1 billion, is almost four times the $850 million that President Clinton originally proposed be directed to small businesses as part of a major economic initiative. Directing just 1 percent of university endowments to small businesses in university communities would provide $739 million to these businesses.

If universities invested only this 1 percent of their endowments in market-rate loans to inner-city small businesses, they could develop at least ninety thousand new jobs (twelve jobs for every $100,000 of investment) and could provide educational opportunities in learning about small business and community development for almost half a million university students.

A mere $500,000 would endow a small credit institution and continuing student projects overseas in perpetuity. It would create new programs for at least forty students per year, and not for just six years, but for the life of the school. It would support sixty jobs in the community, provide direct help to developing countries, and even fund a faculty position.

Universities already offer courses in accounting, business planning, urban sociology and planning, small business development, and a host of related areas. Few if any, however, have developed clinical programs in which the university's own resources are invested directly in the community and in which the university has any real stake in its own surrounding community.

Investing resources in neighborhoods near the university would quickly result in incentives to build actual community development into the social science and professional school curriculum and to incorporate business planning and small business development into the professional school curriculum.

Through an approach like this, it is possible to prepare students with the skills they need to manage and succeed in small businesses instead of just to fit into large organizations. Over the long term, the greater the success of community businesses, the more the university can seek funding from members of the community rather than from large organizations. At the same time, the approach minimizes pressures from those large organizations to prepare docile workers and increases demands from students to be prepared to start their own businesses and improve their own communities. It is an approach that is self-activating.

The advantage of democratic experiential programs overall is that they are probably the best advertisement for increased community support for education. Making students visible in the community, and showing the real benefits of an educational system that is part of the community rather than shut off from it, is a means of attracting financial support from one of the areas in which it has been lacking—from the public.

The fear that any changes in educational methods away from traditional learning would disturb the flow of funds to universities is understandable but not justified. All that is required to see how change in curricula can actually increase a university's fund-raising appeal is a bit of rethinking about how fund-raising has traditionally been done.

Experiential programs sell well because they have high visibility. Members of the community can see them in action and can see positive results. While big donors might question experiential projects because they produce books and front-page newspaper stories and not edifices of stone, that is part of their appeal. They are recognized immediately in the community, and they do not need the same costly overhead as traditional educational programs. They do not require more buildings and office space.

But linking the university financially to the community is just the first step toward remaking the university. The second step is to recognize that democratic experiential courses can save universities money by putting student labors where they count—to university advantage. Internships create a student labor force for service organizations. Democratic education creates a labor force within the universities themselves, with students taking responsibility for their own education.

The economic arguments are compelling enough that a single entrepreneurial university could combine changes in funding with curricular changes and quickly become a leading university, serving as a model for those competitors it would leave in the dust.

Not only do experiential and laboratory approaches train a more productive workforce and an economically adaptive society, but they transmit skills and knowledge much more efficiently— providing faster learning at a lower cost. That is why they can be the hallmark of a new era.

But it still requires one university with the resources and vision to move in this direction. And with almost all of the major universities—those with the greatest resources and the brightest students—mirroring each other in their approaches and inter-linked in a number of ways, that could be difficult.

The real change and "battle" seems to be facing fear itself—the fear of change and the fear of changing outdated views of the world that no longer apply at the end of the twentieth century.

University faculty will be among those who are likely to resist change most strongly. Experiential courses do not need to be taught by faculty (which is one of the reasons they can be taught so cheaply!), and most current faculty do not possess the flexibility, adaptability, and independence of spirit needed to teach them. But in a sense, with adjunct faculty now comprising 30 to 40 percent of university teaching staff and with tenure under attack, universities are already undercutting the power of their own faculty and responding more to economics than to any other goal. While this may be destroying an entire generation of young scholars, the silver lining is that it should ultimately strengthen the arguments for democratic peer learning. It is only a matter of time before univer-sity administrators recognize the economic sense of democratic experiential education and before there will be few faculty left with any power base to oppose them.

Faculty resistance was a problem that blocked the large-scale introduction of experiential courses in the past. "Outsiders" or grad-uate students who developed experiential courses of their own voli-tion or were hired to teach them were not affiliated with departments. They did not have authorization to raise funds or to accredit their programs. They had to rely on faculty in established departments. When political currents changed or funds become scarce, the field programs that did exist were the first to go. But, now, the circumstances have changed. Cost control is taking on added importance.

At the same time, professors can reap the benefits of experien-tial courses. Such courses, even interdisciplinary ones accredited within existing departments, can have a high academic content and can supplement and increase interest in existing offerings. Even if professors do not wish to give up their methods, they can only benefit by the increase in laboratory opportunities and research spin-offs that democratic experiential education would usher in. It is this type of offering that makes the departments and the theory-and-skills courses they offer more attractive to students. Bringing in a new approach can only generate good publicity and more resources. Doing so at the university level would create demands for similar approaches and preparation that would filter through the educational system.

This is the task. However, the individual commitment required for each step is small. As a student, professor, or administrator, you face the same choice that we did. You can stay in the classroom, on one side or another of a desk, being left behind, putting your time in at the university as if it were just another kind of factory labor, where you are just a cog in a machine producing reams of abstractions. Or you can join us in a new kind of experience to widen your horizons outside of the ivory tower and participate in an adventure in democracy and learning.

Resources

A

Sample Contract for Project Participants

All project participants will be bound by this contract (with such modifications as agreed to in writing by all participants at the beginning of the project period) by virtue of their participation in an Unseen America project.

Project Philosophy

Democratic Education

Participants will agree to abide by and actively promote the educational philosophy of democratic experiential education as detailed in project materials.

Participants will take special note of the responsibilities, obligations, and risks that democratic education demands, along with its benefits.

Decision Making

Participants will attempt to make decisions by group consensus and through democratic means, recognizing that such decision making requires additional efforts and commitment of time and energy compared to other forms of decision making.

Participants will also recognize that such decision making is a privilege, and that in the event of time constraints and inability of participants to commit the necessary time and energy, decision making will revert either to majority rule or into the hands of the group leader.

Participants will also recognize that democratic and consensus decision making does not preclude the delegation of responsibilities, including the delegation of certain decision-making authority to a leader.

Group Participation

Members agree to participate openly and honestly in group meetings and to express dissent in a constructive manner to facilitate positive communication among all members over the course of the project.

Before actual research begins, group members will establish a regular schedule of group meetings at which attendance by all team members will be obligatory. Such meetings will not occur at intervals of less than twice per week and will not be for less than 90 minutes per meeting.

In the case of quarrels between any participants that are perceived to affect the other members of the team, any member may, without prejudice, demand that grievances of all parties be openly aired and mediated in the presence of one or more neutral parties.

Any participant will have the right to opt out of this provision for reasons of physical privacy related to gender or on the basis of other criteria subject to group consent. In cases of limitation of rooms or bed space, in which some segregation of the group becomes necessary, allotment will be made on either a random or rotating basis.

In all other travel, research, and dining activities during which segregation becomes necessary or likely due to circumstances (for example, when the whole group does not fit on the same boat) or due to different tastes (for example when some group members would like to try particular foods or tasks and others would like to try different foods or tasks) the same rules will apply.

While this contract recognizes the value of exclusive relationships, the value of democratic experiential projects is in the sharing of one's time, experiences, and emotions with those who are of opposing views and in which compatibility and willingness to exchange ideas may be difficult by definition. Thus, participants agree that any neutral member of the group who is not a party to an exclusive relationship may, without prejudice, make the exclusive relationship and its effect on the group a legitimate topic of group discussion.

Except on personal time (available equally to participants), those participants in an exclusive relationship will agree to abide by the team's decisions regarding their interaction during the project.

In the case of dominant personalities, unwillingness to speak, emotional withdrawal, and the use of slowdowns or withdrawal as a type of veto and a means of increasing one's authority, participants acting in good faith and in full respect for the feelings of the affected party—and recognizing that such behavior may reflect some underlying or repressed unhappiness or insecurity—must accept the responsibility of bringing the issue into the open, either with the affected person alone or before the group, as soon as possible and in a nonthreatening manner.

Goal—Final Product

Participants agree to work toward the production of a written document to be completed at the end of the project period—and/or several short documents at specified intervals—and to be delivered to such parties as the group agrees before research is initiated.

All recommendations made in the written report will reflect the unanimous consent of the participants or will be accompanied by dissenting opinions included in the report, at the option of individual participants.

Health and Safety

The primary concern of the team will be the health and safety of all members. Every member will take responsibility to the maximum extent possible for safeguarding the health of all other team members. No member will take a known risk without the consent of the group or members within the vicinity.

Every participant waives rights to sue project leaders regarding issues of health and safety beyond the normal obligations existing between two persons of mutually equivalent powers and responsibilities. Project leaders will not be regarded as having special knowledge of risks involved in the project.

Each participant retains the right to abstain from any physical activity that he or she feels, in good faith, would jeopardize his or her own personal physical health or safety.

Illegal Acts

Any participant who knowingly undertakes an act in violation of U.S. law or the operating laws of a country or territory visited during the course of the project, whether or not such act is in furtherance of the goals of this project, will be considered to be acting independently and without the consent of any other participants. The member will be considered to have renounced the contract.

Personal Time

For the duration of the project, no participant will pursue any side businesses—income-generating enterprises or contacts regarding future employment or income—unless the individual has the consent of the group.

Extended leaves from group activity will be subject to advance negotiation so as not to disrupt team efforts.

Participants of greater financial means will recognize that their extravagance on personal luxuries and entertainment may create resentment among participants of more limited means, and will pledge to limit the extent of their spending during the project in situations in which it may create such unvoiced or open resentment among other participants.

Expenditures, Costs, and Resources

Participants are responsible for the safeguarding of their own property and, to the maximum extent possible and reasonable, of the personal and joint property of other members of the group.

All costs incurred in furtherance of the project goals will be either:

- Divided evenly among all members of the group.

Or, in the case where an unusual cost is incurred as a result of a project participant's particular research or personal interest:

- Fifty percent covered by the individual incurring the cost and 50 percent divided equally among the rest of the members.

Group consensus will determine under which category any costs fall.

Where there is evidence of disparity in consumption of items that are not directly research related (food costs, for instance), an attempt will be made to equate a participant's costs with his or her consumption.

In the event that an individual does not have immediate access to personal resources, any extraordinary costs incurred by that individual will be covered by the team members, with full reimbursement expected in the case of emergency medical or travel expenses. In cases in which costs were incurred in furtherance of team objectives, with the exception of medical and travel expenses (for example, legal costs or ransom money), the group will divide such costs as equally as is reasonable. The team will seek insurance if members perceive that coverage is inadequate.

All property purchased in furtherance of the project shall remain the property of the organization sponsoring the project.

Deposit

All participants will be required to make a nonrefundable deposit of 30 percent of the projected costs of the project no less than 150 days from the date research is expected to begin on the project, or within 20 days of selection.

All participants must demonstrate prior to beginning travel that they have at their disposal sufficient resources (traveler's checks, accessible bank deposits, and so on) to meet all of their expenses for the duration of the project period.

Provisions for Leaving and Cancellation

No participant will abandon active participation of the project except for reasons of personal health or safety, family or personal emergency, or compelling international circumstances (for example, interests of national or international bodies in which the participant can make a contribution to international welfare and preservation of life on a scale greater than that given through participation in the project). In such a case, the individual will make every reasonable effort to return to the group. Unexcused absence from or abandonment of the project will cause the participant to forfeit all rights to continuing and postproject benefits.

Any participant whose location is unknown to one or more team members for more than twelve hours within an urban area, or more than thirty-six hours in a rural area, will be responsible for notifying the project offices or another agreed-upon contact of his or her location. (If such notification is not received, the participant will be presumed to be in danger, and the group will make every possible effort to locate him or her.)

Postproject Benefits

Any profits over $100 resulting from the use by any participant of raw or processed data, whether written, audio, photographic, or in any other medium, collected during the course of the project will be subject for a period of seven years to equal division among all participants, after accounting for any additional expenses or work product incurred by the participant using the data.

All future work, in publication or use, resulting from the project (including interviews) will accredit the project and other members.

Each member will notify others of possible profit, publicity, recognition, and future opportunities that stem directly from participation in the project.

Publication of Written Group Work

All participants will make their best efforts to seek means of publishing and publicizing the final product of the project team. The order of names on any published work will reflect the efforts of individual participants in achieving publication. Any profits resulting from publication will be divided accordingly: all expenses incurred by members in seeking publication will be reimbursed, with remaining profits to be distributed as above (see "Postproject Benefits").

If any one section of the group product is published, the individual contributing more than 50 percent of the total work will be listed as primary author, with other members either accredited as coauthors or acknowledged as helpers.

Confidentiality

No participant will distribute findings or exchange information with third parties without the consent of the project team.

In conducting research, contact with persons with whom association might damage the credibility of the team's findings, or unfairly favor one segment of the population under study, will be subject to the consent of the team.

In collecting and publishing data, participants will make every effort to protect the rights and privacy of all individuals with whom they come in contact.

In the event that research leads to the discovery of information concerning the violation of any laws or of any ethical beliefs held by participants, the participants will take special precaution to safeguard that information in their conversations in public, in written presentation, and in any communications that could potentially be intercepted.

Participants will avoid accepting any benefits, pecuniary or otherwise, that could create future obligations on behalf of other team members without their prior consent.

Recommendations

Participants are encouraged to take intellectual risks and to attempt to develop skills in areas that may not be their specialties, even though this may detract from the overall quality of the team's final product.

Participants are encouraged to promote the benefits of experiential and democratic education and, when possible, to donate time and money to the future of such projects.

Participants are encouraged to contribute to the strengthening of curricula, goals, and diffusion of ideas, and to suggest ways of reaching future participants and raising funds for future projects.

Acceptance Statement

I have read the Fact Sheet for the project in which I am participating as well as this form contract, and I fully understand all obligations into which I am entering.

I am fully responsible for meeting these obligations. Those individuals or organizations (parents, scholarship sponsors, financial institutions, spouse, or significant other) who provide me with financial support, wholly or from time to time, and/or with whom I consult on major decisions, or who could or would exert pressure on me to change a decision of mine of which they disapprove, have been fully informed of my intention to participate in this project if selected and of the obligations and risks it would entail (as stated in the contract and the Fact Sheet).

Furthermore, while recognizing the importance of my relationships and responsibilities outside of this project—to family, friends, significant others, and ongoing career and business interests—I have made or will make clear to all parties now that my primary commitment during the course of the project will be to the project. I pledge to minimize any disruptions that my continuing relationships and responsibilities outside of the project may have on my full participation.

Dated: _____

Signed: _____

B

Unseen America Projects, Inc.

Unseen America Projects, Inc., is a nonprofit California corporation designed to develop new programs in higher education that are experiential, cooperative, interdisciplinary, and aimed at providing solutions to public policy problems of local, national, and international scope. Student participants develop skills as policy makers, theorists, and independent thinkers with the know-how to establish their own organizations as entrepreneurs in the public and private sectors.

The corporation offers its own programs to university students (usually accredited by the students' home institutions for independent research credit) and provides consultation on techniques for curriculum design and program implementation at established universities.

Past and current successes include the following courses and projects.

The Unseen America: Qualitative Analysis in Social Science Research and Public Policy. This course was first offered at Stanford University in 1985. Since 1989, it has been taught independently by undergraduates at the University of California at Berkeley, where it is now a permanent feature of the curriculum. It has also been taught for a second time at Stanford. At Berkeley, it is sponsored by five departments (more than any other course in the university). Students visit various field sites and consider policy, methodological, and philosophical social science issues.

Social Science Laboratory Courses to Supplement Introductory Social Science Lecture Courses. The Anthropology 3 Laboratory was developed for the University of California at Berkeley to accompany the introductory course in social and cultural anthropology, using the techniques developed in The Unseen America.

The Ecuador Development Project. This project was tested during the summer of 1988 and was open to Harvard and Brown undergraduates. The four student participants and the project leader were affiliated with a think tank in Ecuador but worked independently as a team, meeting with ministry and local government officials, members of the international community, artists, educators, missionaries, volunteers, farmers, indigenous peoples, executives of multinational corporations, and so on.

The group produced a book-length document in Spanish (recently published in English: Lempert, Mitchell, and McCarty, 1995) with recommendations for several areas of domestic policy. The document was organized along the lines of a World Bank, host government, or development agency five-year development plan. The group presented the document personally to the president of Ecuador as well as to a past president of the country and to the heads of several organizations. It received front-page newspaper coverage in Quito, the capital of Ecuador, and was covered on national radio and television.

The Unseen America Nationwide. In this course planned for the future, students will travel across the United States to consider social, political, and cultural issues and to write a book of essays suggesting ideas for "revitalizing America." (Similar projects being planned are *Regional and City Planning* and *Legal Development Teams in Eastern Europe and Other Developing Areas.*)

Community Development Bank/Small Credit Institution. In this course that is also in the planning stages, students will manage a small credit institution to fund small enterprises in depressed areas (in the inner city, rural locations, and overseas) and to study the impact of such aid on the community.

References

Anderson, M. *Imposters in the Temple*. New York: Simon & Schuster, 1992.

Applebome, P. "Employers Wary of School System: Survey Finds Broad Distrust of Younger Job Aspirants." *New York Times*, Feb. 20, 1995, p. 1.

Baltzell, E. D. *The Protestant Establishment: Aristocracy and Caste in America*. New York: Random House, 1964.

Barrow, C. *Universities and the Capitalist State: Corporate Liberalism and the Reconstruction of American Higher Education, 1894–1928*. Madison: University of Wisconsin Press, 1990.

Barber, B. R. *An Aristocracy of Everyone: The Politics of Education and the Future of America*. New York: Ballantine, 1992.

Berle, A., and Means, G. *The Modern Corporation and Private Property*. New York: Macmillan, 1933.

Bloom, A. *The Closing of the American Mind*. New York: Simon & Schuster, 1987.

Blumenstyk, G. "Financial Relationships at Boston U. Said to Be Subject of Investigation." *Chronicle of Higher Education*, Jan. 27, 1993, p. A-25.

Blumenstyk, G. "Campus Cola Wars." *Chronicle of Higher Education*, Feb. 9, 1994, p. A-41.

Bok, D. *Beyond the Ivory Tower: Social Responsibilities of the Modern University*. Cambridge, Mass.: Harvard University Press, 1982.

Boyer, E. *Higher Learning in the Nation's Service*. Washington, D.C.: Carnegie Foundation for the Advancement of Education, 1981.

Brinkley, D. *The Majic Bus: An American Odyssey*. Orlando, Fla.: Harcourt Brace Jovanovich, 1993.

Brooks, P. "Out of the Blue: Perilous Authority." *Yale Alumni Magazine*, Summer 1991, p. 24.

Buckley, W. F., Jr. *God and Man at Yale*. Chicago: Regency, 1951.

Churchill, W., and VanderWall, M. *Agents of Repression: The FBI's Secret Wars Against the Black Panther Party and the American Indian Movement*. Boston: South End Press, Boston, 1988.

Cordes, C. "Debate Flares over Growing Pressures on Academe for Ties with Industry." *The Chronicle of Higher Education*, Sept. 16, 1992, p. A-26.

D'Souza, D. *Illiberal Education: The Politics of Race and Sex on Campus*. New York: Free Press, 1991.

Dewey, T. *Democracy and Education*. New York: Macmillan, 1944.

Diamond, S. *Compromised Campus: The Collaboration of the Universities with the Intelligence Community, 1945–1955*. New York: Oxford University Press, 1992.

Domhoff, W., *Higher Circles: The Governing Class in America*. New York: Random House, 1970.

Dressel, P. L. (ed.). *The New Colleges: Toward an Appraisal*. Iowa City, Iowa: American College Testing Program and American Association for Higher Education, 1971.

Durkheim, É. *The Division of Labor in Society: Study of the Organization of Higher Societies*, 1893.

"Equality to Me, Bias to You," *The New York Times*, Mar. 5, 1995, pp. 14–16.

Fals-Borda, O., and Rahman, M. A. *Action and Knowledge: Breaking the Monopoly with Participatory Action Research*. New York: Apex Press, 1991.

Feldman, J. *Universities in the Business of Repression: The Academic-Military-Industrial Complex in Central America*. Boston: South End Press, 1989.

Freire, P. *Pedagogy of the Oppressed*. New York: Seabury Press, 1970.

Galbraith, J. K. *The New Industrial State*. Boston: Houghton Mifflin, 1967.

Gardner, H. *Multiple Intelligences: The Theory in Practice*. New York: Basic Books, 1993.

Goodman, P. *Growing Up Absurd*. New York: Random House, 1960.

Goodman, P. *New Reformation*. New York: Vintage Books, 1967.

Gross, P. R., and Levitt, N. *Higher Superstition: The Academic Left and Its Quarrel with Science*. Baltimore, Md.: Johns Hopkins University Press, 1994.

Harris, M. *America Now: The Anthropology of a Changing Culture*. New York: Simon & Schuster, 1982.

Hentoff, N. *Free Speech for Me But Not for Thee: How the American Left and Right Relentlessly Censor Each Other*. New York: HarperCollins, 1992.

Hoover, H. *Memoirs*. New York: Macmillan, 1951.

Illich, I. *Deschooling Society*. New York: HarperCollins, 1971.

Jefferson, T. *The Portable Thomas Jefferson*. (M. D. Peterson, ed.) New York: Viking Press, 1971.

Kamin, L. J. "Disputing D'Souza on Political Correctness." *The Chronicle of Higher Education*, May 8, 1993, p. B-3.

Katchadourian, H. and Boli, J. *Careerism and Intellectualism Among College Students: Patterns of Academic and Career Choice in the Undergraduate Years*. San Francisco: Jossey-Bass, 1985.

Keen, M. "The FBI and American Sociology." *ASA Footnotes*, 1992, 20(5), 14.

Kimball, R. *Tenured Radicals: How Politics Has Corrupted Our Higher Education*. New York: HarperCollins, 1990.

LaGuardia, D., and Guth, H. P. *American Voices: Multicultural Literacy and Critical Thinking*. Mountain View, Calif.: Mayfield Publishing, 1993.

Lazarsfeld, P., and Thielens, W., Jr. *The Academic Mind: Social Scientists in a Time of Crisis*. New York: Free Press, 1958.

Lee, H. K. "UC Berkeley Police Go to School." *San Francisco Chronicle*, July 6, 1994, p. A15.

Lempert, D. *A Return to Democracy: The Modern Democracy Amendments*. (Manuscript, taught at Yale Law School in a course by A. Amar and on file with author), 1987, 1993.

Lempert, D. *Business Curriculum Design, Vietnam*. Contract No. RX 2050–665-DL. Washington, D.C.: Government of Vietnam/Georgetown University Center for Intercultural Education and Development, Oct. 1994.

Lempert, D. *Daily Life in a Crumbling Empire: The Absorption of Russia into the World Economy*. (Originally titled *Pepsi-Stroika: The Colonization of Russia*.) Eastern European Monograph Series, 2 vols. New York: Columbia University Press, forthcoming.

Lempert, D., Mitchell, C., and McCarty, K. *A Model Development Plan: New Strategies and Perspectives.* Westport, Conn.: Greenwood, 1995.

Lewis, L. S. *Scaling the Ivory Tower: Merit and Its Limits in Academic Careers.* Baltimore, Md.: Johns Hopkins University Press, 1975.

Lewis, L. S. *Cold War on Campus: A Study of the Politics of Organizational Control.* New Brunswick, N.J.: Transaction Books, 1988.

Lynd, R. S., and Lynd, H. M. *Middletown.* Orlando, Fla.: Harcourt Brace Jovanovich, 1929.

Lynd, R. S., and Lynd, H. M. *Middletown in Transition.* Orlando, Fla.: Harcourt Brace Jovanovich, 1937.

McCormick, C. H. *This Nest of Vipers: McCarthyism and Higher Education in the Mundel Affair.* Chicago: University of Illinois Press, 1989.

McCoy, P. C. "Johnston College: An Experimenting Model." In P. L. Dressel, *The New Colleges: Toward an Appraisal.* Iowa City, Iowa: American College Testing Program and American Association for Higher Education, 1971.

McLuhan, M. *Understanding the Media: The Extensions of Man.* New York: McGraw-Hill, 1964.

Malinowski, B. *Argonauts of the Western Pacific.* New York: Dutton, 1922.

Mason, R. M. *Participatory and Workplace Democracy: A Theoretical Development in Critique of Liberalism.* Carbondale: Southern Illinois University Press, 1982.

Meisler, R. *Trying Freedom: A Case for Liberal Education.* Orlando, Fla.: Harcourt Brace Jovanovich, 1984.

Milgram, S. *Obedience to Authority.* New York: HarperCollins, 1974.

Mills, C. W. *The Power Elite.* London: Oxford University Press, 1956.

National Association of College and University Business Officers *Annual Report.* Washington, D.C.: National Association of College and University Business Officers, 1992.

Oren, D. A. *Joining the Club: A History of Jews and Yale.* New Haven, Conn.: Yale University Press, 1985.

Phelan, J., Link, B. G., Stueve, A., and Moore, R. E. "Education, Social Liberalism, and Economic Conservatism: Attitudes Toward Homeless People." *American Sociological Review,* 1995, 60, 126–140.

Piaget, J. *The Essential Piaget.* (H. E. Gruber, ed.) London: Routledge & Kegan Paul, 1977.

"Policing the Ghetto Underclass: The Politics of Law and Law Enforcement." *Social Problems,* May 1994, 41(2), 177–194.

Resnick, L. B., and Klopfer, L. E. (eds.). *Toward the Thinking Curriculum*. Association for Supervision and Curriculum Development, 1989.

Robins, N. *Alien Ink: The FBI's War on Freedom of Expression*. New York: William Morrow, 1992.

Roszak, T. *Person/Planet*. New York: Anchor Press, 1979.

Sammons, J. L., "Letter to the Editor." *Yale Alumni Magazine*, Mar. 1995, p. 9.

Schrecker, E. *No Ivory Tower: McCarthyism and the Universities*. New York: Oxford University Press, 1986.

Shor, I. *Freire in the Classroom: A Sourcebook for Liberatory Teaching*. Portsmouth, N.H.: Boynton/Cook, 1987.

Shor, I., and Freire, P. *A Pedagogy for Liberation: Dialogues on Transforming Education*. South Hadley, Mass.: Bergin & Garvey, 1981.

Shultz, B., and Shultz, R. *It Did Happen Here: Recollections of Political Repression in America*. Berkeley: University of California Press, 1989.

Slaughter, S. "The 'Official' Ideology of Higher Education: Ironies and Inconsistencies." In W. G. Tierney (ed.), *Culture and Ideology in Higher Education*. New York: Praeger, 1991.

Spock, B. "The Best Way to Teach." *Parenting*, Sept. 1993, pp. 113–116.

Sykes, C. J. *Profscam: Professors and the Demise of Higher Education*. New York: St. Martin's Press, 1988.

"Tech-Transfer and Income on the Rise." *Yale Alumni Magazine*, May 1994.

Toffler, A. *The Third Wave*. New York: Bantam Books, 1980.

Tolstoy, L. *On Education*. Chicago: University of Chicago Press, 1967. (Originally published 1863.)

Tyack, D. *The One Best System*. Cambridge, Mass.: Harvard University Press, 1974.

U.S. Senate, 70th Congress. "Publicity and Propaganda Activities by Utilities Groups and Companies." *Report of the Federal Trade Commission to the Senate of the United States*, 92(81-A). Washington, D.C.: Government Printing Office, 1935.

Warner, W. L. *Democracy in Jonesville: A Study of Quality and Inequality*. New York: HarperCollins, 1949.

Warner, W. L. (ed.). *Yankee City: A Study of a Modern Community*. New Haven, Conn.: Yale University Press, 1947–1959.

Weber, M. *Theory of Social and Economic Organization*. (A. M. Henderson and T. Parsons, trans.) New York: Free Press, 1947.

Whyte, W. F. *Participatory Action Research*. London: Sage, 1991.

Whyte, W. H. *The Organization Man*. New York: Doubleday, 1956.

Wofford, H. "How Big the Wave." In G. MacDonald (ed.), *Five Experimental Colleges*. New York: HarperCollins, 1973.

Yablonsky, L. *Robopaths*. New York: Bobbs-Merrill, 1972.

Name Index

Subject Index